*A*dventure Guide to
Colorado

Steve Cohen

HUNTER
PUBLISHING

Hunter Publishing, Inc.
130 Campus Drive
Edison NJ 08818
(800) 255 0343 Fax (908) 417 0482
e-mail: hunterpub@emi.net
http://www.hunterpublishing.com

ISBN 1-55650-706-2
© 1997 Steve Cohen

This guide focuses on recreation and adventure travel. As all such activities
contain elements of risk, the publisher, author, and all affiliated individuals
disclaim responsibility for any injury, harm, or illness that may occur to
anyone through, or by use of, the information in this book. All information
was correct at the time of publication but, due to the passage of time and
changing circumstances, this guide cannot be entirely up-to-date and accurate. The publisher and author are not responsible for omissions or inaccu-
racies, but welcome readers' comments, corrections, and suggestions for
improvement.

Cover photograph, *Coyote*, by Joe McDonald (Global Pictures)
Maps by Kim André and Lissa K. Dailey

About the Author

An adventure-seeking travel writer and photographer specializing in the
unusual, Steve Cohen's self-illustrated articles appear regularly in dozens of
domestic and international publications, including many of North America's largest newspapers and travel magazines. He lives in Colorado with his
wife, Jodie, and his son, Sean. He is a member of the Society of American
Travel Writers.

Other Adventure Guides by Steve Cohen for Hunter Publishing:

Adventure Guide To Jamaica, Third Edition, 1997.

Adventure Guide To The High Southwest, Second Edition, 1996.

Adventure Guide To New Mexico, 1996, with D.G. Houser and R. Harvey.

Adventure Guide To Arizona, 1996, with Eleanor S. Morris.

Adventure Guide To Utah, 1996, with Madeleine Osberger.

Contents

Introduction

Colorado offers a great concentration of adventurous things to do on a year-round basis. This enormous area includes several national parks, national monuments, tribal and state parks, national forests, wilderness areas, and millions of acres for hiking, biking, skiing, rafting, cycling, fishing, and much more.

The state is bisected by the Rocky Mountains; much of the land area sits far above sea level. The abundance of rugged, virtually primeval terrain lends itself naturally to high adventure.

The territory has also been preeminent among spiritual places to the native people. They were the first to live in the area and their ancient mysteries and modern presence are still evident today.

If you really want to experience Colorado – the land, the people, the history, and the adventures – this book is for you.

The nuts-and-bolts information you need to plan a trip is provided, as well as concise details on adventurous activities. Ride a horse, raft rapids, climb mountains, ski world-class resorts or cross-country to isolated huts, climb through ancient Indian ruins, go on a modern-day cattle drive or soar above it in a glider. From easy ventures to more challenging fare, there's enough to fill vacations for years; it's no surprise that many people return to Colorado again and again.

This adventurous conception of Colorado extends into the metropolitan areas. The mile-high city of Denver, for instance, makes a good home base from which to enjoy an hour of parasailing or an afternoon of snowboarding followed by a great meal, theater, and a nightcap in a brew pub before retiring for the night. Just minutes from any one of Colorado's fascinating cities, nature's geology, flora and fauna are more likely to be on display than the work of man. For those adventurers not seeking to leave the civilized world completely behind, Colorado provides the perfect combination. You can navigate bike trails in the foothills or climb Boulder's Flatirons, all within easy reach of every conceivable amenity. From mild to wild, this book provides the specifics you need to create your own adventure.

This state's many interesting towns will entertain and delight. In Boulder hippies and yuppies mingle. Add a few thousand college students and you have an eclectic mixture you won't soon forget. But it's probably the outdoors that brings everyone together. Hundreds of miles of trails have made Boulder a mountain biking mecca, while its wide-open fields and flowery meadows instill a sense of tranquility to all visitors.

The sleepy Front Range town of Morrison, just minutes from urban Denver, comes alive when you sit and feel the fresh mountain air in its red-rock amphitheatre. Thousands of people converge on this world-renowned concert venue each year to hear their favorite symphonies, orchestras and rock bands play. Nature has created perfect acoustics – better than any an engineer could design, some say. The Red Rocks Theater is even perfect for famous opera singers like Jessye Norman, who sang here several years ago. Wagner has never sounded better. More commonly, rock and pop acts fill the mountain air with their reverberating tones.

Colorado Springs, with its mighty Pikes Peak, waterfalls and *Garden of the Gods* rock formations, also offers the Broadmoor Resort, where you can enjoy every conceivable sport – even skeet shooting. Rock climbing in this area is exceptional. And the booming Colorado Springs Airport is an increasingly popular alternative to Denver International Airport to the north, for travelers seeking lower fares thanks to lower landing fees.

Steamboat Springs caters to true cowboys (visit saddle stores here!) and excels in cross-country ski lessons and downhill racing classes.

The record number of students attending the state university in Fort Collins attests to the fact that this community is no longer a cowtown. Lace up your hiking boots and find what Lory State Park has to offer. Read about Ouray, Silverton, and Telluride, which are known as the *Switzerland of America*. Discover jeep tours that set out into the state's most rugged terrain. Witness young snowboarding daredevils carve dramatic turns on the slopes of Beaver Creek or Vail, Beaver Creek's sister resort, where you can try an Olympic bobsled run. Although this curvy chute is harrowing, anyone with a few dollars can attempt to barrel down the course.

And Colorado's Ski Country USA isn't just for skiing anymore; these areas are alive all summer. Copper Mountain and Winter Park have established themselves as centers for biking, while Breckenridge offers opportunities to shoot the rapids with any number of rafting companies. Look to Aspen to see who and what is in for the season.

This once-isolated region has become incredibly popular in the last few years. It evokes visions of Indians and cowboys, snow-capped peaks, cattle drives, wild rivers, and long sunsets. Colorado has been kept a secret by those in the know. The wide-open spaces beneath clear skies have attracted lovers of the great outdoors for many years.

History

The ancient and now extinct **Anasazi Indians** who first settled this area probably descended from nomads coming across the Bering Land Bridge and down through Canada. Their skillfully constructed and mysteriously abandoned communities are now ruins that can be visited.

The Spanish came upon **Navajos** and other modern tribes in the Southwest in the 16th century while searching for gold. Only in the last 150 years has the area experienced modern civilization. First came gold-, silver-, or copperminers, then ranchers, cowboys, and business people who created small towns – many of which stayed small. Most of the mines are closed now, but ranching and cowboy arts are still widely practiced on vast, open lands. The rugged contours of Western geography haven't changed much. Towns may be few and far between, but they're here.

Colorado Today

In today's rural Colorado the pickup truck is often the vehicle of choice for ranchers. Horses continue to serve cowboys who really do wear pointy-toed boots, broad-brimmed hats or, increasingly, baseball caps advertising farm equipment. Dusty jeans and shirts with pearl snaps – the stereotypical cowboy style – are a pervasive presence here. Except for ceremonial occasions, most Indians wear clothing that looks a lot like cowboy duds. The unlikely blending of three cultures – Indian, Hispanic, and Anglo – along with the remote setting has combined to produce a unique status quo.

Accommodations range from campgrounds and dude ranches – which offer as much time on horseback as you can handle – to deluxe resorts. Dining in the boonies is still mostly unsophisticated. You can now find the odd restaurant serving grilled avocado and mango salsa, but even the better restaurants mostly stick with traditional meat and potatoes. Outside Colorado's big cities or developed resorts, corn dogs and chili, sloppy joes and salad bars continue to reign supreme.

You may be content to gaze at night skies filled with stars, but there are stomping cowboy bars with free two-step lessons and genuine western bands to entertain you. You might even jump on an electric bull here and ride 'em just as they do at Colorado's annual **National Western Stock Show.**

Activities drawing from the terrain and extreme seasons attract the ski crowd in winter; bikers and river runners in spring; campers and hikers in summer; leaf peepers and hunters in fall. Some places, like Vail and Aspen, have been claimed by a young, dynamic, fun-loving crowd. Suntanned hikers and kayakers cruise along in expensive four-wheel-drives with bike or boat racks on the back. Cowboys and Indians ride the range on horseback or in battered pickups with gun racks. By contrast, places like Rocky Mountain National Park are quite serene. Bugling elk gather here during mating season; some have likened it to a religious experience.

Geography

The land remains the dominant force here. Arid and sandy desertscapes characterize southern Colorado. Broad, arroyo-tracked flats stretch to the horizon, broken only by cacti, a rare mesquite tree, or prehistoric seabed rocks rising in wind- and water-carved majesty, seeming to defy gravity. Buttes and mesas, striped in iron-tinged red and orange, and mountains, usually snow-capped, looming beyond are here.

You can go a long way without seeing another human being, but you probably won't get far without finding evidence of deer, elk, pica, ptarmigans, eagles, mountain goats, or hawks. Less frequently spotted are black bears, mountain lions, pronghorn antelope, and bighorn sheep.

This country was created over eons by the geological forces of volcanoes, wind erosion, flowing water, and movements of tectonic plates inside the earth's crust. The results are displayed by improbably shaped land features, such as Sand Dunes National Monument in the south, the serpentine Dolores Canyon in the state's southwest, or the brooding Rocky Mountains, visible from virtually anywhere in the state, crowned by massive thunderheads.

Water, though sometimes scarce, still shapes the land as it flows from melting snow of high mountains. The streams it forms nourish forests and rivers. Even in the deserts a turbulent, impetuous downpour can fill thirsty streambeds in a frightening instant. Flash floods can carry away homes, trees, and cars, then subside as rapidly as they appeared, leaving only a damp testimony to nature's dominance of the land.

Colorado has managed to attract a long line of explorers and settlers. Deserted structures – once dwellings and now ruins or ghost towns – pepper the state and attest to ancient conflicts with drought, crop failures, and ensuing famine. Dusty trails may be all that remain of a once-productive grassland that was thoughtlessly overgrazed and is now desert. Sunbleached mine structures recall expended mineral resources and dreams. Humans are neophytes here in view of geologic forces that have created this country.

Modern researchers believe that nomadic hunter-gatherers were predecessors of the Anasazi, presumed to be the area's first settlers 1,500 years ago. About this time the farming of beans and corn – which became dietary staples – provided the sustenance necessary for settlement in one area. Around 500 years later, another nomadic tribe of Athabascan migrants of Asian descent began its travel south through Canada. The earliest of these arrivals began filtering in 600 years ago – at just about the same time the Anasazi were abandoning their cities and disappearing into the sands of time.

Over a span of some 1,000 years the Anasazi constructed incredible, unassailable cliff dwellings at Mesa Verde in southwest Colorado, sophisticated square and circular towers at Hovenweep on the Utah border, and innumerable hidden monuments. These cultures mysteriously vanished; no one is quite sure whether their demise was the result of drought and subsequent famine, warfare, or perhaps something else altogether.

The largest community in southwestern Colorado is Durango. It has a range of accommodations, 50 or more restaurants, and the famous, coal-fired, steam-powered, narrow-gauge railroad that once carried miners to remote mines. Today it serves tourists, transporting riders through a mountain wilderness to the tiny, tenacious old mining town of Silverton. Silverton's mines are closed now, and it caters mainly to tourists. Either town offers easy access to surrounding national forests that provide attractive environments if you're looking to backpack, ride a bike or a horse, rock climb, or photograph wildlife.

Pinyons and junipers yield to spruce and aspen as elevations increase north of Durango in the San Juan Range. Surprisingly, the weather here is remarkably mild year-round, despite copious snowfall at high elevations. The mountains are always cooler than the deserts, but usually comfortably so, especially in summer when days are warm. But the heat leaves with the sun and a blanket is essential for sleeping at night.

Within Colorado's borders, 1,143 mountains rise to an altitude of at least 10,000 feet above sea level and 1,000 are over two miles high. With 53 often snow-crowned peaks towering above 14,000 feet, the state has more than six times the mountain area of Switzerland. Eleven national parks and national monuments, plus 32 state parks and state recreational areas, provide unsurpassed recreational opportunities to satisfy any outdoor appetite. Also, hundreds of thousands of acres of private land are available to Colorado adventurers who respect the rights of land owners. Seek permission first.

Even if roads are periodically closed, winter travel is still possible in the Rockies, thanks to the many small air carriers that ferry skiers and other visitors in and out of the high country all year. In clear weather, the mountain views from a plane can be astounding. The Rockies stretch below, a jumbled mass of forests, crags, and snow-flecked peaks. The great expanse of Colorado, eighth in size among the states, and the vastness of its wilderness areas (national forests cover one-fifth of the state), are a magnet to adventurous travelers.

Denver, the Mile-High City, is no wilderness area, yet it lays claim to 150 parks.

Close to Denver, the Colorado Audubon Society leads trips in rural Clear Creek County, where ornithologists can walk for many miles, with binoculars and notebooks handy. The state has some 450 bird species, all within 300 miles of the capital. For the more aggressive adventure seeker, there is much more. For example, elite rock climbers from all over the world converge upon the spectacular Flatiron Range 30 miles northwest of Denver.

Seasonal Adventures

Other adventures may be dependent on the weather. A Colorado spring need not begin in March, as per calendar; it could arrive in April, even in early May at over 10,000 feet, or even later in the high narrow valleys of southwest Colorado's San Juan Range. Summit cornices are still snow-covered but the meadows are beginning to come alive. A lot of mud is around though, so do watch where you step.

In late April the earliest pasqueflowers bloom west of Aspen; the sand lilies and mariposa lilies show their white heads in the valleys. Walk among the conifers and you'll notice the fresh yellow clusters. The Engleman spruce show new growth in blue. The rivers are in motion again, their churning waters irresistible to adventurous travelers in Sunrays and kayaks.

Spring is usually a terrific time for late-season skiers seeking uncrowded slopes and bargains. Inhale deeply and snatch a few more runs before stashing away your skis.

Once timid grass begins to sprout through the snow, the first bike racks appear, replacing ski racks on the fleets of sport utility vehicles that ply Colorado's roads and byways. Gliders appear over Colorado Springs and Denver. The first waterskiers, the first anglers, the first backpackers appear in the high regions.

Colorado's state flower, the delicate columbine, spreads its petals like butterfly wings. Elk and deer gingerly approach to feed on crimson-hued shooting stars. In the cities, outdoor markets display their first geraniums, red as traffic lights, little boxes of begonias, sultanas and mums. In some ambitious Denverites' gardens the daffodils, crocus and hyacinths already make their appearance.

The rugged backcountry comes alive, too. There are areas that are as close to primal wilderness as you are likely to find in the lower 48 states. Turbulent whitewater rivers still churn from snow peaks in springtime. After an average winter with more than 300 inches of snow in the high country, rivers may run 40 feet above normal. Rafters float over rocks they would normally be floating under. Of course the rivers retreat, eventually hardening into blistered, parched lowlands under the unforgiving summer sun.

Summer is the main tourist season in Colorado, followed by the ski crowd in winter. *Caution: Skiing through waist-deep soft powder in the high, dry air on a typical sunny winter day may be addictive!* The sun always comes out after a storm, so skiers sans jackets by noon are a common sight.

The Nature Of Adventure

In the last few years, adventure travel has come into its own. It is no longer considered only for daredevils seeking the classic hang-by-your-teeth adventure, although that sort of trip is surely available in abundance out here. You probably won't have to cheat death unless you choose to, but if you sample some of this book's activities, you may have a life-affirming experience.

Inside this book you'll find extensive information on a range of activities, many of which will provide challenges relating to climate, altitude, remoteness, and physical fitness. Others may not be physically stressful, but confront your cultural perceptions. From easy-to-accomplish soft adventures, family and seniors' trips, to daredevil ventures that will really get your adrenalin pumping, you can find them here. There are activities you can pursue for an hour, a day, a week, or a month. Whatever your inclination may be, the payoff is in the remarkable regenerative power of a classic **river trip**, a **cattle drive**, an **Indian ceremony**, or an **archaeological dig.** Colorado offers thousands of miles of maintained trails for you to **hike, bike,** and **ride** on horseback. If you're a water lover, river trips in canoes, kayaks, and whitewater rafts are calling. There are evocative backroads to explore by jeep and mammoth vistas to gaze upon from the gondola of a hot-air balloon. You can visit historic and modern Indian and cowboy sites. You can travel by dogsled in winter, raft wild rivers in springtime, climb cool mountains in summer, and explore canyons and high desert in fall.

How To Use This Book

This book divides the state of Colorado into regions, beginning with the major gateway, Denver. You could, however, easily trace the same route from Colorado Springs, only 70 miles from Denver, and the state's other main air gateway.

Each chapter starts with an introduction to the region. This gives information on climate, history and culture, along with the main sites and activities. It is followed by a short section called *Getting Around*, which outlines the main roads and transportation options as well as the general route the chapter will follow. Each region is then broken down into touring sections listed in the same order as they appear on the selected route. These sections provide information and useful contact numbers, such as chambers of commerce, regional United States Department of Agriculture Forest Service offices, Bureau of Land Management offices, National Park Service offices, and airline and rental car companies.

After the general touring sections within each chapter, a separate section detailing specific *Adventures* within each region follows. These include options for independent travelers as well as those seeking guided tours. There are numerous activities to choose from, and many more limited only by your imagination. For example, you can experience an enjoyable hike on a listed bike trail, or bike on a jeep road. The following is a brief description of the range and nature of activities covered under the *Adventures* categories.

ON FOOT

Whether you want to venture off on your own or with a guide, this category will show you where to go and how to do it. There are hundreds and hundreds of miles of hiking trails in Colorado. Some are strenuous, requiring specialized rock climbing skills and equipment, others are a walk in the park. It is impossible to list them all, but you will find a cross-section of the hikes for all levels of ability, from short walks over easy trails to multi-day routes through mazelike canyon networks.

When hiking the backcountry, the more popular trails are usually well worn and marked, but it's still remarkably easy to get lost. Don't head out into the wilds on your own without some preparation. Figure out where you want to go, then consult the Forest Service, BLM, Park Service or local guides for up-to-date topographical maps and information. Discuss with them the difficulty of various trails and technical climbing skills or specialized equipment that may be required. Some adventures in this area can be easily accomplished, while others require special gear, permits, and expertise. If you're short on equipment or in doubt about your skills, seek help from the professionals before attempting a demanding adventure. If you question going it alone then you probably should not. Even if you know what you're doing there's no substitute for direct contact with people whose business is understanding the areas and activities you're pursuing. Numerous local contacts are provided in this book. The Forest Service suggests that all users of the backcountry remember the following:

❏ Take no chances. Assistance can take hours or days.

❏ Be aware of conditions. Varied terrain exposes you to hypothermia, dehydration, and lightning on exposed ridges. There can be snow fields in early summer.

❏ Start hiking early in the day – mornings are generally clear. Later in the afternoon you may encounter storms. An early start gives you time to get to your destination and set up camp in comfort.

❏ Travel with a companion. File a hiking plan with someone who is staying behind and check in with revisions so you can be found if something goes wrong.

❏ Be in shape. Don't push your limits. Allow time to acclimate to altitude.

❏ Always take fresh water with you, especially in the desert where heat can be deceiving and water may not be available. A gallon of water per person, per day is advised for summertime desert travel.

❏ Pack extra food just in case you're out longer than planned.

ON HORSEBACK

If you prefer not to be burdened with packs but want to travel into some of the most improbable terrain imaginable, try hiking with pack stock. Llamas are available through several operators. They're not strong enough to carry the weight of an adult, but they are prodigious hikers and can easily tote 100 pounds of food and equipment in spe cially designed packs. Other hiking trips with horses or mules to carry the gear are also available.

Without weight restrictions imposed by the strength of your own back, you can experience deep backcountry with a case of beer or a few bottles of wine, an extra pair of shoes, and other heavy and awkward items.

Harder on your bottom than your feet is horseback riding. Horses are still common out here and trips on well-trained, tractable mounts or high-spirited animals are easily arranged for an hour, a day, or over-night. A number of guest ranches and resorts offer horseback riding. These are listed under *Accommodations*.

If you'd like to try your hand at being a cowhand, working ranches often accommodate guests who may participate in all ranch activities, such as herding and branding, actual cattle drives – moving a herd from one place to another over several days. Ten to 12 hours a day in the saddle, moving at a slow pace is hard work, but it is, for some, the ultimate Western adventure.

ON WHEELS

There are several short train trips offered in Colorado through scenic landscapes on historic rail lines.

A jeep or other four-wheel-drive may sometimes be the only motor-ized vehicle able to negotiate the hundreds of miles of remote, mini-mal roads. Please stay on established roads and don't ruin the backcountry by carving your own route.

It's not unusual to see an old-fashioned horse-drawn wagon lumber-ing down a road. What is unusual is that some of these operators will take you along for a ride. One fellow even builds authentic old-fash-ioned stagecoaches. He offers a variety of trips when the equipment isn't being used for a movie or commercial shoot.

Mountain biking has really blossomed as a mainstream activity throughout the West. New high-tech bikes with 18, 21, or more speeds make it possible for just about anyone to negotiate some of the terrain. Mountain bikers move faster than hikers, and knobby tires can transport you into regions where motorized vehicles cannot go.

Throughout the region, the topography for biking is testing and picturesque. The assortment of logging roads, jeep routes, and single-track trails on public lands is immense, offering something for everyone, from paved bikeways to world-class backcountry excursions.

It would be impossible to include all the great biking routes here. The selection offered in this book will suit all skills and abilities, along with information sources for further exploration. Suggested operators will generally handle the logistical arrangements that an independent rider would have to manage alone. Most guided tours provide a sag wagon if you can't make those last few miles. On a tour or on your own, every rider needs to carry extra food and water, a head lamp, maps, and rain gear. A helmet is essential.

Local bike rental operators, repair shops, and tour resources are included throughout the text. Valuable sources of information are the experts in local bike shops who know the terrain.

Although bike riding is generally supported in Colorado, continuing access to backcountry trails is partly dependent on the goodwill you and other outdoor folk engender. The International Mountain Biking Association has established rules of the trail to help preserve mountain bikers' trail rights:

❏   Ride on open trails only. Respect trail and road closures, private property, and requirements for permits and authorization. Federal and state wilderness areas are closed to cyclists and some park and forest trails are off-limits.

❏   Leave no trace. Don't ride on certain soils after a rain, when the ground will be marred. Never ride off the trail, skid your tires, or discard any object. Strive to pack out more than you pack in.

❏   Control your bicycle. Inattention for even a second can cause disaster. Excessive speed frightens and injures people, gives mountain biking a bad name, and results in trail closures.

❏   Always yield. Make your approach known well in advance to others using the trail. A friendly greeting is considerate and appreciated. Show respect when passing by slowing to walking speed or even stopping, especially in the presence of horses. Anticipate that other trail users may be around corners or in blind spots.

☐ Never spook animals. Give them extra room and time to adjust to you. Running livestock and disturbing wild animals is a serious offense. Leave ranch and farm gates as you find them, or as marked.

☐ Plan ahead. Know your equipment, your ability, and the area in which you are riding and prepare accordingly.

☐ Be self-sufficient at all times, keep your bike in good condition, carry repair kits and supplies for changes in weather. Keep trails open by setting an example of responsible cycling for all to see.

As for the terrain, even routes classified as easy by locals may be strenuous for a flatlander. Most downhill trails will include some uphill stretches. Pay particular attention to your personal limits if you're on your own.

ON WATER

Around mid-May to mid-June rivers rise dramatically and the flows are at their highest, fastest and coldest. Sometimes by August things are pretty sluggish. It all depends on the winter snowfall, spring rains, and summer thunderstorms.

At high or low water levels, an experienced hand is needed to negotiate the rivers. Unless you really know what you are doing, you might consider a river tour, rather than an independent trip. Tour operators also handle the permits that are necessary for certain popular stretches, permits that may only be offered through lottery drawings and are therefore hard to come by. Some stretches of whitewater, such as Colorado's Upper Animas River with continual Class V rapids for two days, can be deadly to all but highly experienced kayakers. Participants are required to take a pre-trip physical fitness test by all tour operators running this stretch. Down below, on the Lower Animas through Durango, half a dozen tour operators sell one- and two-hour raft trips through town to anyone who comes along. There is a river trip for just about everyone, but your enjoyment may be marred if you try to take on more adventure than you can handle.

CLASSIFYING WHITEWATER RAPIDS

Class I	Easy
Class II	Intermediate
Class III	Difficult
Class IV	Very Difficult
Class V	Exceptionally Difficult
Class VI	Impossible

For any river trip, the smaller the vessel, the bigger the ride. Be sure to inquire about the size of a raft and how many people it holds. Ask if you'll need to paddle or simply ride along while guides do the work. Listings that mention paddle boats mean you will have to paddle. Oar boats mean a guide does the work. Kayaks accommodate one person, who will obviously have to do all the paddling.

With these things in mind, floating gently through ancient gorges decorated with vegetation and Anasazi rock carvings, called petroglyphs, or racing along rugged whitewater rivers pouring out of the high country has become justifiably popular. Tours are available for an hour, two hours, a half-day, full day, or overnight for up to several weeks.

Lakes and reservoirs throughout the state sometimes offer boat ramps for your vessel. Larger bodies of water feature marinas where you can rent a rowboat, a canoe, a motorboat, a windsurfer, and other equipment.

If you're seeking fishing waters rather than rapids, lakes and reservoirs are suitable for canoe and boat excursions. In addition, there are innumerable places to fish from the shores of streams, rivers, and alpine lakes. Many waters are well-stocked with a variety of fish, including several species of trout, kokanee salmon, northern pike, large- and smallmouth bass, crappie, bluegill, and channel catfish.

ON SNOW

You'll find the most reliable and sophisticated downhill skiing operations in the world in Colorado. This is Ski Country, USA – the big time in terms of terrain and facilities. From much-improved Purgatory and Telluride in the more remote southwestern part of the state, to areas closer to Denver, such as Winter Park or Vail, the skiing and snowboarding is fantastic and the reason why many "locals" moved here in the first place.

Cross-country skiing areas are generally more peaceful and less crowded than developed downhill areas but, unless you plan to stick to the groomed trails, it is wise to know what you are doing. You can ski the backcountry for an hour or for days, but conditions are often unstable and avalanches are a danger in some areas or under certain conditions. To help match your abilities with appropriate terrain, it is highly recommended that you consult with ski shop personnel or regional information sources.

The listings in each chapter are some of the safest cross-country routes. Remember that conditions are completely unpredictable and depend entirely on weather conditions that can and do change rapidly. For current snowpack and wind conditions, on-the-spot research is essential before any backcountry ski trip. Dress warmly and carry high energy foods. Though less physically demanding, the same rules apply if you're snowmobiling or dogsledding.

Ice climbing requires special equipment and skills, not to mention appropriate terrain. You can find it all in the listings under this heading.

IN THE AIR

If you think Colorado looks impressive from the ground, then you might want to consider seeing it from the air on a scenic flight. A range of options are available, including fixed-wing aircraft, helicoptors, gliders, and balloons.

ECO-TRAVEL & CULTURAL EXCURSIONS

This catch-all category includes trips and tours that don't quite fit any of the categories above, but that are worth your attention.

WHERE TO STAY & EAT

Although not necessarily an adventure, finding good places to stay and eat can be a challenge in certain parts of the state.

In some remote areas, there may be only a campground with a fire grill, or a single, shabby motel for many miles. In other places you'll find a number of excellent establishments. All listings are subjective and are included for some good reason, whether for exceptional service, ambiance, great food, originality, or good value. Rates range from inexpensive to deluxe. Because these services can change rapidly, local information sources may come in handy for updates.

CAMPING

Public campgrounds and information sources are included in this section, along with details about camping on Indian reservations and remote backcountry campsites. See pp. 74-75 for more information about camping throughout the state.

Travel Strategies & Helpful Facts

Colorado is a large, spread-out area. If you've booked a multi-day outfitted trip, the operator may be able to meet you at the closest airport. Otherwise, a car will be needed. Rentals are available in many places, including DIA (Denver International Airport), the Colorado Springs Airport, Grand Junction's Walker Field, Aspen/Pitkin County Airport, Eagle County Airport, Durango's La Plata Field and other airports. Among airlines offering service directly to rural communities are **United Express-Mesa Airlines** (☎ 800/MESA-AIR), **Frontier** (☎ 800/4321-FLY), and **America West** (☎ 800/235-9292). New commuter airline service, via carriers such as Mountain Air Express, Air 21, and Western Pacific, is expected to be the trend as airlines sign on to serve ski resorts. The larger resort communities are also served by major airlines running direct flights from all over the United States, as well as charter flights during the prime ski season.

United Express is by far the best bet for air travel to places like Durango, Crested Butte and Steamboat. Larger carriers, Frontier for instance, offer flights to these smaller destinations only during peak travel and ski seasons.

An important factor to consider is Colorado's burgeoning popularity. In many resorts visitations have doubled in the last five years and the effects on privacy and the environment have resulted in controls being placed on access to certain public lands at certain times. Consider traveling outside the traditional summer season or the peak winter months. The state is busiest from the 4th of July through Labor Day. If you're here to ski, you may want to schedule trips in early December or between mid-January and President's weekend, instead of March, when the resorts can be overrun with students and spring-breakers.

To enjoy uncrowded spring skiing, when the snow is deepest, the weather warmest, and many skiers' thoughts are already turning to cycling and kayaking, visit after the third week of March.

CLOTHING & GEAR

Colorado is a casual place. Shorts and t-shirts are fine for summer days, but long pants and a sweater or jacket may be needed at night, particularly at higher elevations, where it has been known to snow every month of the year. Because conditions can change very quickly, layering your clothes is the best idea.

Sneakers may not be sturdy enough footwear for backcountry hiking; heavier, lug-soled boots are recommended. A broken-in pair of cowboy boots may be a good idea for extended horse travel. Hiking boots with heels to catch your stirrups will probably do for short trips of a few hours to a day.

Find out in advance everything you can about your destination, such as water supplies, restroom facilities, fireplace availability, and restrictions on camping, group size, fires, and wood cutting. Plan your gear accordingly; bring shovels, cook stoves, water jugs, or saws as needed.

Outfitters and tour operators can usually supply any special gear that may be required for specific activities, so check with them about rental equipment before buying expensive items.

Always carry extra food and water on any backcountry excursion. You never know when these things may come in handy.

Depending on your activities special clothing and gear may be needed. Rafting in spring may call for a wetsuit. In winter, if you're cross-country skiing hut-to-hut, special touring skis with metal edges are highly recommended. Cross-country skiing produces a lot of heat so you can easily work up a sweat, but when you stop moving you will feel how cold it really is out there. Again, layers are the answer. Even in mid-summer on a backcountry bike ride you might start out in 80° weather, then run into a thunderstorm that drops the temperature dramatically. If you always plan for the most severe conditions you will be able to handle these changes in fine form.

The sun can be quite strong. Wear a hat, sunscreen, and bring sunglasses to prevent snow blindness in winter when the glare can be oppressive. Insect repellent is a good idea in the summer, particularly at lower elevations.

DRIVING

To get out and really experience the rugged backcountry and mountains of Colorado you need a car, and some of the best places to go are not on main roads. Always inquire of locals about current backroad conditions. Some of these may be marked for four-wheel-drive vehicles only. Do not test local wisdom or challenge these signs in your sportscar. You will be in deep trouble if you travel several hours down an ultimately impassable dirt road and discover you cannot turn around. After rains, dirt roads can become dense, muddy tracks from which there is no easy escape. Snow frequently closes main Highways in winter (though generally for short periods) and unmaintained backroads may disappear until spring.

A truck or a four-wheel-drive with high ground clearance are clearly the vehicles of choice but, with or without one, precautions are essential. The farther you plan to go, the more important it is to carry spare fuel and water for your radiator. Top up the gas tank wherever you can; the next gas station may be 100 miles away. Smart backcountry winter travel means good snow tires, windshield wipers that work, a couple of blankets, and a shovel in your car.

Local people understand the conditions and will probably help you out if you have trouble, but there may be nobody around for many miles or many hours. A cellular phone or CB radio could make a big difference in getting help. Up-to-date, reliable maps are available from offices of the AAA, the Forest Service or BLM. Outdoors stores are also good sources.

THE WEATHER

The diverse topography causes wide variations in climate. The kinds of activities you wish to pursue may dictate the season when you visit, but be aware that summer is not necessarily the most comfortable time. Summer weather is considerably milder the higher you go into the mountains, and certainly quite spectacular on an 80° blue-sky day in the San Juans.

Certain outfitting or adventure tour businesses are only open during particular seasons; some lodgings even close during the winter. Parts of Mesa Verde are closed in winter, although that needn't prevent you from snowmobiling or cross-country skiing on unplowed park roads, and having the open ruins to yourself.

If you come in the spring to raft rivers, be prepared to deal with mud in the lowlands, or dust storms in the deserts. Fall is considered by many to be the perfect season. The air is cooler, but not yet cold. Desert areas are once again tolerable after the scorching summer, while mountains boast colorful foilage and fewer crowds.

At Colorado's Great Sand Dunes National Monument, count on day-time temperatures near 100° by July and August. A fine time to visit is May or late October/early November, when other attractions are bogged down by snow or brisk temperatures. While the Sand Dunes may be scorching, it's likely to be a comfortable 70-80° in Durango or Telluride. A temperature drop of 30-40° after the sun goes down is common throughout the region. January through March may be cold, even well below freezing in the high mountains.

☞ Always check with local offices of the Colorado State Patrol and the National Weather Service for current road conditions. Don't be lazy about this. Just because it looks okay where you're standing does not mean it's going to be that way where you're going. Conditions can change quickly. Anticipation is the key to success on any wilderness trip.

Special Concerns

The areas covered in this book are here for all to enjoy and special care should always be taken to insure their continued existence. Some remote regions are designated wilderness areas with enforced rules of etiquette, including restricted access limited to those on foot or with pack animals only. Throughout the state, fishing and hunting are subject to state or tribal law. Certain forests have restrictions on campfires and, even where fires are allowed, dry weather may lead to prohibitions on open fires. It's always safest to cook on a campstove. If you need to make a fire, do not cut standing trees but burn dead wood only.

Do not be tempted to pocket an arrowhead or a pottery shard you may find on your travels. Think of the next person who'll be coming along, and remember that artifacts are protected by strictly enforced laws. Legend also claims that the spirits react quickly and violently to pilferers of native artifacts.

Take only photographs and leave only footprints. Before leaving a campsite, replace rocks and scatter leaves and twigs to restore the area to a near-natural condition. Pack out all your garbage and any other trash you may find. Bury human waste 100 feet or more from any water source and not near possible campsites. Use only biodegradable soap and, whenever possible, wash from a bucket of water far from running sources.

Do not travel into a fenced area as the Forest Service or BLM may be protecting it for revegetation or protecting you from dangerous conditions, such as extremely wet roads. Private landowners do not need a reason to keep you out; respect private property. Cross streams only at designated crossings.

Watch for lightning. Avoid exposed mountain summits above the treeline during thunderstorms. If you get caught in a thunderstorm, don't hide under a tree or in your tent. Get into your car or look for a cave or a deep protected overhang. If none of these options are available, crouch down as low as you can and hope for the best. Avoid narrow canyons during rainy weather; check weather reports for thunderstorm predictions. Disastrous flash flooding is a real danger.

The water is fine for swimming. But drinking the water in lakes, rivers, and streams is not the same wilderness treat it once was. Now it's more likely to contain *giardia lamblia*, a tiny protozoan that can cause medical problems. Animal waste in many water sources can give you diarrhea and violent stomach cramps, requiring medical attention that could be far away. To avoid problems, make sure you always carry adequate fresh water. On longer trips this usually means boiling all lake and stream water for 20 minutes or carrying effective water purification paraphernalia. You can buy this equipment from area sporting goods stores.

Information

The Bureau of Land Management (BLM) administers millions of acres of public lands. For the good reason that these lands are enormously diverse, these extensive holdings are divided into various regions. Regional headquarters can refer you to local offices, many of which are listed throughout the book. The following general sources can be a big help in getting you started before you make up your mind about exactly what you want to do. Most provide free information.

☞ For information on all aspects of touring the state, go to the Colorado Web site at *http://colorado.com*. Here you will find town-by-town details on hotels, restaurants, parks, entertainment, events, and much more.

FOR MORE INFORMATION

Colorado Road Conditions, ☎ 303/639-1111.

Colorado Division of Wildlife, Central Regional Office, 606 Broadway, Denver, CO 80216. ☎ 303/296-1192. Information on fishing licenses and regulations through out the state.

US Forest Service, PO Box 25127, 11177 West 8th Ave, Lakewood, CO 80225. ☎ 303/236-9431. Information on travel, camping, hiking, and other activities in national forests.

US Bureau of Land Management, 2850 Youngfield St, Lakewood, CO 80215. ☎ 303/236-2100. Information about recreation on BLM land.

National Park Service, PO Box 25287, Denver, CO 80225. ☎ 303/969-2000. Information on all aspects of travel within national parks, national monuments, and recreation areas.

Colorado Division of Parks and Outdoor Recreation, 1313 Sherman St, Denver, CO 80203. ☎ 303/866-3437. Offers information on state parks and recreation areas.

US Geological Survey, 1961 Stout St, Denver, CO 80294. ☎ 303/844-4196. Provides topographical maps.

Colorado Outfitters Association, PO Box 32438, Aurora, CO 80041. ☎ 303/751-9274. Offers listings of backcountry outfitters.

Colorado Campground Association, 5101 Pennsylvania Ave, Boulder, CO 80303. ☎ 303/499-9343. Offers information on private campgrounds.

Colorado Parks & Outdoor Recreation, 1313 Sherman St, Denver, CO 80216. ☎ 303/866-3437.

Cortez Area Chamber of Commerce, Box 968, Cortez, CO 81321. ☎ 970/565-3414, or 800/346-6526.

Durango Area Chamber Resort Association, PO Box 2587, Durango, CO 81302. ☎ 970/247-0312 or 800/535-8855.

National Forest Service, Rocky Mountain Region, 11177 West 8th Ave, Lakewood, CO 80225. ☎ 303/236-9431.

Ouray Chamber of Commerce, PO Box 145, Ouray, CO 81427. ☎ 970/325-4746.

Silverton Chamber of Commerce, PO Box 565, Silverton, CO 81423. ☎ 970/387-5654.

Southwest Colorado Tourism Center, ☎ 800/933-4340.

Telluride Chamber Resort Association, PO Box 653, Telluride, CO 81435. ☎ 970/728-3041.

Denver

In 1858 Denver was a small Indian village with buffalo to hunt on the plains to the east and a variety of game and fish in the mountains to the west. The tranquility of the area was permanently changed when Green Russell, a Georgian prospector married to a Cherokee Indian, found small amounts of placer gold on the banks of Cherry Creek where Denver now stands.

That same year gold was also discovered near Dry Creek in what is now the Denver suburb of Englewood. Word of the finds spread eastward, and some 150,000 people began the trek across the wide plains in wagons and on foot.

By 1859 the Gold Rush was in full swing. Denver soon had dry goods stores, blacksmith shops, real estate agencies, doctors and lawyers. Rich diggings were found, and the city continued to grow in size and culture. When the gold ran out, silver replaced it. Railroads and the cattle industry – and later tourism – guaranteed Denver's place as the hub of the West.

The city also owes much to General William Larimer, often credited as Denver's founder. His log cabin, built in 1858 at what has become the downtown intersection of 15th and Larimer streets, was one of the town's first. (Nearly everyone else lived in tents.) Although the front door was made of an old coffin lid, his place was Denver's first to have a genuine glass window. It was Larimer who jumped the claim of an older "town corporation" across the Platte River and named the resulting settlement *Denver City* in honor of the territorial governor, General James W. Denver.

Denver has been called the "Queen City of the Plains," "the Mile-High City" (the elevation is 5,280 feet), and the "Climate Capital of the World."

The Colorado capital of today is a far cry from the cattle country of a generation ago. Indeed, anyone who knew Denver even a few decades ago wouldn't recognize it today. The growing city with a small-town ambiance has become a full-fledged metropolis. The Denver Center for the Performing Arts, for instance, is nearly as big as New York's Lincoln Center.

Denver is the center of finance and commerce in the Southwest, the nation's fastest growing region. The new families have reclaimed old downtown neighborhoods, such as historic Capitol Hill; they restored the old brick and frame homes, and have made the area thrive again. Meanwhile, young professionals made the daring new LoDo (Lower Downtown) a huge success. But more about that later.

The new Denverites have brought with them their favorite shopping, dining, and entertainment from around the world. Department and specialty stores offer wares from antique clothing to Oriental jade, computers, even Greek and Thai groceries. The modern glass-enclosed Shops at Tabor Center rivals malls in the country's largest cities for elegance and variety. Just outside downtown, the Cherry Creek Shopping Center boasts high-quality retailers such as Neiman Marcus, Saks Fifth Avenue, Burberry and Coach that draw shoppers from throughout the West. The most recent addition to the retail scene is Park Meadows, located off Interstate 25 and County Line Road, featuring the state's first Nordstrom department store and Crate & Barrel home goods.

Lovers of haute cuisine will find their pleasure in scores of restaurants, such as the award-winning Wellshire Inn or the Palace Arms, which might surpass standards set by prestigious restaurants on both coasts.

Indeed, the visitor to the Mile-High City can now find any ethnic dining experience: French, German, Swiss, Italian, Spanish, Greek, Mexican, Vietnamese and assorted Oriental cooking. You'll even discover Afghan and Moroccan food. Indian food is also gaining a strong following. Denver's ethnic cuisine reflects its varied population.

Thanks to an increasingly sophisticated public, the Colorado state capital also excels in cultural offerings. There are numerous colleges and several large universities, with their libraries and lectures. The Colorado Symphony and the Denver Theatre Company are at home in ultra-modern performance halls in the heart of downtown. The Denver Art Museum hosts top international exhibits, and galleries are here en masse. Foreign motion pictures garner large audiences. Denver is no longer an unsophisticated cowtown, as critics used to claim. In some circles the city of Denver is now rated among the more sophisticated cities in the US. It is obviously more than a gateway to the rugged outdoors.

The Queen City of the Plains has retained some of her Western flavor, however. Much of Denver's heritage remains in the shape of historic buildings, fine museums, and old mansions. The analysis of a piece of quartz for mineral content, the tanning of leather, the hand-polishing of Indian silver still go on with great expertise. Denver is the ideal place to acquire Western wear and saddles of all varieties. Many city parks contain statues of cowboys. The annual National Western Stock Show has been a popular local event for almost a century and now also draws a national crowd. Several chop houses boast some of the finest buffalo and elk steaks to be found anywhere.

Because of its size and fierce competition, the Mile-High City offers choices to visitors traveling on a budget. Hundreds of acceptable restaurants with reasonable prices dot the city; low-cost accommodations are equally varied and abundant. Many museums and galleries are free, and theaters often offer discounted tickets. The mild climate gives tourists ample opportunities to discover Denver's many parks and other green areas.

The city's tourist attractions are, fortunately, close together in or near the downtown area and can be visited on foot. You can easily walk to the United States Mint, the State Capitol, the Colorado History Museum, the Civic Center, the exciting Museum of Western Art, and all kinds of shops and eateries.

Like many large cities, Denver has a number of suburbs. While the population of the actual city is around 600,000, the greater metropolitan area boasts approximately two million residents. The "burbs" and Denver are interconnected, with boundary lines zig-zagging like the pieces of a jigsaw puzzle. Aurora, which lies to the east and southeast, is the fastest growing and largest suburb.

Getting Around

Denver International Airport is the gateway to Colorado for many travelers. It is currently the largest airport in the world and is appropriately served by practically all major lines and numerous air carriers. DIA is a hub for United Airlines (☎ 800/241-6522), which offers the most daily flights. Other lines include American (☎ 800/433-7300) and Delta (☎ 800/221-1212). In addition, major national and international car rental firms, as well as local ones, operate from offices at the airport. Public transportation is also available, with bus and limo service providing connections to Denver, Boulder and other parts of the state. For complete information contact the Denver Metro Convention & Visitors Bureau (☎ 303/892-1112) at 225 W. Colfax Ave.

Denver's streets are arranged simply: north/south streets and east/west avenues form a grid. Street addresses start in both directons from Broadway, avenue addresses from Ellsworth. Street names fall in alphabetical order west of Broadway and east of Colorado Boulevard.

In the heart of downtown Denver, thoroughfares run diagonally to the normal grid. Numbered streets are in this section; in the balance of the city it's the avenues that are numbered. (17th Street, for instance, is immediately downtown, whereas 17th Avenue is not.) A good orientational aid when driving in Denver is to remember that the mountains lie to the west.

Luckily, the most exciting parts of Denver's hinterland – and the famous outdoorsy four-season resorts – are connected by air, occasionally by rail and certainly by Highway Interstate 70 roars uphill and west into the high country. Interstate 25 goes south toward beautiful Colorado Springs and north toward Fort Collins and Greeley.

Denver is enhanced by an easy-to-reach backcountry road system that provides access to scenery, fast ski runs, resort towns, sky-piercing peaks, wildflowers, and idyllic picnic spots.

With the Rocky Mountains in its backyard, Denver is also the sports capital of the West. The Colorado capital boasts more sporting goods stores per capita than any other city in the nation, as well as the world's largest sporting goods store – the Sports Castle at 10th and Broadway. An artificial snow surface even lets fledgling skiers sample the sport without leaving the store. Nearby, within city limits and in the suburbs there are opportunities for cross-country skiing, tennis, sailing, waterskiing, swimming, hiking, jogging, and even river running.

Touring

The suggested route for touring Denver and its many attractions begins at **Sloan's Lake** at 17th Avenue and Sheridan Boulevard. Travel south on Sheridan to West Colfax Avenue, then proceed eastward towards Speer Boulevard. Following Speer Boulevard north, you'll find **Elitch Gardens** straight ahead. A right turn off Speer and onto Larimer Street takes you through the **Historic Larimer Square District** and into the bustling **LoDo** (Lower Downtown) shopping areas. Crossing Larimer Street is the **16th Street Mall**, a 12-block-long pedestrian-only walkway surrounded by stores and eateries on all sides.

Denver

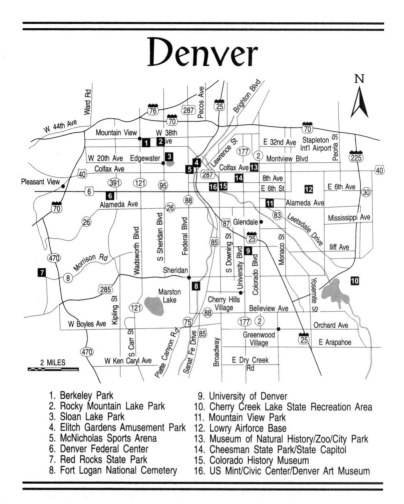

N

1. Berkeley Park
2. Rocky Mountain Lake Park
3. Sloan Lake Park
4. Elitch Gardens Amusement Park
5. McNicholas Sports Arena
6. Denver Federal Center
7. Red Rocks State Park
8. Fort Logan National Cemetery
9. University of Denver
10. Cherry Creek Lake State Recreation Area
11. Mountain View Park
12. Lowry Airforce Base
13. Museum of Natural History/Zoo/City Park
14. Cheesman State Park/State Capitol
15. Colorado History Museum
16. US Mint/Civic Center/Denver Art Museum

Following Speer Boulevard south for a block, and then turning east onto 14th Street, you'll find the **Denver Art Museum**, the new **Denver Library**, and the **Colorado History Museum**. They are all within walking distance of one another.

Continue east on 14th to York Street, another crossroads on the Denver tour. Turning north onto Josephine Street will take you by **City Park**, home to the **Denver Zoo** and the **Denver Museum of Natural History**. Turning south onto York Street brings you to **Cheesman Park** and the **Botanical Gardens** and, further south still, to the **Cherry Creek Shopping Area**. Continuing south on Josephine to westbound Louisiana, you pass **Washington Park** before reaching Interstate 25. Taking

Interstate 25 north, you reach Colfax Avenue, where this scenic tour of Denver began.

Light Rail is Denver's newest addition to its mass transit system. This $70 million, six-mile track system whisks both easygoing travelers as well as intent business people to points all over Denver in record time. Whereas buses average only eight mph in the central downtown area, light rail vehicles average 15-18 mph. And they're safe, too. Each train is equipped with cameras.

Light rail can be boarded at any of 25 terminals from Aurora Campus, past the new convention center, over the 16th Street Mall and throughout the eastern portion of downtown Denver to 30th and Welton. For information, ☎ 303/299-6000.

The Denver Public Library at 1357 Broadway, ☎ 303/640-6200, is worth a visit since its massive expansion. The librarians not only dispense books and magazines, but also organize an incessant round of free programs. These include videos and films of every kind, story hours, lectures, and exhibits. Visit the handsome Western Room. It has one of the best Western history sections in the US.

The Molly Brown House, home of the "unsinkable Molly Brown," at 1340 Pennsylvania, ☎ 303/832-4092, recreates Denver's rich Victorian past. Molly, a survivor of the *Titanic* disaster, bought the house in 1894. It has been beautifully restored. Directly south of Molly's place is another famous residence, the **Colorado Governor's Mansion**, at 8th Avenue and Pennsylvania, 400 East 8th Avenue, ☎ 303/866-3682. It is surrounded by terraced gardens and ancient elms. Free summer tours are given by the Colorado Historical Society.

The Civic Center, Colfax and Bannock, actually encompasses a three-block area of lovely lawns, gardens and trees. The familiar "Bucking Bronco" statue sits amid all the greenery. The Denver City and County Building, as it is referred to by locals, houses Denver's most important courts and various offices. An open-air Greek-style theater serves various artistic, musical, folk-dancing events in summer. At Christmas, the building is adorned with huge colored yuletide decorations and lit up in rainbow colors. Some Denverites make it a habit to drive up and see the lights; others feel that the huge amount of money for the decorations could be used for better purposes.

Some 400,000 visitors a year head for the **US Mint** at 320 West Colfax Avenue and Cherokee Street, ☎ 303/844-3331. The fortress-like build ing actually contains the largest depository of gold bullion outside of Fort Knox; there is no admission charge to see the day's production of pennies (some 18,000,000) or the other coins. Tours lead along catwalks above the roar of stamping machines and coins being cut out from huge sheets. The tours depart every 15 minutes.

LoDo, bounded by 20th and Speer Boulevard on the east and west, and Market and Wynkoop streets on the south and north, this area boasts more than 50 restaurants, several brew pubs, a couple of dozen art galleries, and plenty of shops, all housed in one of the finest collections of turn-of-the-century buildings in America. Indeed, there is enough shopping and sightseeing here to keep most travelers entertained for hours, perhaps days.

Thrill seekers might head to the newly transplanted **Elitch Gardens Amusement Park,** South Speer & Elitch Drive, ☎ 303/571-9451. This reinvented 70-acre theme park is situated on the banks of the South Platte River. The park's move from its old location cost a few flowers but added views, convenience and new rides. The rides have exciting names such as *Sky Flyer, Run-Away Train, Sea Dragon,* and *Tilt-A-Whirl.* Dangle upside down on the *Avalanche,* whiz through an aerial loop on the *Sidewinder* or, for the less adventurous, take the elevator up the 250-foot *Total Tower* to observe the serene beauty of the distant Rocky Mountains.

The Famous Denver Mall. Perhaps you'd rather observe. The 16th Street Mall, Denver's ultra-modern $76-million pedestrian thorough-fare is the best people-watching spot in the city – a place where you can be entertained by a juggler or classical violinist, shop in small exclusive shops, or just sit on one of hundreds of benches and watch Denver go by. A dozen fountains, festive banners, 200 red oak trees, and a lighting system straight out of *Star Wars* make this mile-long mall an attractive shopping and entertainment street.

While there, check out the **Overland Sheepskin Co.,** 1512 Larimer, ☎ 303/534-7717. They provide a large selection of Western wear, specializing in sheepskin. They also have hats and other leather products.

Parks

The city of Denver boasts over one hundred named parks of various sizes and shapes that stretch in every direction. If you visit the Denver Civic Center, for instance, you'll at once notice the many well-tended lawns and trees.

The citizens' fondness for their greenways cannot be denied. Each year, Denverites go in for lawn contests to decide who has the prettiest one. Every day, the newspapers print advice on lawn care. A wail goes up if a city father hints at the possibility of rationing the water used for sprinklers. Stores keep large stocks of fertilizer and commerce is brisk in garden tools, boxes of petunias and geraniums that embellish even the most humble Denver gardens.

On weekends, Denverites head for the public parks, which must be among the most well kept and varied in the nation. Each of the city's parks has its own subtle characteristics depending on location, size and activities.

Begin with Denver's largest, **City Park**. You reach it from downtown in 10 minutes of driving (enter the gates at West 20th Avenue and York Street). Keep in mind that you could spend a full summer day and evening here without a moment of boredom. A family may while away many hours at the **Denver Zoo**, ☎ 303/331-4100, where 1,500 animals are housed on some 70 acres. Take the children to *Monkey Island*, where monkeys swing and leap all summer (in spring you'll find these critters still in the Primate House). A special glass edifice contains dozens of colorful chirping, singing, and talking birds. Other natural habitat areas are for polar bears, llamas, turtles, baby elephants, rhinos, giraffes, and more. A special zoo designed for small children is popular. Here you'll find ducklings, lambs, chickens and other farm animals. The zoo is open from 10AM to 7PM. Active visitors will welcome the City Park's large tennis complex (no charge for playing).

The main entrance to the City Park and zoo is on East 23rd Avenue, but you can also get in from East 17th Avenue.

Any day – rain, snow or shine – is a good day for those hardy runners or cross-country skiers who're drawn to **Washington Park**, at South Downing and East Virginia, not far from East Alameda Avenue. This wide expanse is almost unknown to tourists, despite all the delights here: elderly gentlemen play a summer game of *boccie* on a well-kept lawn; executives in white slam tennis balls across one of the many free courts. Bring a lunch basket and relax. Watch as people walk their dogs and children enjoy the swings.

On your way from downtown to the mountains, consider the greenery surrounding **Sloan's Lake Park** at West 26th and Sheridan (or reach it from West Colfax Avenue). In the right light, the mountain backdrop can be stupendous. Denverites patronize this lake for expert waterskiing, sailing, motorboating (no swimming), fishing, bicycling, tennis (courts on both sides), or simply walking around. The circle walking tour takes about one hour.

Actually, Denver's municipal parks cover 2,800 acres; to these, you may add another city-owned 14,000 acres in the foothills. Other parks you might consider include the following:

Cheesman Park, East 8th Avenue and Franklin Street, is perfect for a restful hour or so. You can enjoy mountain views and plan your conquest of Colorado's "Fourteeners."

Eisenhower Park, South Colorado Boulevard and East Dartmouth, offers a swimming pool, indoor tables for serious ping-pong players, and a hiking trail.

Congress Park, East 9th Avenue and University, has an outdoor pool for lap swimming, tennis courts and playgrounds.

Bear Valley Park weaves and curves along West Dartmouth near South Sheridan. A bike trail follows a small river.

Museums

Denver's many museums will arouse your curiosity and are of special interest to older children.

Forney Historical Transportation Museum, 1416 Platte Street, ☎ 303/433-5896. The museum sits in all its massiveness at the Valley Highway and Speer Boulevard (Exit 107). Here you can see some 250 vehicles, including 1915 Cadillacs, 1905 Fords, various old surreys, locomobiles, ancient electric cars, carriages of all sorts, bygone cycles, rail coaches, steam engines, and old airplanes. The notable exhibits include Theodore Roosevelt's Tour Car, Aly Khan's Rolls Royce, and Amelia Earhart's Gold Bug Kissel.

Larimer Square, between 14th and 15th on Larimer, is not precisely a museum in the ordinary sense, although it has long been designated as Denver's Historic District. Twenty pre-1900 buildings reflect the romance of the last century's dramatic Victorian flair, but don't expect 100% Victoriana within the square itself. The shops, restaurants and galleries are much in tune with 20th-century sophistication. It's a pleasant place to spend a Saturday browsing – to eat a leisurely lunch in one spot followed by a scrumptious dessert in another.

Denver Botanic Gardens, 909 York Street, ☎ 303/331-4000. Another suggestion for a cold day: A marvelously warm greenhouse. This is Denver's pride and joy with plants from the South Sea Islands, India, and Madagascar, including African Palms. It features indoor displays of tropical trees and shrubs, along with outdoor gardens and a conservatory showcasing beautiful arrangements of native and exotic plant life. Memorable architecture, too. Visit the special Alpine section. Admission free on Sundays.

The Denver Museum of Natural History, 2001 Colorado Boulevard, ☎ 303/322-7009, sits on the east side of City Park. It has exhibits of animals and plants of North and South America, collections of geological material, and extinct mammals and ancient reptiles. The life zone groups, with panoramic backgrounds 40 feet in length, are unique. They depict animal and plant life of the West from the tops of the highest mountains to the deserts.

Among the outstanding exhibits are great meteorites from Canyon Diablo crater, crystalline gold from the Colorado hills, and the bones of a 75-foot marine reptile.

Colorado State Museum is just south of the Capitol at 200 14th Avenue, ☎ 303/892-2069. Four floors of exhibits depict the history and development of Colorado through dioramas, artifacts and illustrations. See cliff-dwelling pueblo people at Mesa Verde. The Baby Doe Tabor and Eisenhower exhibits are popular.

Denver Art Museum, at 100 West 14th Avenue, ☎ 303/640-2793, completed in 1971, is the largest art museum between Kansas City and Los Angeles. Works by Da Vinci, Rembrandt, Picasso and Renoir, among others, grace the museum. It also features pieces from the Orient, Europe, America (including American Indian cultures), the Pacific Islands and Africa. There is a museum shop and restaurant.

The Colorado State Capitol, ☎ 303/866-2604, stands exactly a mile above sea level; a plaque on the 15th step marks the spot that is exactly 5,280 feet (1,609 m) high. The dome is covered with 200 ounces of pure gold and there is a beautiful view from the rotunda of the entire Front Range, from Pikes Peak all the way north to the Wyoming border, a distance of over 150 miles (241 km). Free tours of the attractive rooms are given by appointment on weekdays.

The Museum of Western Art, 1727 Tremont Place, ☎ 303/296-1880, has the third largest collection of Western art in the nation, with classic Frederic Remington and Charles Russell paintings. It is all housed in a restored Victorian building that was once Denver's classiest bordello and gambling hall. Artists exhibited include Thomas Moran, Albert Bierstadt and Norman Rockwell. Highlights of the museum include an authentic #1 *Bronco Buster* bronze by Frederic Remington, one of the most famous sculptures in Western art, and Georgia O'Keeffe's *Cow's Skull on Red*.

Colorado Railroad Museum, 17155 West 44th Avenue, Route 58, ☎ 303/279-4591. To get here, you can use Interstate 70 to Exit 64 and then travel west on 44th Avenue. Or you can find your way to West

44th Avenue from Federal Boulevard. This museum always fascinates families. It is housed in a replica of an 1880 railway depot complete with old station and carts for the baggage, ancient benches for waiting, rusty water towers and so on. In all, visitors can roam some 12 acres of displays and inspect the old tracks, the various narrow-gauge locomotives and see many old pictures and papers.

Sports

FOOTBALL

By August, football can easily dominate the small talk in the Denver area. At this time the majority of football fans are turning their attention to five-time AFC (American Football Conference) champs, the Denver Broncos.

The Broncos' grip on the city may be best measured by the sellout crowds at **Mile-High Stadium** (it seats 76,000-plus). On any given Sunday cheers from hoarse throats and spirited waves roll through a sea of orange and blue. Indeed, some fans have been known to take Bronco-mania to new heights by painting their bodies and dyeing their hair in the official team colors – a true sign of devotion, or psychosis, depending on your point of view.

Mile-High Stadium is at 2755 West 17th Avenue. For information, ☎ 303/433-7466.

Top-drawer college football teams can be seen at several locations in the Front-Range area of Colorado. Visitors are limited only by the distance they are willing to drive to see a game.

Handiest to Denver, of course, is **Folsom Field**, home stadium of the University of Colorado's Buffaloes in Boulder, about 25 miles from Denver via I-25. You can also come by bus from downtown Denver. ☎ 303/492-8337.

BASKETBALL

When giants like LaFonso Ellis take to the basketball court and easily swish a three pointer to the delight of the crowd, you know you're watching the Denver Nuggets in their home court, **McNichols Arena**, 1635 Clay Street, ☎ 303/893-3865.

The Nuggets, who've set some precedents in willingness to search out and pay for outstanding players, give the hometown a show with fast-paced shoot outs against teams like the Portland Trailblazers and Utah Jazz. Tickets can usually be purchased before games.

College basketball involves two major teams, Boulder's University of Colorado, and Colorado State University in Fort Collins.

Be forewarned: In these venues the bleacher seating sometimes tests the endurance of fans and visitors. Bring a pillow for comfort! Tickets are available at the ticket offices of both institutions. University of Colorado, ☎ 303/492-8337. Colorado State University: ☎ 970/491-7267.

HOCKEY

The Colorado Avalanche won NHL's Stanley Cup playoffs in 1996. They play home games in McNichols Arena (see above, under *Basketball*). Unless the team takes a turn for the worse, tickets can be among the toughest in town to secure.

The University of Denver Pioneers, who helped their school rise to near-top rankings in total NCAA titles in a decade through their prowess on the ice, often provide a hard-fought match and a display of talent.

Home games for the Pioneers are played in the 5,000-seat **Denver University Arena**, about six miles from the heart of downtown Denver at East Jewell Avenue and South Gaylord Street, ☎ 303/871-2336. Here you can watch the teams of the University of Notre Dame, the University of St. Louis, Michigan State, Michigan Tech and others.

And for a sampling of the college atmosphere at the arena, check out the cheap seats, or "Creature Bleachers," as they're aptly called. In this section of student seating, beer and enthusiasm abound. Whereas in other parts of the arena a flying puck will cause a spectator to take cover, here it's cause to get up and get rowdy.

BASEBALL

After enduring more than 75 years of minor league baseball, the region was finally awarded a major league franchise, the Colorado Rockies, in 1993.

A beautiful new stadium, **Coors Field**, (20th and Blake Street) was built to accommodate the team, which annually draws more spectators than any other baseball team in the country. Go extra early, like five hours before game time, to secure cheap seats in the Rockpile, a section that draws colorful characters reminiscent of Wrigley's Field's "Bleacher Bums." Otherwise, there's a plethora of different priced tickets. The Rockies have sold every ticket to every game they've ever played. Plan far in advance for the dates you seek, if at all possible.

Due to Denver's high altitude, baseballs tend to travel farther; hence, Coors Field has earned a reputation as a hitter's ballpark. It's also an eater's ballpark, with plenty of opportunities to buy gourmet fare that transcends well beyond franks, brats and popcorn.

Order tickets by calling ☎ 800/388-ROCK or 303/ROCKIES.

FOR MORE INFORMATION

Contact the **Denver & Colorado Convention & Visitors Bureau**, 1555 California Street, Denver, CO 80202, ☎ 303/892-1112, for more information.

Adventures

On Foot

The **Beaver Brook Trail**, on Lookout Mountain, can be accessed from Denver by car via I-70 (take Lookout Mountain Exit). Drive past Buffalo Bill's Grave until you see the sign on your left. Varied flora, fauna and terrain. The trail can be icy in winter.

Belmar Park, at West Ohio and Wadsworth Boulevard, provides an hour's worth of foot trails through undulating wildflower and sedge meadows. Canada geese occupy an attractive lake here, and a small outdoor "museum" of old farm machinery adds a pastoral note to the landscape. Barns and sheds round out the picture. Good for runners and, in winter, cross-country skiers.

Soda Lakes, 13411 Morrison Road, is pleasant for walking sun-worshippers; there are few trees bordering these trails and you receive the brunt of the sun. The air is fresh, though, and the foothills make a pretty picture.

For tourists short on time, there is the **Willow Springs Trail**. Take Wadsworth Boulevard south to Belleview, follow the signs west toward the reddish foothills. Belleview turns into Highway 48 and leads to the peaceful Willow Springs Country Club. Proceed uphill through the club as far as you can go, park, and head for an open gate (motorized vehicles are banned beyond that point). The trail sets out past a whale-shaped rock and moves uphill through the meadows on an old wagon road. Leafy trees hug the little valley, and the birds sing as you tramp up hill and down dale. There are no cars or Highways in sight, and Denver's skyscrapers are far, far below you.

On Water

Denver and its immediate surroundings offer plenty to the action-minded water enthusiast. The season lasts from April to the beginning of October.

Cherry Creek Reservoir, 4201 South Parker Road and I-225, is part of a 4,000-acre state park. Especially in summer, the water surface here comes alive with sailboats, motorboats, and noisy jet skis; the slight hilliness makes the terrain interesting to bikers in summer and cross-country skiers in winter. Windsurfing and fishing are other options here. The water is a bit too muddy for swimmers.

Chatfield Reservoir, off the Chatfield Exit on South Wadsworth Boulevard, is larger and quieter than most lakes in the area. The marina (with boat ramp) sees waterskiers and sailboats of various sizes. There is even a model airplane launching area. Bring sandals; beaches are rocky.

Sloan's Lake, West 26th and Sheridan, is somewhat smaller and doesn't allow swimming, but you will see a lot of waterskiers.

Among other somewhat busier summer swimming pools and lakes are: **Aloha Beach Congress Park**, East 9th Avenue and University Boulevard; **Eisenhower Park**, East Dartmouth Avenue; **Columbus Park**, West 38th Avenue and Navajo Street; **Curtis Park**, 32nd and Curtis Streets; **North Jeffco Recreation District**, 9101 Ralston Road; and **Del Mar**, East 6th Avenue and Peoria Street.

FOR MORE INFORMATION

Contact the **Department of Natural Resources**, 1313 Sherman Street, Denver, CO 80203, ☎ 303/866-3437.

On Horseback

For those wanting to be a part of nature and partake of the true Western experience, horseback riding may be just the thing. Below are listed a few of the more reasonable local stables.

FOR MORE INFORMATION

Both **Hampden Farms**, 8440 West Hampden Ave, Lakewood, CO, ☎ 303/980-1949, and **Longview Stables**, 2400 East Exposition Ave, Aurora, ☎ 303/366-7892, offer English and Western riding lessons in indoor or outdoor arenas.

High Prairie Farms, 7522 Pinery Pkwy South, Parker, CO, ☎ 303/841-5550, has spacious, state-of-the-art facilities, including 11 arenas and an events center. Group lessons are available here.

In the Air

There are two ballooning companies eager to please should you want to float above it all for a while.

FOR MORE INFORMATION

Looney Balloons, Inc., PO Box 621166, Littleton, CO 80162. ☎ 303/979-9476.

The Life Cycle Balloon School, Ltd., 2540 South Steele St, Denver, CO 80210. ☎ 303/759-3907.

Eco-Travel & Cultural Excursions

The **Denver Performing Arts Complex**, at 15th and Curtis Street, ☎ 303/640-2862, is the second largest performing arts center in America. The complex is entered under an 80-foot-high, block-long glass arch that leads to nine theatres offering over 9,200 seats. Highlights of the center include the 2,800-seat **Buell Theatre**, home to top Broadway road shows such as *Phantom of the Opera*; **Boettcher Concert Hall**, the first symphony hall in-the-round in the nation; and the **Helen Bonfils Theatre Complex**, which has four theatres and the West's largest resident acting company. The complex also includes the world's first voice research laboratory, where scientists are studying methods to help actors and singers prolong the use of their voices.

☞ **Tattered Cover**, 2955 East 1st Avenue, ☎ 303/322-7727, is one of the most unusual bookstores anywhere. This huge establishment has four stories and stocks 500,000 titles. Tattered Cover also has its own European-style café, an international restaurant, a staff of 300, and a self-service newsstand. Customers can read all day and all evening while relaxing on the sofas, chaises, and settees scattered throughout the store. No one bothers you while you immerse yourself in the literature of adventure. Tattered Cover has a second location at the corner of 16th and Wynkoop, downtown, ☎ 303/436-1070.

FOR MORE INFORMATION

The Cultural Connection Trolley offers an unexpected bus connection between all the major sightseeing stops, including Victorian homes, assorted museums, a stroll around Larimer Square, an inspection of the renovated Denver Public Library and other points of interest. For more information, contact **Regional Transportation District**, 1600 Blake St, Denver, CO 80202-1399. ☎ 303/299-6000.

Gray Line, 5855 East 56th Ave, Denver, CO 80022. ☎ 303/289-2841, sells tours lasting two to five hours. They offer a special six-hour tour of the Denver Mountain Parks.

The Mile-High Adventure Club, 7373 South Alton Way, Englewood, CO 80112, ☎ 800/489-4888, takes visitors to explore the Rockies through "light" adventure. River running, horseback riding, hot-air ballooning, casino gambling and more can be arranged on easy day-trips from Denver.

BREW PUBS

With more brew pubs than any state in the nation, Denver practically invented the microbrew craze that is now sweeping the country. There's even a brew pub inside Coors Field, where the Rockies play. At these microbreweries, the brewery is on site and, in most cases, a visible part of the decor. LoDo contains many notable pubs. Among the best ones are the following.

Wynkoop Brewing Co., 1634 18th, ☎ 303/297-2700, was the first microbrewery in Colorado, established in 1987. Here you can sip eight types of beer at any given time, making Wynkoop the largest micro-brew producer in the nation. Pale ale, fruit beer, and chile beer are among the selections. Free tours available on Saturdays.

Breckenridge Brewery, 2220 Blake, ☎ 303/297-3664, also offers many styles of beer. You can buy their offerings by the case to take with you, or you can sample it all at an area set up with tables and booths and a standard bar atmosphere. This facility specializes in limited edition beers, such as the "Popus Visitus," available while the Pope was visiting Denver.

Rock Bottom Brewery, 1001 16th Street, ☎ 303/534-7616, emphasizes food as well as beer. You can dine on salmon while you sip. Rock Bottom usually offers an average of six beers at any one time. In the summertime, there is live entertainment on the patio.

FOR MORE INFORMATION

Call the microbreweries directly or contact the **Association of Brewers**, PO Box 1679, Boulder, CO 80306-1670, ☎ 303/447-0816.

Where To Stay & Eat

Accommodations

You could do worse than to spend a night in the Mile-High City, to sample its restaurants, go out on the town, and do some shopping before you take off for the mountains. Many people earmark a full day for Denver. It's the air travel gateway, and the best place to rent a car.

Hotel and motel rates vary, but you'll always pay less than you would in Chicago or New York City. Our accommodation listings are designed to suit all pocketbooks, including hotels for budgeteers.

The Brown Palace Hotel, 321 17th Street, ☎ 303/297-3111, dates back to 1892 and remains one of Denver's most historic yet up-to-date hotels. It offers an excellent location in the heart of the city, close to libraries, business offices, the financial district, art galleries, Denver

Mall, and restaurants. The "Brown" has not only fame in its favor but offers an unmatched ambiance, a prestige address, and understated elegance. Deluxe rates.

The Oxford, 1600 17th Street, ☎ 303/628-5400. This supremely renovated, historic building is downtown. A small grand hotel near Union Station. 82 rooms. Restaurant, bar, entertainment. Quiet and tasteful with many original touches. Deluxe.

Adams Mark Denver Hotel (formerly Radisson), 1550 Court Place, ☎ 303/893-3333. A large establishment downtown catering to Colorado's major conventions. The block-long second floor lobby is unusual. Five dining areas and a handsome cocktail lounge. Heated pools, saunas, TV, radios, barber, beauty shops, and drugstore. An airport bus is available. Underground parking. Upper stories yield views of the Rockies. Expensive.

Westin Hotel, Denver Tabor Center, 1672 Lawrence Street, ☎ 303/572-7213 (800/228-3000). Denver's luxurious 430-room, 19-story superhotel in downtown. Seventy shops, plus access to the mall. Suites and meeting facilities. Expensive.

Castle Marne, 1572 Race Street, ☎ 303/331-0621 or 800/92-MARNE, is a beautifully restored 1889 mansion in a prime downtown location, now operating as one of Denver's finest bed & breakfasts. Stone balconies and stained glass, ornate woodwork, original fireplaces and a four-story turret. Expensive.

Queen Anne Inn, 2147 Tremont Place, ☎ 303/396-6666 or 800/432-INNS, is another historic downtown bed & breakfast, even older than nearby Castle Marne, dating to 1879. Rooms come with piped-in chamber music and fresh cut flowers. Expensive.

Stouffer Renaissance Denver, 3801 Quebec, ☎ 303/399-7500, sits close to the old Stapleton International Airport. It's one of the newer and bigger ($15 million) investments in Denver's hotel world. The nine-story hotel has 404 guest rooms and suites, plus a good restaurant. There's also an indoor swimming pool and sauna. Two buses shuttle every 15 minutes between the new DIA airport and the hotel. Popular with winter vacationers. Ample free parking. Expensive.

Denver Marriott Hotel, I-25 at Hampden, ☎ 800/228-9290. Excellent location en route to Colorado Springs. All the modern amenities, 605 quality rooms, convention facilities, indoor-outdoor pool, restaurants. Recommended. Deluxe.

Embassy Suites-Southeast, 7525 E. Hampden Avenue, ☎ 303/696-6644. Offers not only huge rooms but free breakfast and complimentary early evening cocktail hour. Top-notch service and a quiet setting put this chain hotel a notch above some others. Conveniently located to shopping and good restaurants. Deluxe.

Executive Tower Hotel, 1405 Curtis Street, ☎ 303/571-0300. A downtown skyscraper hotel, popular with convention guests. Health and athletic club on premises. Ballroom. Restaurants. Expensive.

Regency Inn, 3900 Elati Street, I-25 at West 38th Avenue, ☎ 303/458-0808. A large hotel in north Denver, popular for conventions. Two pools, saunas, exercise rooms, barber and beauty shops, gourmet restaurant and cocktail lounge. Less expensive than the downtown hotels. Deluxe.

Sheraton Denver Tech Center, Tech Center, 12 miles southeast of downtown Denver, ☎ 303/779-1100. Built in 1980. 627 rooms, plus conference and banquet facilities. Deluxe.

The **Super 8 Motel**, 58th and Valley Highway, ☎ 303/296-3100, is a good choice for traveling families. The furniture and comfort are worth more than the price. Free parking. In midsummer all 100 units are teeming with tourists, so reserve ahead. Inexpensive.

Anchor Motel, at 2323 South Broadway, near Evans Avenue, ☎ 303/744-3281. The Denver shopping centers, Englewood and Littleton areas are easily reached from this location. South Broadway can't match the silence of the Colorado forests and there's lots of traffic outside your windows, but the rates are right. Reserve in advance. Inexpensive.

The Motel 6 on Highway 6 at 480 Wadsworth Boulevard, ☎ 303/232-4924, is the great motel bargain in Colorado. But unless you write or phone long beforehand you will find it near impossible to rent one of the 120 units. The reason is evident – bargain rates. Don't expect "grand hotel" treatment, however. Clean, nondescript, but modern rooms with TV and free local calls. Inexpensive.

Holiday Chalet, East Colfax at High Street, in East Denver, ☎ 303/321-9975. Small apartment hotel. Moderate.

Haus Berlin, 1651 Emerson, ☎ 303/837-9527, is listed on the National Register of Historic Places. Good Capitol Hill location. Bed & breakfast with four rooms. Moderate.

FOR MORE INFORMATION

For more information on Denver's accommodations, contact the **Denver Metro Convention & Visitors Bureau**, 1555 California, Suite 300, ☎ 303/892-1112.

Restaurants

The restaurants of Denver and its large metropolian area are often underestimated. A tourist can find every type of fare from fancy haute cuisine to the simplest cowboy meals. Foreign restaurants proliferate, Western steak houses are abundant and you can get excellent mountain trout practically everywhere. Prices range from a few dollars for a full homestyle meal to $25 per person for an entrée. Denver's restaurants are more informal than those in eastern cities. At a good restaurant a man needs no tie and rarely even a jacket; women are welcome in slacks.

At the peak of the tourist traffic during summer, reservations become essential, especially for better dining. Dinner business also becomes brisk on Fridays and Saturdays.

FOR BIG SPENDERS

Wellshire Inn, 3333 South Colorado Boulevard, ☎ 303/759-3333. Elaborate international-Polynesian menu served against a baronial manor backdrop. Grandiose Victorian setting. Overlooks golf course. Brunch, lunch and dinner. Specialties include rack of lamb, spinach salad, fresh fish, vegetables, chowchow, and chicken with almonds. Outdoor service in summer. Well worth the price.

The Palace Arms, at the famed Brown Palace Hotel, 321 17th Street, ☎ 303/297-3111, was General/President Eisenhower's favorite – especially the rack of lamb. Filet mignon, duck and other specialties. Expensive but no longer dressy.

Ellyngton's, at the same hotel, draws wealthy business people, lawyers, and politicians for lunch or brunch. Reservations a must. Closed for dinner.

The Manor House, 14432 West Ken-Caryl Avenue, ☎ 303/973-8064. Stately, historic mansion. Hard to find and hard to forget for its old-fashioned elegance and elaborate American meals, which were designed for the era before cholesterol awareness.

McCormick's Fish House & Bar, 1659 Wazee, ☎ 303/825-1107, is a classy dining area at the historic Oxford Hotel. Three meals a day, all interesting, especially the fish dishes.

Strings, Casual Contemporary Cuisine, 1700 Humboldt, ☎ 303/831-7310. Serves lunch and dinner. Charisma and local reputation are enhanced by the chef taking food seriously. Specialties include roast lamb, veal chops, duck breast, fresh fish and more.

Morton's, 1712 Wynkoop, ☎ 303/825-3353, serves up some of the largest pieces of beef you'll find. Everything is big here, including the chops, lobsters, salads, potatoes and desserts. Their kitchen is ultra-attentive to detail, so expect your meat to be cooked just the way you requested. Bring your appetite and be prepared to pay through the nose for a meal not likely to be forgotten.

Augusta Room, Westin Hotel, 1672 Lawrence Street, ☎ 303/572-7222, offers dramatic Denver downtown views and classic interior architecture with lunches and dinners to match. House specials include lobster, veal, and fresh salmon. Elaborate wine list. Be sure that the tab fits your expense account budget. The Augusta Room is *expensive.*

The Normandy Restaurant at East Colfax and Madison Street, ☎ 303/321-3311, stands for checkered red tablecloths, smiling waitresses, and a nice French Provincial menu that features tender veal dishes, an excellent coq au vin, French sweetbreads, a bouillabaisse and dozens of other tasty items. (For appetizers, try the homemade pâté maison or the hot snails.) Noted wine cellar and house wines. Expensive.

AMERICAN & WESTERN

Wuthering Heights, 7785 West Colfax, ☎ 303/238-7774, a block west of Wadsworth on westside. Old World atmosphere created by armored knights, red lamps, carpets, fireplaces, and pewter. Classic American menu, and near-perfection in the kitchen. Famous for combinations such as lobster and prime rib or crab legs and steaks. Large selection of entrées and good house wines. Recommended despite lack of lighting. Deluxe.

The Denver Buffalo Company, 1109 Lincoln Street, ☎ 303/832-0880. Buffalo served in the Buffalo Room from the restaurant's own ranch. Other entrées available, too. A Denver institution. Good location on edge of downtown Denver. Western decor. Expensive.

A very hungry traveler will find solace at the **Northwoods Inn**, 6115 South Santa Fe Drive, ☎ 303/794-2112, with an old Lumber Camp atmosphere. Enormous portions at moderate prices. Large succulent steaks. Remember: Some of the best beef originates in Colorado. Good value.

Lazy H Chuckwagon, 18301 West Colfax Avenue, Building L, Heritage Square, Golden, ☎ 303/278-1938. BBQ beef or chicken breast with cowboy beans, baked potatoes plus country Western music, songs, even poetry. Well worth the drive to the Denver foothills.

ITALIAN & MEXICAN

Josephinas, 1433 Larimer, ☎ 303/623-0166. Roaring Twenties ambiance on Larimer Square. Excellent Italian lasagna, spaghetti, pizza, and chicken. Bar. Historic building. Moderate.

Casa Bonita, West Colfax at JCRS Center, ☎ 303/232-5115. Mexican food in a multi-tiered restaurant decorated with murals that tell the history of Mexico. Busy and entertaining. Table service in the evening. Moderate.

Old Spaghetti Factory, at 1215 18th Avenue, ☎ 303/265-1864, is a downtown pasta outpost in the old Denver Cable Car Company building. Lively and crowded. Enormous portions. Great value.

El Noa Noa, 722 Santa Fe Dr., ☎ 303/623-9968, is the true Mexican restaurant with all the expected *platos*, Mexican beers, even guitars being strummed and, on occasion, flamenco dancers. Slow service. Outdoor patio in summer. Inexpensive.

Dino's Italian Food, 10040 West Colfax at Kipling, ☎ 303/238-7393. Great home-made lasagna, manicotti, rigatoni, and ravioli. Long tradition. Recommended. Good value.

Blue Bonnet, 475 South Broadway, ☎ 5303/778-0147. Unpretentious neighborhood café and bar with Mexican food. Watch out for the green chile; it's hot. Inexpensive.

CHINESE, VIETNAMESE & THAI

Imperial, 431 South Broadway, ☎ 303/698-2800, is being emulated by competitors for its Oriental decor, versatility (Mandarin, Hunan, Cantonese) and originality. Efficient and expensive.

The Empress Seafood Restaurant, 2825 West Alameda Avenue, ☎ 303/922-2822, has long been adopted by the local Chinese community for its appetizer carts and (bewildering) variety of dishes. Try the duck. Expensive.

Mr. Panda Gourmet Buffet, 6206 West Alameda, features 50 items, self-service style, hot and cold, sweet or sour, salty or in a pepper sauce. Eat all you want. Surprisingly low price.

Red Coral, 1591 South Colorado Boulevard, ☎ 303/758-7610, is the best bargain among Mandarin restaurants, giving the largest portions of consistently good quality. Enormous menu; good value.

T-Wa, 5555 S. Federal Boulevard, ☎ 303/922-4584, specializes in the fresh ingredients and lighter fare for which Vietnamese cuisine has become well-known. This family spot, offering a wide variety of seafood, chicken, pork and beef dishes, is modestly decorated and moderately priced.

INDIAN

India's Restaurant, 3333 S. Tamarac, ☎ 303/755-4284, is unobtrusively set in the rear of a shopping center. Once inside, decor from the Moghul era takes over. Delicate spices permeate the vegetarian and meat dishes that are carefully prepared at lunch and dinner. Expensive.

Delhi Darber, 1514 Blake Street, ☎ 303/595-0680, is the city's original Indian restaurant and, for many, still the favorite. Lunch hour buffets provide a chance to sample the myriad tastes; they may include tandoori-cooked dishes, lentil entrées or shrimp and chicken specialties. Dinner features larger versions of the lunchtime favorites. The sweet and unusual Indian tea perfectly complements the delicate spices. There is an ample wine list. Moderate.

INEXPENSIVE/GOOD VALUE

White Fence Farm, 6263 West Jewell Avenue, ☎ 303/935-5945, is between South Sheridan and Wadsworth Boulevards. Nestled in a meadow en route to the mountains. (Car needed.) Great American food with a Southern accent – ham, turkey, chicken, and ribs, prepared Colonial style and served by girls in historic dress. Freshly baked goods. Liquor. Excellent food. Mostly local clientele. Dinner only. Inexpensive.

Country Harvest, Villa Italia Shopping Center, West Alameda, ☎ 303/937-3730. Buffet-style for gluttons or the hurried. Self-service; you're usually in and out in 30 minutes. Satisfying food but no liquor. Open seven days a week for lunch and dinner plus Sunday brunch. Inexpensive.

Boston Market, 1100 South Colorado Boulevard, ☎ 303/759-9575, is the reborn "Boston Rotisserie Chicken," among the best in town.

Wonderful vegetables and potatoes. No beer or wine, but the food is good and cheap.

Camping

Denver has several commercial campgrounds and RV parks that cater especially to those looking for an outdoor experience with a few added luxuries.

Barr Lake Campground, 17180 East 176th, Brighton, is one of the closest campgrounds to Denver. Here there are full hook-ups, laundry and showers. What's more, it is just minutes from **Barr Lake State Park & Bird Sanctuary**. Tenters welcome. For more information, ☎ 303/659-6180.

Chief Hosa Lodge and Campground is Denver's closest mountain campground, reached via Exit 253, off I-70, ☎ 303/526-0364. This 56-acre campground has 150 spaces among the shade of tall pines. Additionally, such amenities as hot showers, a pool and an athletic area offering volleyball and horseshoes are available.

Denver North Campground at 1600 North Washington, ☎ 303/452-4120, offers camper cabins as well as pull-through sites.

FOR MORE INFORMATION

USDA Forest Service (national forests), PO Box 25127, Lakewood, CO 80225, ☎ 303/275-5350.

National Park Service (national parks), 12795 West Alameda Pkwy, Lakewood, CO 80225, ☎ 303/969-2000.

Colorado Division of Parks and Outdoor Recreation (state parks), 1313 Sherman St, #618, Denver, CO 80203, ☎ 303/866-3437.

Colorado Association of Campgrounds, Cabins & Lodges (privately owned campground information), 5101 Pennsylvania Ave, Boulder, CO 80303, ☎ 303/499-9343.

Just Beyond Denver

Boulder, Golden,
Idaho Springs & Central City

The elevator zooms up one of Denver's many new skyscrapers. Step off on the 40th floor. The hall window faces west yielding Denver's famous view: wave after wave of mountain peaks, the highest crests flecked with eternal snow under the blue Colorado sky.

You get a sense of Denver's surroundings when you have lunch at the Westin Hotel. From 18 stories up, you see those vast Rocky Mountains beckoning all adventure sports enthusiasts.

Highways lead west to the great outdoors: Highway 6 to Golden and Lookout Mountain, Central City and Idaho Springs; Highway 36 to Boulder; Highway 285 to Morrison. This remarkable network of roads can be seen from many hiking trails.

The traffic is impressive when you consider the history of the area. These environs were still wilderness a few hundred years ago, a home for buffalo herds, mountain lions and deer or elk.

Colorado's earliest European influence came with the Spaniards, who established outposts north of Mexico as early as the 1650s. Tree rings tested from old mineshaft timbers suggest dates from the early 1700s.

The Spanish left their language throughout Colorado. Streets are named *Mariposa* (butterfly) and *Tejon*, pronounced "tay-HOHN," (badger). There are also the San Juan and Sangre de Cristo mountain ranges.

After 1800, the pace picked up in Colorado, especially in the foothills and higher up, in Central City and Black Hawk.

"Go West, Young Man, Go West!" wrote famed *New York Tribune* editor Horace Greeley. And go west they did, lured by tales of golden fortune in the Rocky Mountains. Greeley himself undertook the perilous journey in May of 1859, enduring a stagecoach accident and

Just Beyond Denver

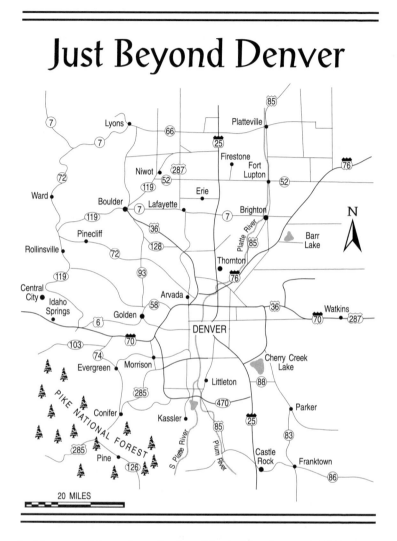

primitive conditions for a firsthand look. He observed 5,000 miners furiously working claims in Central City and reported to his readers, "We have this day personally visited nearly all mines and have seen the gold plainly visible in the riffles of nearly every sluice, in nearly every plain."

This article, printed in an extra of the fledging *Rocky Mountain News*, was picked up by almost every newspaper in the United States. The future of Colorado was secure. A wave of emigrants hit the trail towards the "richest square mile on earth."

Camps grew overnight, as 20,000 "boomers" spread out over the mountains, staking claims in Boulder, South Park and other sites. Shopkeepers, barbers, carpenters, bankers, teachers and preachers, many of them industrious German immigrants, brought the trappings of civilization. But life was not easy in the 1870s. Houses were log or plank, with dirt floors and no windows. Gambling halls, saloons and a red light district prospered, while desperados terrorized the community, and fires and floods raged.

The Union Pacific Railroad bypassed the area, much to the consternation of her proud citizens. Governor John Evans raised money to finance the Pacific Railroad. Many people turned out to watch Evans drive the symbolic last spike. Unfortunately, a silver spike donated by miners for the occasion had been pawned by its bearer in a drunken spree. An ordinary iron spike was pushed into Evans' hand with the words, "Hurry up and drive it – no one will know." A new era began as the iron horse made the area truly accessible.

Land speculators, investors and adventurers poured into the still-untamed prairie. Horace Greeley returned for an update, poet Walt Whitman and President Ulysses S. Grant visited, and asthmatic patients came to the dry climate for the "camp cure." A large slice of humanity, from Chinese and Irish mountain men to rich European tourists, mingled in the streets.

Isabella Bird, a proper but plucky Englishwoman, traveled through Colorado in 1873 on her horse Birdie. She noted in her journal, "It is a busy place, the *entrepot* and distributing point for an immense district, with good shops, some factories, fair hotels, and the usual deformities and refinements of civilization."

Miners came down from the hills periodically to blow their hardearned wages on booze, gambling and loose women. Crime flourished and Central City, among other towns, earned a widespread reputation for lawlessness. Police and city officials were paid off regularly to ignore gambling and prostitution. Bordellos or "parlour houses" were big business, and the best madams became very wealthy. Nowadays, prostitutes and their johns are arrested.

Getting Around

Because of Colorado's burgeoning Highway system, you can reach the attractions on the outskirts of Denver via many routes; some offer more scenic views, some just the Highway.

Interstate 25 is the best take-off point. To reach Boulder, drive I-25 north to the Boulder Turnpike (Highway 36).

All other towns are more of a straight shot from I-70. Take I-25 north to the I-70 Exit. Proceed west on I-70. You will shortly run into Morrison. Next will be Golden. Both Idaho Springs and Central City can be accessed from Golden by taking a Highway that follows the old Colorado Central Railroad bed, Highway 6. Past Golden on I-70 is the El Rancho Exit. Take this exit to Highway 74, which will lead to the pretty mountain town of Evergreen.

Touring

Boulder

Boulder, Colorado, is the pleasing result of blending Western down-to-earth life with a sophisticated and academic culture. The University of Colorado was Boulder's growth catalyst, and the city's location drew interesting people from many different backgrounds.

Its location 22 miles northwest of Denver on US 36 means that you can get there in about half an hour on the Boulder Turnpike. The Flatirons, huge slabs of reddish flagstone lifted by the same geological forces that created the Rocky Mountains, tower high above the city and have become its trademark. The Flatirons challenge rock climbers all summer despite the hot stone.

Hiking trails invite you into the wilderness, and nearby trout streams and lakes lure anglers into these hills. Boulder draws its sweet drinking water from Arapahoe Glacier on the Continental Divide, 28 miles west of town.

As you approach Boulder, you will see the much-photographed reddish sandstone formations known as the Flatirons, the abrupt border between the plains and the Rocky Mountains. The Flatirons are also a gateway to webs of popular hiking trails in the hills that rise behind the college town. Rock climbers favor these rocks.

CULTURE

Macky Auditorium, on the University campus, hosts performances by the Boulder Philharmonic, the College of Music, visiting musicians participating in the Artists Series, and concerts by nationally known groups. For information, contact Campus Box 285, University of Colorado, 80309. ☎ 303/492-8424.

The University Drama and Dance Departments offers performances year-round. Write to them at Campus Box 261, 80309. ☎ 303/492-7355.

The mood of Boulder can be felt on the **Pearl Street Pedestrian Mall.** Locals and visitors wile away the day and browse in boutiques, dine on an outdoor patio or simply hang out and people-watch (always an interesting prospect in Boulder). As you stroll along on warm evenings, you will encounter musicians, jugglers and other street performers – some quite talented. The outdoor, brick-paved mall was first closed to car traffic in the mid-seventies and has since become one of the nation's finest examples of a thriving pedestrian mall.

More ambitious? **The Walking Tours of Boulder** is a self-guided stroll with an accompanying pamphlet outlining places of note. Contact the **Bureau of Conference Services and Cultural Affairs**, 1001 Canyon, 80302. ☎ 303/442-1109.

Scientists will be interested in the **National Center for Atmospheric Research**, 1850 Table Mesa Drive, ☎ 303/497-1000. Tours of this southwest Boulder facility are offered Monday-Saturday. Brochures, exhibits, and trail maps for the center's nature preserve are available.

BOULDER FESTIVALS

Mid-June through July sees the yearly **Colorado Music Festival** in Boulder. Visiting performers and composers lend their talents and energy to the celebration. You will need reservations. Write to the Boulder Festival, 1245 Pearl, Boulder, CO 80302 for details. ☎ 303/449-2413.

Boulder's tree-lined campus is worth a visit for the **Colorado Shakespeare Festival** each summer. Three Shakespeare plays are performed in repertory from mid-July through mid-August. Actors are chosen from national auditions and quality is high. Write University of Colorado Department of Theater & Dance, Campus Box 261, 80309, ☎ 303/492-7355.

FOR MORE INFORMATION

The Boulder Chamber of Commerce, 1001 Canyon Blvd., Boulder, CO 80303, ☎ 303/442-1044.

US Forest Service. Boulder Ranger District, 2995 Baseline Rd., Room 110, Boulder, CO 80303, ☎ 303/444-6600.

Red Rocks & Morrison

More than 100 million years ago, the area surrounding Red Rocks bordered the Western Interior Seaway, a vast inland sea that covered most of Colorado and Kansas. The seaway gradually receded, preserving dinosaur tracks in the gray shale where only mud used to lie. Today, clues of the predators who once roamed the area can be seen from the road. Fish scales are found within the sandstone.

RED ROCKS AMPHITHEATRE

Red Rocks Amphitheatre is one of the unforgettable places in Colorado and an acoustic and geologic wonder.

Towering walls of 400-foot-high red sandstone shoot up from a modern stage and provide nearly perfect acoustics for the artists who perform there and up to 10,000 lucky fans.

From the Beatles to Bruce Springsteen, world-class orchestras to opera stars, 8,000-seat Red Rocks has hosted its share of famous names. It has seen a virtual who's who of the music industry, from the most mundane to Grateful Dead or Jessye Norman singing Wagner.

Red Rocks is about 15 miles west of Denver, near the town of Morrison. The drive there is an easy 30 minutes via West Alameda and Alameda Parkway. An alternate route uses Highway 285 to CO 470.

RED ROCKS PARK & DINOSAUR RIDGE

Red Rocks Park is just 10 miles from the cozy little community of Morrison, with its antique stores and cafés. And Morrison shouldn't be missed by adventure-bound folks in search of sights. Consider: **Dinosaur Ridge**, 16831 W Alameda Pkwy, Morrison, CO 80401, ☎ 303/697-3466. What looks like a run-of-the-mill hill from the Highway is, on closer inspection, a world-renowned outdoor paleontologi-cal museum – a dino delight – for those so inclined.

Dinosaur Ridge contains more than 100 iguanodon and ostrich-like dinosaur tracks that were discovered in 1937 when Alameda Parkway was being constructed over the ridge. But this is not the area's only connection with dinosaurs. In 1877, alosaurus, brontosaurus and the world's first stegosaurus bones were discovered right here. These startling findings right outside the sleepy little town of Morrison were responsible for the subsequent rush of paleontologists to the West.

Visitors can walk the two-mile round-trip trail and read the interpre-tive signs. On Open Ridge days, Alameda is closed to traffic and the Friends of Dinosaur Ridge, a nonprofit group dedicated to education about the ridge, conducts tours. Either way, it is a fascinating walk through a Jurassic Park of sorts.

MORRISON NATURAL HISTORY MUSEUM

The Morrison Natural History Museum, 501 Highway 8, ☎ 303/697-1873, is a natural outgrowth of the area's rich paleontological past.

The museum concentrates mostly on explaining the discoveries that have been made in the Morrison area. However, there is also informa-tion on the more recent major dinosaur findings in New Mexico and Utah.

The museum has many attributes of big natural history museums, with professional exhibits and roaming staff to answer questions. Unlike many of its larger counterparts, this museum is not stuffy. This casual facility rewards curiosity and encourages discovery: signs read, "Please Touch!"

The museum is full of other unexpected treats. One added bonus is the display of the Morrison stegosaurus bone, where you can work on the actual stegosaurus bone found in the area in 1877. Like real paleontologists, visitors don goggles and break sandstone into fila-ments to expose the fossil. What's more, you can even take a little sample of your learning home. In addition to the usual commemora-tive t-shirts, the Morrison Natural History Museum has iguanodon tracks and small fossil casts for sale.

This museum is neither big or fancy, but it definitely has its rewards.

Golden & Lookout Mountain

The air above Lookout Mountain sparkles. You get here via Highway 6; turn left on SR 68 and head uphill.

As you drive up to Lookout Mountain, you may see an unexpected sight: a hang glider circling above calmly, quietly like an eagle. Stop the car and you'll learn that this 7,000-foot mountain is the gateway for these daredevils. Do they belong to a club or organization? Apparently not. They're simply individuals who enjoy paragliding.

SITES & ACTIVITIES

From curvy SR 68, you also reach the six-mile **Beaver Brook Trail,** which crosses a variety of rocks, scree, and sand. It was partially built by the Colorado Mountain Club (see address at end of this section). The trail's charm is the meadows on both sides, with flora galore, in a myriad of colors, including lavender, crimson, blue, bright white, butter yellow, and pink. The first sign of spring brings forth a rush of Easter daisies, mountain marigolds, wild sweetpeas, fairy trumpets, pink rock hill phlox and others in many hues. The trail is also home for a variety of conifers, aspen trees, bushes and ferns.

Once on Lookout Mountain you may wish to use I-70 and briefly visit the **Mother Cabrini Shrine**. There is no charge to visit the little chapel, devoted to Saint Francis Xavier Cabrini. The setting includes a large number of fields, surrounding forests and quite a few steps that will make devout walkers happy, though the site hardly qualifies as an adventurous one.

For a taste of a small-scale western theme park, and one less adventurous than either of Denver's bigger amusement parks – Elitch's or Lakeside – consider a trip to **Heritage Square** in the Golden area, just one mile west of the intersection of US 6 and 40. The rustic artisan and entertainment village was built on the 1860 townsite of Apex, another mining boomtown. Metalsmiths, jewelers, candymakers, and more make and sell their wares. Horseback rides, a narrow-gauge train trip, and a large melodrama theater will keep you busy in this town of tree-lined, lamplighted streets. Plenty of free parking.

Seekers of unusual action will spot Heritage Square's **Alpine Slide**, where you race downhill toboggan-style with brakes. Or perhaps you'd like to bungee jump. Here it's safe. The tower is permanent and the employees are well trained.

For more information, contact Heritage Square, Golden CO 80401, ☎ 303/279-2789.

The biggest attraction in Golden is synonymous with Colorado in the minds of many travelers – the **Coors Brewery**, 13th and Ford Streets, 80401, ☎ 303/277-BEER. Each year more than 300,000 visitors take the 30-minute tour of the world's largest brewery, which ends with a free glass of brew.

CULTURE

Other points of interest in Golden include the following:

Foothills Art Center, 809 15th Street, 80401, ☎ 303/279-3922. Originally a Presbyterian church built in 1892, the center now houses regional arts and crafts. Open Monday-Saturday, 9-4.

Colorado School of Mines' Geologic Museum is nearby at 16th and Maple. The 1940 structure displays mineral ore, fossils, mining equipment, meteorites, and even a replica of an old gold mine. The museum's hours are 9-4, Monday-Saturday, Sunday 1-4. ☎ 303/273-3823. Free.

The Colorado Railroad Museum, at 17155 W. 44th Avenue, has an 1880s-style depot, historical exhibits, old narrow-gauge locomotives, railroad and trolley cars. Hours are 9-5 daily. ☎ 303/279-4591.

Time permitting, you could also ascend SR 68 from Golden for an excellent view of the town and its famous brewery. Some people conquer the Highway on their mountain bikes. Shortly, you reach the **Lookout Mountain Nature Center**, 910 Colorow Road, Golden, 80401, ☎ 303/526-0594. The displays of stuffed birds and various Colorado dried plants are of special interest to children. The center is open Tuesday through Sunday, 10AM to 4PM (no charge). Incidentally, you can also get to this nature museum on foot via the Beaver Brook Trail (see above). After the one-hour hike, you'll appreciate the Nature Center's water cooler.

In the same general vicinity, atop Lookout Mountain you'll see the signs for the **Buffalo Bill Memorial Museum**, Golden CO 80401, ☎ 303/ 279-1584. Located just a few feet from his grave site high on top of Lookout Mountain, overlooking the plains of Denver and eastern Colorado, the museum follows Cody's life from his early childhood to his death in Denver in 1917.

Col. William F. Cody was a superstar. From 1883 to 1913, he and his show, *Buffalo Bill's Wild West – A Dramatic Exposition of Life on the*

Plains, toured the globe, performing in over a thousand cities in a dozen different nations.

At its height, the show made more than a million dollars a year in profit, played before the crowned heads of Europe, criss-crossed America in a special train of 52 box cars (10 more than the great Barnum and Bailey Circus), featured the third largest buffalo herd in existence and employed over 640 cowboys, Indians, vaqueros and rough riders.

It is estimated that over 25 million words were written about Cody during his lifetime, including 557 dime novels. His face was plastered on hundreds of thousands of posters, so much so that even today his silver hair and distinctive goatee are more recognizable than the features of the presidents, kings and generals who frequently honored him.

To many he was a living legend, a Pony Express rider, cavalry scout, Medal of Honor winner and buffalo hunter; a tall, handsome, soft-spoken man who was the living embodi ment of all the glory and romance the West had to offer. The history, the legends and the myths about this remarkable man come to life at the Buffalo Bill Memorial Museum. It has an outstanding collection of posters and memorabilia from Buffalo Bill's Wild West, including exhibits on the women of the Wild West such as Annie Oakley, Goldie Griffith and Lulu Parr. Some of Cody's elaborate costumes, saddles and guns are on exhibit, as well as original paintings of the famous scout.

From the museum, it's a two-minute walk through Colorado blue spruce trees to the top of the mountain where Buffalo Bill was buried in 1917. Over 25,000 people turned out for the funeral procession, the largest in Colorado's history.

From the grave site, there are panoramic views of the plains to the east, and the snow-capped Rockies to the west, a fitting resting spot for the man President Theodore Roosevelt called "an American of Americans."

FOR MORE INFORMATION

Golden Chamber of Commerce. 507 14th St., Golden, CO 80401. ☎ 303/279-3113.

Idaho Springs

Stroll along Idaho Springs' short main street. Step into a leather shop selling beaver hats or a little rock store that also sells gems and beads. Explore Idaho Springs' old gold mines. **The Mount Evans Highway** leads from downtown Idaho Springs to the top of North America's highest automobile road atop 14,264-foot-high Mount Evans. Mountain goats and bighorn sheep graze here. Although the road is crowded on summer weekends due to its close proximity to Denver, it is far less so than its more famous counterpart to the south, Pike's Peak, which can be seen from here. The surrounding Mount Evans Wilderness Area offers thousands of acres for hiking, camping, fishing and horseback riding in summer, cross-country ski trails in winter. The last 10 miles or so of the road are open to automobiles only season ally; heavy snow closes the road much of the year.

Near Idaho Springs, there is a patch of eternal snow which, while not a real glacier, attracts summer skiers. **St. Mary's Glacier** can be climbed with ease even by flatlanders and you require no special equipment except good boots. Also make a note of a well-regarded horseback operation in the Idaho Springs area: **Glacier Mountain Adventures**, Glacier Road, Idaho Springs, 80452, ☎ 800/555-3581. Trips follow a historical trail, departing from Glacier Station in the old mining district of Alice CO. The trail goes from gold mine to gold mine until it ends on Yankee Hill. You ride on trails once walked by prospectors and along the way stop for gold and silver ore samples, pictures and perhaps get a glimpse of the eagles soaring overhead. You may see deer and elk grazing through the delicate flowered tundra, fragrant forests of spruce, colorful aspens, or 1,000-year-old bristlecone pines which cover the mountain. You can also opt for a one- or two-hour ride.

At the **Phoenix Mine**, PO Box 3236, Idaho Springs, 80452, ☎ 303/567-0422, you can try your hand at the craze that brought thousands of men to Colorado back in the 1800s, gold panning. Here you will see real miners push gold and silver ore from the mine in rail carts. Take the guided tour and dig your own gold ore sample. At this mine, they even let you keep what you find.

FOR MORE INFORMATION

For more information, call the **Idaho Springs Info Center**, ☎ 303/567-4382.

Central City

From Idaho Springs, traffic signs invite you to Central City via CO 119, a trip of scarcely more than half an hour. A lot of tourists flock to this historical town, especially in summer when the opera is in session. But you see busloads of people heading up to Central City in fall and winter as well. The reason? Gambling. Some folks here call it the ultimate adventure and you're likely to see them lose their monthly paycheck or gamble away a Social Security check.

GAMBLING

The excitement of slot machines, poker and blackjack returned to Colorado's high country in October 1991 when limited-stakes casino gambling was once again legalized for the historic mining villages of Central City and Black Hawk.

When gambling was legalized through a state-wide referendum, no one anticipated the activity would become so popular. Original predictions guessed that a few casinos would open, but that it would take a half-dozen years before any large number of gaming devices were located in the towns and that most of the gaming would be confined to a slot machine or two in gift shops and saloons.

Instead, a boom that rivaled the original Gold Rush was started. By July of 1992, just 10 months after gambling was legalized, Central City and Black Hawk boasted a total of 26 casinos with over 3,100 slot machines and 90 blackjack and poker tables.

To be sure, not everyone is enamored with Central City. Parking space is difficult to find and the access roads are too narrow. The casinos themselves are claustrophobic, hectic, noisy and full of cigarette smokers. And, while do you hear the clatter of a 25¢ slot machine surrendering a few dollars, few win any money. (If you must gamble, you'd be wise to pocket your small winnings and get out for a mountain walk instead.)

HISTORY

Representing an important period of Colorado history, Central City dates back to May 1859 when John Gregory staked his claim to the first gold lode found in the Rockies. A reputed half-billion dollars of precious minerals were taken from the ground.

On December 15, 1872, the first train from Denver rolled into **Black Hawk** and six years later the rail line was extended into Central City. The railroad was a great success, although Isabella Bird complained in her 1875 book, *A Lady's Life in the Rocky Mountains*, that she had never seen "such churlishness and incivility as in the officials of that railroad." The train traveled up a grade that rose 200 feet per mile through spectacular Clear Creek Canyon with thousand-foot black rock walls rising on either side. Today, Highway 6 follows the same route and you can still see some of the old railroad bed as it cuts through the rock walls along rushing Clear Creek.

Statehood in 1876 was greeted with wild celebrations in Central City. Progress soon followed in the form of horse-drawn streetcars, gas lighting, telephone service, home mail delivery, and a fire department. Mining fever swept Colorado once again in 1877 when various sites poured forth their silver lode and many of the new "Silver Kings" sank their fortunes into local real estate.

In 1893 silver prices dropped and fortunes were lost in mountain towns like Central City and Black Hawk. Hundreds of homeless people camped along the banks of the South Platte River. True to form, Colorado gold saved the day. Central City area has long been a National Historic Landmark of the Department of the Interior and the National Park Service. Much of its colorful history revolves around the Opera House and the Teller House.

The **Opera House**, restored and re-opened in 1932, is widely known as a gem of a theater and as the scene of classic operas and hit plays, starring leading singers of the Metropolitan, the New York City Center, and top actors from Broadway and Hollywood. Seating at the Opera House is tight. Designers hesitate to add more seats for fear of changing the acoustics. The neighboring **Teller House** first opened over 100 years ago as a luxury hotel when the town consisted mainly of tents and wagons. Today, the rooms are still furnished with authentic period pieces.

Central City and Black Hawk are one mile apart, with frequent free shuttles running between them. They are 34 miles west of Denver.

FOR MORE INFORMATION

Central City Opera House Association, 621 17th St., Suite 1601, Denver, CO 80293. ☎ 303/292-6500.

Visitor Information Central City, PO Box 249, Central City, CO 80427. ☎ 800/542-2999.

Adventures

On Foot

BOULDER

The hiking and backpacking terrain west of Boulder offers epic opportunities for mountain travel on a variety of public grounds operated by various agencies. These include the excellent and extensive holdings of the **City of Boulder, Mountain Parks**, 9th and Baseline, 80302, ☎ 303/441-3405. Public lands in the Roosevelt National Forest and the Indian Peaks Wilderness Area are administered by the **Boulder Ranger District Office**, 2995 Baseline Road, 80303, ☎ 303/444-6600.

In addition to hiking trails, the Boulder area is also well-known throughout the world for the rock climbing walls found in nearby Eldorado Canyon.

For starters, the following are several easy hiking trails:

The Mesa Trail, one of Colorado's most pleasant, can be quickly reached by car. From Denver, drive the Boulder Turnpike (#36) until you get to the Superior Exit; Highway 170 will take you toward Eldorado Springs. Slow down until you notice the picnic tables and a small parking area on the right. The Mesa Trail is well marked. You cross a little bridge and soon zigzag through a landscape of sumac bushes, ferns, and sedges. The uphills are gentle enough, leading you into impressive pine forests, with glades to view the Flatiron citadels. (Here you see climbers on summer weekends.) The trail winds up in Boulder's Chautauqua Park. Many people opt to start their hike here and walk the route in reverse.

The seven winding, wooded miles of the **Boulder Creek Path** make their way across town from Eben G. Fine Park, at the base of Boulder Canyon, to 55th Street on the east side of town. There are underpasses at each intersection so, whether you're walking, biking, running or rollerblading your way across town, you need not worry about car traffic. Along the way, you will find xeriscape gardens, a children's fishing pond, and a fish observatory. The trail follows the creek west of town along a beautiful mile-long stretch of Boulder Canyon. Seven more miles up the canyon are the picturesque Boulder Falls. If you are interested in renting rollerblades or bicycles, inquire at **University Bicycles**, 839 Pearl St., ☎ 303/444-4196.

Boulder is an extremely health-conscious town; joggers and bicyclists may be seen pumping away even in the worst of weather. Thanks to the rocky terrain, serious rock climbing is B-I-G in Boulder. **Bob Culp**, Box D, Eldorado Springs, 80025, ☎ 303/499-1185, is a reliable instructors. Culp features half-day or full-day courses, plus private guiding.

MORRISON & GOLDEN

Golden Gate Canyon State Park, 3873 Highway 46, Golden, 80403, ☎ 303/592-1502, is 14,000 acres of forested hiking trails, fishing streams, and wintertime cross-country ski trails within a 45-minute drive of Denver. There are several campgrounds.

Red Rocks Park in Morrison, ☎ 303/575-2637, offers a number of hiking trails winding through 400-foot sandstone monoliths.

IDAHO SPRINGS

Special caution is advised of hikers in these areas. The number of old and abandoned mine shafts found throughout the backcountry in these parts makes any hiking an iffy proposition. The **Mount Evans Wilderness Area** close to Idaho Springs is a much better bet for many miles of hiking terrain, such as a challenging trail from Echo Lake to Mount Evans covering 12 miles one way. For information contact the **Clear Creek Ranger District Office**, PO Box 3307, Idaho Springs, 80452, ☎ 303/567-9404. The office is a block south of I-70 on Highway 103.

On Wheels

BOULDER

Boulder is actually a little too popular with mountain bikers; riders are no longer allowed on trails in the Boulder Mountain Parks.

MORRISON

Mount Falcon Park can be reached by taking Highway 285 west to Parmalee Gulch Road. Turn right onto Picutis and follow the signs. The park pays homage to John Brisben Walker, who owned over 4,000 acres of land in this area during the early 1900s. It was here that Walker, a wealthy land speculator and owner of *Cosmopolitan* magazine, began to act upon his dreams.

He built an elaborate mansion on Mount Falcon while planning the construction of what would be a second home for the Presidents of the United States, a "Summer White House." Bad luck, bad investments and bad timing would eventually topple Walker's dreams, though. His home burned in 1918 and American involvement in WWI along with his waning fortune halted the Summer White House project at the foundation.

Although Walker's dreams faded, all is not lost to the mountain biker. The crumbling ruins of the two edifices make intriguing backdrops as the miles of multi-use trails wind and meander around them.

The trails offer a little something for riders of all abilities. A seasoned veteran might try the **Castle Trail**, part of which carried Stanley Steamers in Walker's time. This fairly steep rock and loose gravel trail challenges at one point with a series of narrow switchbacks.

Two-Dog Trail is good for intermediate riders. At .2 mile, it is a mellow ride that offers breathtaking views of Denver.

GOLDEN, LOOKOUT MOUNTAIN & RED ROCKS

There's too much vehicular traffic for good biking around here.

IDAHO SPRINGS & CENTRAL CITY

Biking down from the **Mount Evans Highway** is a relatively easy, no-pedaling trip through truly spectacular scenery. The **Oh My Gosh Road** between Idaho Springs and Central City is another good bike route, though steep in parts.

On Water

BOULDER

Clear Creek Rafting, Heritage Square, Building U-3, 18301 US Highway 40, Golden, 80403, ☎ 303/277-9900 or 800/353-9901. Just 30 minutes from Boulder, Clear Creek Rafting is conveniently located.

Being a university town full of action-ready students means some unique offerings. Consider the **Boulder Outdoor Center**, also known as the BOC, where you can take kayak and canoe lessons. Technique and safety are important to the BOC. Contact the Boulder Outdoor Center at North 47th Street, 80301, ☎ 303/444-8420.

Paddle Shop, 1729 15th St., Boulder, 80301, ☎ 303/786-8799. Paddling instruction for all levels. Also offers river rescue courses and rentals.

EVERGREEN

Summer means boating and fishing in this upscale bedroom suburb situated west of Denver in the mountains, but when temperatures drop in mid-December and the snow flies, lace up your skates and taste a true winter wonderland.

The sight of Evergreen Lake conjures up thoughts of Norman Rockwell paintings: nestled among tall pines, mittened children and adults gliding over the slick but imperfect surface of nature's skating rink.

Rentals are available at the icehouse. The open skate hours make this a convenient site. They're open from early morning through the moonlight hours. **Evergreen Lake**, 29614 Upper Bear Creek Road, Evergreen, 80439, ☎ 303/674-0532.

On Snow

IDAHO SPRINGS, GOLDEN & BOULDER

Snow sport areas close by include Golden Gate Canyon State Park, Mount Falcon Park, and the Mount Evans Wilderness Area, where you can even ice fish on Echo Lake. West of Boulder, near Nederland, a winter sports area, including a small downill ski slope with lights, is at Lake Eldora. Contact **Eldora Mountain Resort**, PO Box 1378, Nederland 80466, ☎ 303/440-8700, or the Boulder Visitors Bureau.

Where To Stay & Eat

Accommodations

BOULDER

Aspen Lodge Ranch Resort, 6120 Highway 7, Allenspark 80517, ☎ 303/586-8133. Set at 9,100 feet. Open year-round. Moderate-expensive.

Best Western Boulder Inn, 770 28th Street, Boulder, 80302, ☎ 303/449-3800. Across from University of Colorado. Restaurant, bar, pools, 100 attractively furnished rooms, private baths, restaurant. Moderate.

Best Western Golden Buff Motor Lodge, 1725 28th Street, Boulder, 80302, ☎ 303/442-7450. Established motel convenient to University of Colorado campus. Large, well-decorated rooms, heated pool, exercise room, putting green. Moderate.

Boulder Victoria, 1305 Pine St., Boulder, 80302, ☎ 303/938-1300. Victorian bed & breakfast offering plenty of food when you awake as well as afternoon tea. Central location. Expensive.

The Briar Rose, 2151 Arapahoe Avenue, 80302, ☎ 303/442-3007. The Briar Rose offers comfort and attentive service in an English Country House atmosphere. The nine guest rooms are furnished in period antiques. Moderate-expensive.

The Broker Inn, 555 30th, Boulder, 80302, ☎ 303/444-3330. Near University of Colorado. Pool, meeting room. Elegant Old West Restaurant is on premises. Expensive.

Clarion Harvest House Hotel, 1345 28th Street, Boulder, 80302, ☎ 303/443-3850. Resort in its own right, with Nautilus equipment, two pools, 14 tennis courts and more. Moderate-expensive.

Peaceful Valley Lodge & Guest Ranch, Box 2811, South Star Route, Lyons 80540, ☎ 303/747-2881. Moderate-expensive.

ĢOLDEN

Golden Motel, 24th and Ford, Golden, 80401, ☎ 303/279-5581. Clean, 15-unit motel. Inexpensive.

Antique Rose Bed & Breakfast Inn, 1422 Washington Avenue, 80401, ☎ 303/277-1893. Moderate.

The Jameson Inn Bed & Breakfast (Innkeepers: Mark & Peggy Shaw), 1704 Illinois Street, 80401, ☎ 303/278-0351. Moderate.

IDAHO SPRINĢS

Late-hour drivers should keep in mind that the local motels, while not fancy, are among the lowest priced in Colorado.

Indian Springs Resort, 302 Soda Creek Road, 80452, ☎ 303/623-2050. Old resort hotel with mineral pool, baths, exercise room, small café. Moderate.

CENTRAL CITY

Golden Rose Hotel, 102 Main, 80427, ☎ 303/825-1413. Small, Victorian. Expensive.

Shamrock Inn, 351 Gregory Street, Black Hawk, 80427, ☎ 303/582-5513. Within walking distance of casinos. Bed & breakfast featuring private bath and cable TV. Moderate.

Restaurants

BOULDER

José Muldoon's, 38th and Arapahoe, ☎ 303/449-4543. Great Mexican food and beer. Moderate.

Flagstaff House, 1138 Flagstaff Road, ☎ 303/442-4610. On Flagstaff Mountain, with fine views of the city and mountains. The award-winning continental/American menu includes their own oven-smoked salmon, venison, duck, and Alaskan king crab. Prime rib is the house specialty. Cocktail patio, free appetizers. A treat in summer. Longtime owner on premises. Upscale prices. Deluxe.

Boulder Dinner Theatre, 55th and Arapahoe, ☎ 303/449-6000. Cheerful young actors, singers, dancers regale you after a well-cooked supper. Expensive.

Red Lion Inn, Boulder Canyon Road, four miles west on State Route 119, ☎ 303/442-9368. Continental and American menu includes prime rib, elk, antelope, and duck à l'orange. Cocktail lounge. Good wine list. Reservations required. Expensive.

Cypress Cafe, 726 East 2nd Avenue, ☎ 970/385-1920, serves some of the healthiest food in town, good salads with lots of unusual green things in them, pastas and, in summer, fresh herbs and vegetables grown in their own garden. The food is briskly seasoned and tasty. Dining on the small outdoor patio is especially pleasant on a warm summer day, and is sometimes accompanied by live jazz.

RED ROCKS & MORRISON

The Creekside, 401 Highway 74, Morrison, ☎ 303/697-1700. Don't expect fine dining here. The decor of this tiny café is a hodge-podge of the old and the new: a classic bank vault door that doubles as the entrance to a walk-in supply closet, an antique ceramic tile ceiling, rattan chairs and formica tables. But what Creekside lacks in style, it more than makes up for in fresh, nourishing fare.

Two must-tries on the menu are the calzones and the hogback sandwiches. Both are served piping hot and are filled with mountains of fixins. Reasonable prices.

The Morrison Inn, 301 Bear Creek Avenue, ☎ 303/697-6650, serves up standard Mexican food: chimichangas, rellenos, burritos. What they're really known for, though, are the margaritas. Expect a crowd on Fridays and Red Rocks concert nights. Moderate.

Tony Rigatoni's, 215 Highway 74, ☎ 303/697-5508, is one of the newer additions to the town and packs a crowd most nights. This Italian restaurant offers a pleasant atmosphere with an attractive bar and pictures of old Italy covering the walls. Occasionally, a strolling accordion player makes an appearance. Portions are large. Moderate.

The Fort, 19192 Highway 8, Morrison, ☎ 303/697-4771, near Morrison on Highway 285, fits into this rocky country with its adobe architecture. Western food served here includes buffalo steaks, deer meat, carne asada and many other well-spiced dishes. Start with guacamole and wash it down with a margarita or Mexican beer. Expensive.

GOLDEN

Actually this is Lakewood, but it's on the Golden border. Gigantic chops, sizeable steaks and all the trimmings are what **Simms Landing,** 11911 West 6th Ave. Lakewood, ☎ 303 237-0465, has been serving up for decades. Also popular is the Sunday brunch.

IDAHO SPRINGS

If you reach these mountains in the evening and your stomach is yearning for food, try **Beau Jo's Pizza**. This outfit is well known for its varieties; you compose your own pizza here. Beau Jo's, 1517 Miner, ☎ 303/573-6924. Inexpensive.

The **Buffalo Bar**, 1617 Miner St., ☎ 303/567-2729, also serves up wholesome Colorado-style fare. Try any of the buffalo entrées. Salads are fresh and good. Inexpensive.

Also consider a stop at **El Rancho Colorado**, 18 miles west of Denver on I-70 (Exit 55A). This spacious, gracious mountain restaurant offers a ponderosa pine interior, wood-burning fireplaces, and tender steaks. Try the trout. The cozy bar is graced with a fireplace, a come-as-you-are atmosphere, and is popular with skiers. ☎ 303/526-0661. El Rancho also has guest rooms. Moderate.

CENTRAL CITY

Make a note of **Black Forest Inn**, a mile below Central City in Black Hawk, ☎ 303/279-2333. Authentic German food. Cozy and pricey.

Camping

BOULDER

Roosevelt National Forest, west of Boulder, offers numerous tent camping opportunities. ☎ 303/498-1100.

Kely-Dahl Campground, three miles south of Nederland on Highway 119, has 48 sites. ☎ 303/498-1100.

Boulder Mountain Lodge, 91 Four Mile Canyon Road, 80302, ☎ 303/444-0882, has motel rooms as well as creekside campsites.

MORRISON

Bear Creek Lake Park, 13411 Morrison Road, Lakewood, 80226, ☎ 303/697-6159, is part of a 2,458-acre open space. The campsites are short on trees, but there are lush creek beds and woods within walking distance. Fishing is close by at **Bear Creek Lake**. Amenities include picnic shelter, BBQ grills, sandpit volleyball courts and horseshoe pits. Rarely crowded.

GOLDEN

Dakota Ridge RV Park, 17700 W. Colfax, Golden, 80401, ☎ 303/398-1625 (or 800 398-1625) has plenty of pull-through sites, a meeting area, playground and a convenience store. Great proximity to Red Rocks Park.

IDAHO SPRINGS

Echo Lake, SR 103, 80452, ☎ 303/567-2901, features beautiful views and sites surrounded by spruces. The area is near numerous hiking trails. There's fishing, and close proximity to forests and backcountry of the Mount Evans Wilderness Area.

CENTRAL CITY

Columbine, County Road 279, 80427, ☎ 303/567-2901, has 47 sites spread over four acres. This area is short on luxuries.

I-25 North

Greeley & Fort Collins

Interstate 25 runs through the Denver suburbs and then north toward Wyoming, straight as an Indian's arrow. To the west, you see the gleaming profile of the Continental Divide with its limitless recreational possibilities; to the east the fertile fields of sugar beets, barley, dry beans, and potatoes. Cattle quietly seek shade from the summer heat. This is the approximate area where Mark Twain joined a buffalo hunt in 1862. "It was noble sport galloping over the plain in the dewey freshness of the morning," Twain wrote.

West of I-25 are roads to the canyons and rivers like the Big Thompson, where kayakers shoot the white-capped rapids. Here, too, are the dude ranches that provide excellent vacations for horse lovers.

Touring

Greeley

About an hour north of Denver on I-25, exit onto Highway 34 to Greeley. This attractive community was named after Horace Greeley, that great promoter of the West, newspaper editor and traveler. Greeley was sufficiently impressed with this region that he and his agricultural editor, Nathan Meeker, purchased 12,000 acres of land and began to interest Easterners in establishing a colony. In 1870 Meeker arrived with 50 families and their cooperative Union Colony became a reality.

Interstate 25 North

CULTURE

Visit the **Meeker Memorial Museum**, 1324 9th Avenue, 80631, ☎ 970/350-9221, formerly the home of Nathan Meeker. It contains many of his furnishings and the plow that turned the first sod in the Union Colony. It's listed in the National Register of Historic Places.

Another point of interest in Greeley is the **University of Northern Colorado**. James Michener is one of UNC's famous alumni. This institution has grown to some 11,000 full-time students, plus 6,000 part-timers who take continuing education courses.

SPECIAL EVENTS

Greeley's inhabitants believe in action. For instance, the **Greeley Independence Stampede** is held the first week of July. It features six rodeos, parades, fireworks, and events on all downtown plazas. The rodeos are at Island Grove Park, 14th Avenue and A Street.

The **Weld County Fair** takes place the first week in August, with horse shows, livestock displays, and various contests.

If you come to Greeley in spring, you should try to attend the **Greeley Jazz Festival**. Many college musicians from the plains and the Rocky Mountains west come to town for three days of clinics and performances by the top names in the field. The weekend always includes gigs by UNC's own student groups, which are among the best in the West.

FOR MORE INFORMATION

Greeley Convention & Visitors Bureau, 1407 Eighth Avenue, Greeley, CO 80631, ☎ 970/352-3566.

Greeley Chamber of Commerce, ☎ 970/352-3566 for details, or write Box 1464, Greeley, CO 80631.

Fort Collins

With its 80,000 residents (including 20,000 students at Colorado State University), this is no doubt the most important city in northern Colorado. An active visitor will find a complete gamut of recreation and entertainment in this neck of the woods.

Fort Collins exudes a youthful feeling; it's full of tanned and sparkling young people who race by on their cycles or rollerblades or come jogging down the pike. Fly-fishing for trout has become a major sport in the Fort Collins area, which is honeycombed with mountain parks.

SITES

Fort Collins Mountain Park, set in a broad, wooded valley, is a beautiful recreational area. If you have the time, you can drive west through 10,285-foot Cameron Pass in the Medicine Bow Range, or north to West Lake Campground, at 8,300 feet, close to the lovely Red Feathers Lakes. Return to Stove Landing, east of the scenic Big Narrows, and turn south on the unnumbered forest road passing Buckhorn Mountain and Masonville, then turn left on US 34.

You should also visit the **Roosevelt National Forest**, which is laced with scores of mountain trails used by hikers and bikers. It consists of some 800,000 (yes, 800,000) acres of mountain playground west of Fort Collins. Continue through Bellvue, pass the **State Fish Hatchery**, and head into the hills via the "Route of the Trout." Route 14 follows the Cache La Poudre River through Poudre Canyon. This canyon takes you into Roosevelt National Forest, named in honor of Theodore Roosevelt. It is a "multiple-use forest," with appropriate areas designed for cattle grazing, timber cutting, wildlife protection and recreation. Some of the best fishing streams in the state are located back from the Highway.

FOR MORE INFORMATION

Fort Collins Convention & Visitors Bureau, 420 S. Howes Street, Fort Collins, CO 80522, ☎ 970/482-5821.

Adventures

On Foot

GREELEY

Some of the best hiking and biking trails can be found at the US Forest Service's **National Grasslands**, a 20-minute drive north of Greeley. The area is mostly flat, but extremely spacious. From Greeley, take Highway 85 north, then head east via Highway 14 to your destination.

Golf is available at Highland Hills, 23rd Street and 54th Avenue. **Tennis** is offered at four different municipal parks: Centennial Park; Farr Park; Sherwood Park; and Sunrise Park. Bittersweet Park offers **jogging** tracks at 35th Avenue and 13th Street. Many **bike paths** circuit the town.

FORT COLLINS

Thanks again to the Forest Service, the area bustles with trails that get heavy spring, summer and fall use by students; the trails often double as cross-country ski terrain. Among the popular sites are the easy-to-reach **Horsetooth Mountain Park** and **Red Feather Lakes**, where a footpath circles the blue water. Get here via Colorado 14 from Fort Collins. **Roosevelt National Forest** is replete with trails for hikers. Ditto for **Lory State Park**.

On Wheels

FORT COLLINS

While in Fort Collins, pick up the free map, "Tour de Fort." This pocket guide illustrates the 56 miles of local bike trails, lanes and routes. You can find it at any Fort Collins bicycle shop.

Within the **Colorado State Forest**, 70 miles west of Fort Collins, the Never Summer Nordic Yurt System offers unique opportunities to cyclists. Consider staying in a yurt here. Yurts are portable, round dwellings first used by nomadic Mongols in Central Asia. They sleep six comfortably and make good push-off sites for some great rides.

One such bike trip is the **Grass Creek Loop**. It's a tough 16-mile round trip. Along the way you will pass the North Michigan Reservoir and the 10,000-foot Gould Mountain. For more information, contact **Never Summer Nordic Yurt System**, PO Box 1254, 80522, ☎ 970/484-3903.

Lory State Park offers great single tracks for more advanced riders. This former ranch of John Howard is now a 2,400-acre park that tempts bikers with challenging mountain biking almost year round; snow is frequent in winter, but abundant sunshine keeps the Lory State Park trails relatively clear. Just beyond the park entrance at the Timber Recreation Area is the **Timber Trail**. This single track route is not terribly technical, although loose gravel adds a challenge.

On Water

GREELEY

Swimming can be enjoyed at three city parks: Centennial Pool, 23rd Avenue and Reservoir Road; Island Grove, at 14th Avenue and A Street; and Sunrise Pool, at 4th Avenue and 12th Street.

Fishing is permitted in the lakes at Bittersweet, Sanborn, Allen and Glenmere parks.

Boyd Lake State Park, 3720 North County Road 11-C, ☎ 970/669-1739, has launch ramps for waterskiers and a beach for swimmers. Wildlife and birdwatching are popular here.

FORT COLLINS

The Fort Collins region is also well-known for its nearby fly-fishing possibilities. Among other rivers, you might head up the **Poudre Canyon** and the **Poudre River,** which is uniformly praised by serious anglers in search of trout.

For swimming and boating, there is the **Horsetooth Reservoir** west of town. Horsetooth has nearly 4,000 acres of water and attracts huge summer crowds with swimming, boating, waterskiing and windsur-fing.

City Park, Mulberry at Sheldon, is a large park with a lake, jogging tracks, and ice skating in winter.

Unlike the mass amphibious assaults of some companies, **Adrift Adventures of Colorado, Inc.,** 1816 Orchard Place, 80521, ☎ 800/824-0150, or 970/493-4005, runs small trips that manage to preserve the serenity of the backcountry. Their Yampa River trip, in northwestern Colorado, is a true wilderness journey on Colorado's last free-flowing river, using rafts and kayaks.

The company also offers a fishing trip on the **Gunnison River,** which has little tourist traffic.

For serious whitewater, they head to the **Upper Cache La Poudre,** a Wild and Scenic River that is Class V at high water. Raft-supported kayak trips are also offered.

On Snow

FORT COLLINS

Cross-country skiers with little time might like the **Beaver Meadows Cross-Country Center** west of town. Contact them at Box 2167, 80522, ☎ 970/482-1845.

For more ambitious downhill skiers – those who're unafraid of altitudes – there awaits the **Rocky Mountain National Park,** which you reach via Highway 34 and Estes Park. At the visitor's center, you will be directed to the lofty trails circling Bear Lake and Fern Lake, among many others.

The **Blue Lake Trail**, 10 miles northwest on Highway 287, then 53 miles west on Highway 14, will also get you away from crowds and into the backcountry. This 6½-mile trail is best for intermediate skiers, as it has some steep, uphill sections. Skiers here will be rewarded with vistas of the Mummy Range and Rocky Mountain National Park.

Where To Stay & Eat

Accommodations

GREELEY

Best Western Ramkota Inn, 701 8th Street, ☎ 970/353-8444. 148- room hotel. Small indoor pool. Moderate.

Cherokee Park Ranch, Box 97, 80536, ☎ 800/628-0949, sits at 7,200 feet. Open May 13 through September 30. Moderate.

Heritage Inn, 3301 W. Service Road, Evans, 80620, ☎ 970/339-5900. It has 59 units, restaurant, lounge, heated pool, outdoor recreation, cable TV. Moderate.

FORT COLLINS

University Park Holiday Inn, 425 W. Prospect Avenue, 80521, ☎ 970/482-2626. A convention facility offering dining and deluxe accommodations. Expensive.

Fort Collins Marriott Hotel, 350 E. Horsetooth Road, 80521, ☎ 970-226-5200 (Denver ☎ 303/629-0484). Every room has a view of the Front Range. Two restaurants and a full-service lounge. Convention facility. Expensive.

Edwards House Bed & Breakfast, 402 W. Mountain Avenue, 80521, ☎ 970/493-9191. Expensive.

Sky Corral Ranch, 8233 Old Flowers Road, Bellvue, 80512, ☎ 970/484-1362. Sits at 7,800 feet. Open all year. Expensive.

On the banks of the Big Thompson River, sits the **Sylvan Dale Guest Ranch**, 2939 N. County Road 31D, Loveland, 80538, ☎ 303/667-3915, a working ranch with a large haying operation. Run by the Jessup family since the 1940s, Sylvan Dale features wholesome country meals plus riding on the expansive terrain in this area surrounding Alexander Mountain. Expensive.

The **Lovelander Bed & Breakfast Inn**, 217 W. Fourth Street, Loveland, 80537, ☎ 970/669-0798. Moderate.

Restaurants

GREELEY

Eat'n Place, Greeley-Eaton, ☎ 970/464-3636. Unexpectedly plush restaurant. Corn-fed beef, chicken, fish. Expensive.

Village Inn, 2729 8th Avenue, ☎ 970/353-5187. Huge portions. American cuisine featuring egg dishes, sandwiches, and steaks. Moderate.

FORT COLLINS

Nico's Catacombs, 115 South College Avenue, ☎ 970/484-6029. A downtown restaurant. Extensive menu. Continental-style restaurant with seafood and wild game. Expensive.

Old Chicago, 147 South College Avenue, ☎ 970/482-8599. Steaks and pasta dishes. Moderate.

Camping

Nearly six million people stay in Colorado's hundreds of campgrounds each summer. A $10 pass gives you entrance to campsites at all 32 state-supervised outdoor areas; otherwise, per-night fees range from $2 to $14. The same prices are found in Colorado's national parks. At both, check with rangers for camping regulations.

A $25 "Golden Eagle" passport allows you and anyone in your vehicle to enter many national parks and recreation areas during a full calendar year. The passport doesn't cover all areas, nor does it include special fees. A "Golden Age," $10 passport provides free park access to those 62 years of age or older.

Information and applications are available from any office of the Forest Service, Bureau of Land Management, and at most ranger stations, or you may write to the National Park Service Headquarters (see below).

At Rocky Mountain National Park, campsites are scarce during the high summer season. First-come, first-served basis. Inquire at Park Headquarters, ☎ 970/586-2371.

Colorado's 300 privately owned campgrounds offer almost 14,000 vehicle and tent sites in the state. For a free directory, write the **Colorado Campground Association** (see below) or check with any Chamber of Commerce.

FOR MORE INFORMATION

Colorado Division of Parks/Recreation, 1313 Sherman St., #618, Denver, CO 80203, ☎ 303/866-3437.

National Park Service (Regional Office), PO Box 25287, Lakewood, CO 80225, ☎ 303/969-2000.

National Park Service Headquarters, Room 1013, US Dept. of the Interior, 18th & C Streets NW, Washington, D.C. 20240.

Colorado Campground Association, 5101 Pennsylvania Street, Boulder, CO 80303, ☎ 303/499-9343.

GREELEY

Greeley RV Park and Campground, 501 E. 27th Street, 80631, ☎ 970/353-6476, has 89 sites spread over 10 acres. Amenities include flush toilets, playground and recreation room.

FORT COLLINS

Crags Campground, 66 miles west of Fort Collins on Highway 14, offers 27 campsites amid a stunning forest backdrop. RVs and trailers should not attempt the rugged road; best for tent campers. ☎ 970/498-2770.

Ansel Watrous Campground, just off Highway 14 west of Fort Collins, is in Poudre Canyon. Close proximity to the Poudre River. It only has 19 sites, so you should get there early. ☎ 970/498-2770.

Glen Echo Resort, 31503 Poudre Canyon Drive, Bellvue, 80512, ☎ 970/881-2208, is a private campground 41 miles west of Fort Collins. Because of its location in the Poudre Canyon, ample fishing is available.

Horsetooth Reservoir, three miles west of the city, offers numerous sites off US 287. Watersports, including fishing and boating, are popular all year round (see under *Adventures*, above). Park permits are necessary.

FOR MORE INFORMATION

Parks and Recreation Dept., 145 E. Mountain Avenue, Fort Collins, CO 80524, ☎ 303/221-6640.

I-25 South

Colorado Springs, Cripple Creek, Pueblo, Trinidad & Walsenburg

Geography

Some 65 miles south of Denver, Colorado Springs dazzles the visitor. This city is also known as "The Springs." The trip by car takes less than an hour and the rewards are plentiful. This is Colorado's second largest and most handsome city. The well planned community is a boon to the eye, a pleasant accident of nature – the Rocky Mountains rise to 14,000 feet just beyond the spacious, clean streets. The lower mountains are mauve beauties while the highest summit – Pikes Peak – resembles a spectacular Swiss Alp. To top it all, Colorado Springs is blessed with a great number of truly remarkable sightseeing attractions. It's the perfect place to spend a week – especially if you like action.

History

Colorado Springs started as "Colorado City" in 1859, organized by a party of Kansas prospectors. The town advertised its free highway to the gold fields, mineral baths, and the Garden of the Gods (a dramatic assembly of sandstone monoliths). The gold eventually ran out and a decline in Western travel during the Civil War sent Colorado Springs into a period of decline. A flood washed away some of the settlement.

Then, in 1871, General William Palmer's railroad company purchased nearly 10,000 acres. Palmer had discovered the site of Colorado Springs at the foot of Pikes Peak while scouting for the railroad. It was the ideal location for his dream: an elite city, a cultural oasis for the well-to-do. Palmer and friends incorporated in 1872. The General and his partners made it clear that mills, smelters, saloons, gambling houses, and similar edifices would be confined to boisterous "Colorado City." The new community of Colorado Springs planned broad, elm-lined thoroughfares with Indian, French, and Spanish names. Lots were set aside for schools and churches, and an extensive park system projected. Cash and 20 acres of land were donated for the founding of Colorado College. Written into all land deeds was a clause prohibiting the manufacture or sale of intoxicating liquor on the premises, a restriction enforced for many years.

THE BROADMOOR

Other factors influenced the area's development, too.

During the 1850s, Spencer Penrose and his partner Charles Tutt decided that the region needed a European-style luxury hotel. As world travelers, the two Easterners knew what they wanted: a regal Renaissance-style hotel. The stone was specially quarried in Italy, the outside frescoes painted by artists imported from Siena and Florence and on the walls there were French lithographs – Toulouse-Lautrecs, no less.

The Broadmoor Resort is like none other in Colorado. It appeals especially to the action-oriented person. Sports of all sorts proliferate. It's the only hotel in Colorado that offers skeet and trap shooting. It has the largest tennis program in the state (with famous instructors); several 18-hole golf courses; a lake for waterskiing, canoeing, row-boating; paths for bicycling; trails for riding; shuffleboard and fishing. The Broadmoor has its own zoo, its own ski slope, shops of all kinds and award-winning restaurants.

You'll stride past genuine Renaissance fountains, bronze and mahogany statues, and curtains and carpets from Venetian palaces. The hotel has eight dining rooms and a pub brought from England, stick by stick.

Guests staying here dress up in the evenings, hence the enormous closets. Most windows look out at Pikes Peak, its head sometimes in the clouds, its flanks mantled by snow.

Is it adventurous? Hardly. Is it impressively unique on its own pampered terms? Definitely. And you can be sure that it's all very expensive, too.

For more information contact **The Broadmoor**, PO Box 1439, Colorado Springs, CO 80901, ☎ 719/634-7711.

The "Springs" founders planned a community to attract and hold people of means and social standing, a citizenry of "good moral character and strict temperance habits." They made it clear that manufacturing establishments were not wanted. General William J. Palmer, who made and unmade towns by directing where railroad tracks should be laid, was impressed with this site so near the mountains, foothills and canyons.

From the beginning, the railroad promoted the region as a scenic wonderland and health resort. Pikes Peak was already a national landmark. Physicians extolled the dry air and bright sunshine, and several TB sanitariums were established. The town grew rapidly.

When new gold and silver finds – especially in nearby Cripple Creek – brought these mountains to life again in the 1880s, Colorado Springs boomed, too. Within a few months of the first strikes, five mining exchanges had opened. Promoters and financiers rushed to Colorado Springs from across the nation. Bonanza kings invested part of their fortunes in substantial office structures and palatial houses. Between 1890 and 1900, the population increased from 11,000 to more than 23,000. During the next decade Colorado Springs became one of the wealthiest cities per capita in the United States. The town never lacked patrons who contributed materially to its development.

Wealthy tourists and settlers, many of them British, were drawn to the area's natural beauty. For awhile Colorado Springs had the nickname, "Little London." Tuberculosis patients came for sanatorium treatments and some stayed. In 1909, the Garden of the Gods, 1,000 acres of spectacular red sandstone formations, became a city park.

Spencer Penrose, a Philadelphian, acquired a mining claim while visiting friends, and eventually made a vast fortune. Penrose stayed on in Colorado Springs and shared his wealth with the community. The Pikes Peak auto road, Cheyenne Mountain Zoo and the Will Rogers Shrine were some of his projects. Penrose turned a one-time dairy into the Broadmoor Hotel, which became a five-star resort.

Touring

Colorado Springs

Colorado Springs is easy to get around. I-25 south crosses downtown and the outlying areas and also connects with attractions. A network of smaller roads take you to your destination. For instance, The Broadmoor is an easy drive off I-25 on Highway 85-87, while the Air

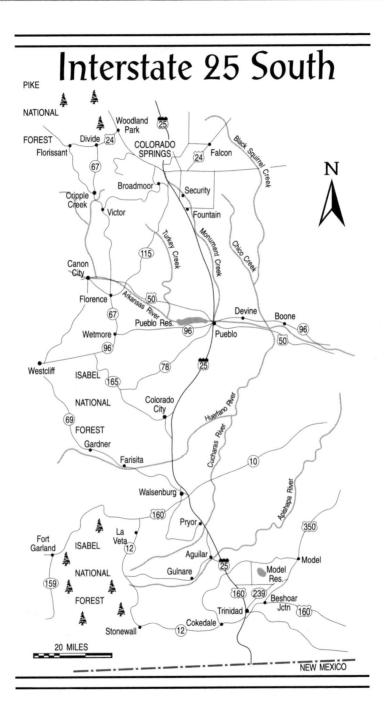

Interstate 25 South

Force Academy has its own exits from the interstate. For more details, see the individual attractions.

Colorado Springs is still rated as one of America's most beautiful cities by European travel agents. For many tourists, Colorado Springs *is* the Rocky Mountains. It offers a variety of attractions.

SITES

The **US Air Force Academy**, 11 miles north of town on I-25, welcomes visitors all year. The visitors' center provides details on exhibits, films, parades, and activities, which are all free. Much of the architecture is extraordinary and the landscaping is attractive, with buildings neatly tucked away among 18,000 acres of pine, spruce and fir forests. Behind the academy rises the impressive Ramparts Range. Earmark at least half a day for your visit.

Among things to see are exciting glider take-offs and landings, and a stunning cadet parade (weekdays at noon), complete with marching band. You can visit the superbly run 560,000-volume library and to the Planetarium, which offers periodic free shows and doubles as classroom for astronomy, physics and navigation.

The architecturally bold chapel is part of a 75-minute walking tour – a summer feature that shouldn't be missed. The stroll includes numerous other buildings – all of them well-conceived and blending into the scenery. Apart from the daily parades of the 4,000 spic-and-span cadets (including females), you can watch air shows, and see a 30-minute introductory film. If you happen to be here in June you may witness the graduating ceremonies when hats fly into the air and newly minted Air Force officers are at last ready for their careers.

Academy grounds are open to the public year round from 6AM to 7PM. Many buildings open at 9AM and close at 5PM.

For more information contact the **US Air Force Academy**, USAF Academy, 80840, ☎ 719/472-2025.

Cheyenne Mountain contains the bomb-proof headquarters of the North American Air Defense Command, NORAD. Here, 90 computers and a million miles of communication lines watch the horizons for enemy missile attacks. More than 1,700 people populate a small city deep inside this hollowed-out mountain, where the 15 buildings are supported on 1,319 steel springs weighing 1,000 pounds each. Rock reservoirs hold six million gallons of water and steel blast doors protect the complex. (In case of a nuclear attack, these 25,000-pound gates can be closed in 30 seconds.)

There are two public tours daily, each limited to 40 people in good health (lots of walking and stair-climbing), plus films and exhibits. Positive identification is required, and no cameras or tape recorders are permitted. Tours may be reserved up to six months in advance. Tour days are Monday, Tuesday, Wednesday and Friday from 7-3. Tours are free.

The Garden of the Gods is world-renowned. More than two miles of paved roads meander among towering red sandstone cliffs, balanced rocks, and other dramatic formations. Once sacred ground to natives, the 1,350-acre park was donated to the city by private owners. The trading post offers refreshments and use of telescopes. Horseback tours available, ☎ 800/874-4515. Open all year (winter hours 9-5).

The Garden of the Gods is best reached by taking US 24 expressway (I-25 Exit 141) to the Manitou/Garden of the Gods Exit. After exiting the freeway, follow the signs to the Garden of the Gods Road.

Above the Broadmoor Resort, you can visit the **Cheyenne Mountain Zoo**, where giraffes, bears, elk, deer, penguins, and other creatures are kept in a modern environment.

To reach Cheyenne Zoo from I-25, go south on Nevada Avenue. Turn right on Lake Avenue to the Broadmoor. Turn onto Mirada Road and follow signs. ☎ 719/632-9555.

Nearby **Seven Falls** cascades 300 feet through a deep canyon. The entire area is beautifully lit at night and at Christmas, making this the only completely lighted canyon in the world. Located seven miles southwest of town on Cheyenne Boulevard, ☎ 719/632-0741.

Nature worshippers will want to see the **Cave of the Winds**, past Manitou Springs off US 24, atop scenic Serpentine Drive. Natural formations here were first discovered in 1880. Forty-minute guided tours are offered every 15 minutes throughout the day.

The 14,110-foot **Pikes Peak** towers above everything and you have several options to reach the summit. You can take your own car; just follow US 24 west on Colorado Avenue. It takes about four hours to make it to the mountaintop that way. (A toll gate will extract a fee from you.) You can also hike to the lofty heights. Each July 4, the **Pikes Peak Auto Hillclimb** attracts world-class race drivers who try to beat each other's time to the top.

CULTURE

The **Colorado Springs Fine Arts Center**, 30 West Dale Street, 80903, has an excellent reputation for its contemporary art and for special exhibits of paintings and sculpture. The modern building has been praised by architects. Closed Monday. ☎ 719/634-5581.

FOR MORE INFORMATION

☎ 719/474-2241, ext. 2239, or contact the **Colorado Springs Convention and Visitors Bureau** at ☎ 800-DO VISIT (368-4748).

Cripple Creek

Cripple Creek, built on the side of a mountain, is beginning to revive its mining industry thanks to rising gold prices. This rebirth comes in concert with the 1990 legalization of "limited stakes gambling" in three of Colorado's historic mining towns – Cripple Creek, Black Hawk and Central City – and on the Indian reservations near Ignacio and Cortez, in southwest Colorado. A year after legalization, slot machines were ringing and blackjack tables jammed with card sharks.

Gambling isn't new to Colorado mining towns. Around the turn of the century miners were known to stake their entire earnings in hopes of getting rich quick. Back then Cripple Creek's thriving red-light district was Myers Avenue. There were two opera houses, countless saloons and the town's very own version of the New York Stock Exchange.

Today, casinos have pushed out the mom-and-pop tourist businesses along Bennett Avenue; still, in the neon glow of the evening, Cripple Creek recalls very much its Wild West past.

Mining at the end of the 20th century doesn't rival the old days when a half-billion dollars of the precious metal was dug from the surrounding hills. In those boom days – from 1890 to World War II – Cripple Creek was America's rough-and-tumble "promised land." Everyone came here: A young Jack Dempsey fought all comers for $50 a match; the late Groucho Marx, stranded between engagements, arrived in a grocery wagon; journalist Lowell Thomas grew up in the neighboring town of Victor. By 1900, Cripple Creek had 40 stock brokers, 60 doctors, 39 real estate brokers, and eight newspapers.

Today, Cripple Creek's permanent residents cash in on both tourism and gambling.

Visitors come to ride **Cripple Creek and Victor Railroad**, a four-mile, 45-minute excursion in open cars through mining country. Guides provide a good narration. You climb aboard from the station at the end of Bennett Avenue, PO Box 459, ☎ 719/689-2640. There are photo stops at trestles and in mountain valleys. The tiny **Cripple Creek District Museum** is housed in the once-busy railroad terminal. Exhibits recreate the city in which 25,000 people once worked, brawled, got rich, or lost everything.

The **Imperial Hotel** here has received a major sprucing since gambling's introduction. Built in 1896, the three-story brick inn was restored in the late 1940s and again in 1992. Not all rooms have baths, but the decor is authentic 1890s frontier. The basement **Gold Bar Room Theater** offers a summer-long performance schedule of the Imperial Players. Their melodrama is accompanied by honky-tonk piano (famed ragtimer Max Morath got his start here). After the show, the actors put on an old-fashioned collection of skits and blackouts. *Time* magazine once called the Imperial "the Old Vic of American melodrama." Don't miss it.

Pueblo

Pueblo, population about 100,000, is some 40 miles south of sophisticated Colorado Springs. By contrast, Pueblo is a worker's town, thanks to large steel mills, factories and agricultural fairgrounds. In fact, the yearly **Colorado State Fair and Exposition** is one of the biggest events in the state. Every summer, the 17-day fair is an action-packed experience for all who visit.

The Colorado State Fair is unique. Witness the variety of activities planned, from the PRCA championship rodeo to the largest carnival and midway in the state. There are hundreds of lambs, steers, hogs, horses, and other animals to see and touch, a popular children's barnyard, parks with all types of free entertainment, along with scores of exhibits, creative arts, and evening performances by some of the nation's top entertainers.

For details contact **Colorado State Fair**, State Fairgrounds, 81004, ☎ 719/566-0530.

You get to the fair by exiting I-25 at Central Ave.

The **El Pueblo Museum**, 324 West 1st Street, ☎ 719/583-0453, displays Native American clothing, buffalo skins, and gold panning equipment, along with artifacts integral to Colorado's early history.

Of particular interest here, though, is the thigh bone of a prehistoric mammoth. This eons-old fossil was stumbled upon during a reconstruction project in downtown Pueblo. After spying the old bone, you can't help but imagine this giant plodding down mainstreet.

Royal Gorge, 50 miles southwest of Colorado Springs on Highway 115, features a 1,200-foot-deep chasm. The gorge stopped Zebulon Pike's westward expedition; he just couldn't make it across. Today, travelers plumb the rocky canyon depths via a steep incline funicular, or drive across a mighty suspension bridge – one of the world's highest. In addition, they can also use a 35-passenger tram. In the terminals, about 100 tons of concrete and steel anchor the big cables. Also, a miniature narrow-gauge passenger train carries passengers along the chasm rim for a closer look. More adventurous types can make a raft trip down the Arkansas River as it splashes through the floor of the gorge. Details from **Royal Gorge Rafting** in nearby Canon City, ☎ 719/275-7507.

Be sure to visit **Buckskin Joe**, a Western hamlet named for an old mining camp. The log cabins and rough-timbered shacks that line the street were found in ghost towns and abandoned mining camps, disassembled, and rebuilt here. Buckskin Joe has been used as a set for scores of Western movies and television programs (John Wayne worked here frequently). Between filmings, the town promotes fake shootouts, as well as stagecoach rides. It has gift shops and exhibits. Refreshments are available.

FOR MORE INFORMATION

Contact **Pueblo Chamber of Commerce**, 302 North Santa Fe, PO Box 697, CO 81002. ☎ 719/542-1704.

Walsenburg

Walsenburg is another exit from I-25 south. This one heads west, allowing the driver to see Colorado peaks as well as the La Veta Pass. To the east is Colorado's fertile land. Walsenburg is a worthwhile stop for museum lovers. There are two of them: the **Mining Museum**, 101 E. 5th Street, Walsenburg, ☎ 719/738-1107, and the **Fort Francisco**, US 160, La Veta, ☎ 719/742-3474.

Trinidad

Trinidad is still further south, with more museums and mountain vistas. Both communities offer a quiet night's sleep to the traveler. Trinidad is the region's touchstone for culture and accommodations. Visit the **A.R. Mitchell Museum of Western Art**, 150 E. Main Street, ☎ 719/846-4224.

FOR MORE INFORMATION

Trinidad Chamber of Commerce, 309 Nevada Avenue, Trindad, CO 81082, ☎ 719/846-9285.

Adventures

On Foot

COLORADO SPRINGS

The inhabitants of Colorado Springs are blessed with walking paths of all kinds. Short footpaths criss-cross the spectacular Garden of the Gods. The ambitious hiker will welcome the long **Barr Trail** to the top of Pikes Peak (14,110 feet). Walkers interested in a brief outing should consider the **Cheyenne Canyon** trails.

The US Air Force Academy Falcon Trail is approximately 12 miles long and is open to all hikers. It has been designed to give you a good look at the natural and man-made beauty of the academy.

The start and finish point for the trail is immediately south of Building 5132 (the Youth Center building), which can be identified by its large blue sign. Some groups may prefer to start and end their hike at the academy camping areas.

The **Falcon Trail** is home for many different types of plants and animals. As you hike the trail, note the various plant communities, animal habitats and geological areas. A good field guide will help.

Short llama treks are the perfect way to see Colorado Springs and its environs. The llama carries your pack while you explore trails lined with wildflowers, spacious meadows and icy streams. All that remains for you is to breathe in the pure mountain air and take in the vistas.

One company, **Adventures Out West**, PO Box 38512, Colorado Springs, 80937, ☎ 719/578-0935, offers llama "walkabouts." Their planned hikes range from easy to challenging and will last two to four hours.

On Wheels

COLORADO SPRINGS

One of the quickest ways to reach the summit of Pikes Peak is by the world-famous **Pikes Peak Cog Railway**. The railway, which first made it to the top in 1891, was the dream of Zalmon Simmons. Simmons, an industrialist, was determined to trade his mule for more comfortable transport to the summit. He was reported as saying, "I'm going to ride up this beautiful mountain in the grandest comfort science can provide."

His legacy lives on in the Swiss-made trains used here. Today, passengers rave about the comfort and warmth that the trains provide. Pikes Peak can be more than 30° cooler than Colorado Springs.

The 46,158-foot railway is truly a wonder. You climb from 6,571 feet at the station to 14,110 feet at the summit. This represents a vertical gain of 847 feet per mile.

Once on top, visitors may stay just the half-hour interval between cars or stay as long as they please. A restaurant at the Summit House serves excellent lunches plus snacks and soft drinks. There is also a picturesque picnic park with ovens, tables, wood and water. You may hike over countless scenic trails to the many lookout stations that offer exciting photo views.

At night, thousands of twinkling lights spread out in the valley below in the shape of a huge question mark. A breathtaking scene.

Trips leave the Ruxton Avenue station in Manitou Springs every half hour from 9:30AM to 5PM, between late May and October. During July and August the cable cars operate until 9PM daily, including holidays.

For more information contact **Mount Manitou Incline**, 515 Ruxton Ave, Manitou Springs, 80629, ☎ 719/685-1045 (May through October).

On Water

COLORADO SPRINGS

The Broadmoor. A European-style spa has been added to the Broadmoor's many facilities. Muscle-relief baths, relaxation hydrotherapy, German-style mud baths, and massages are all available. The Broadmoor features an attractive outdoor pool with country club-type restaurant al fresco. The resort has also introduced a summer fly-fishing school led by experts. Small classes. ☎ 719/634-7711.

For sportier types and true daredevils, **American Adventure Expeditions** organizes raft trips and kayaking in various nearby rivers. Write Box 1549, Buena Vista, 81211, ☎ 719/395-2409. About a zillion other rafting operators line the Arkansas River near Canon City, and farther west, around Salida.

CRIPPLE CREEK

The locals say that **Eleven Mile Canyon** offers some of the best brown and rainbow trout fishing in Colorado. Here, the choppy waters of the South Platte cut through a narrow canyon. Even on a day when the fish don't bite, the scenery remains unforgettable.

To get here, head north on Highway 67 to Highway 24. Drive to Lake George and look for the canyon turn-off.

PUEBLO

Pueblo State Recreation Area and Reservoir offers a multitude of water adventures, with over 60 miles of shoreline. Fishing is good here. Expect to catch trout, walleye, small- and largemouth bass, as well as the usual crappie and sunfish.

Rock Canyon Swim Area. Swimming is strictly prohibited in the reservoir, but a sandy beach below the dam is provided for just this purpose. Lifeguards on duty.

The **Arkansas River,** which flows through town, is inviting if you'd like to float along on a sun-drenched day. The Arkansas beckons mostly canoers, as the white-capped waves have diminished significantly by the time the water reaches Pueblo.

TRINIDAD

Trinidad State Recreation Area can be found just four miles west of Trinidad. Here, Trinidad Lake offers boating, waterskiing and, of course, fishing. ☎ 719/846-6951.

In the Air

COLORADO SPRINGS

Thanks to an adventurous, enterprising population, Colorado Springs offers balloon flights of various lengths for four to eight people. Contact **Adventures Out West,** Box 38512, 80937, ☎ 800/755-0935.

Where to Stay & Eat

Accommodations

COLORADO SPRINGS

Colorado Springs has a tremendous number of good hotels and motels, plus every type of restaurant.

Colorado Springs Marriott, 5580 Tech Center Drive, 80919, ☎ 719/260-1800. This hotel enjoys an excellent location. It has 310 guest rooms and suites with mountain views. Expensive.

Doubletree Antlers Hotel, 4 S. Cascade, ☎ 800/222-TREE. The perfect hotel for people who want to be downtown, close to business and shopping. Expensive.

The Palmer House, I-25 and Fillmore, ☎ 719/636-5201. Longtime hotel-motel overlooking I-25, close to sightseeing. Moderate.

Lost Valley Ranch, 29555 Goose Creek Road, Box 70, Sedalia, 80135, ☎ 719/647-2311. Moderate.

Elk Mountain Ranch, PO Box 910, Buena Vista, 81211, ☎ 719/539-4430. Sits at an elevation of 9,435 feet. Nestled among aspen and evergreen. Expensive.

Black Forest Bed & Breakfast, 11170 Black Forest Road, 80908, ☎ 800/890-9901. Moderate.

Cheyenne Canon Inn, 2030 W. Cheyenne Boulevard, 80906, ☎ 719/633-0625. Moderate.

Holden House – 1902 Bed & Breakfast Inn, 1102 W. Pikes Peak Avenue, 80904, ☎ 719/471-3980. Moderate.

PUEBLO

Pueblo has the usual, reliable Holiday Inns, Best Westerns and other chain motels. For travelers in search of more intimate and interesting quarters, there is the **Abriendo Inn**, at 300 W. Abriendo Avenue, Pueblo, 81005, ☎ 719/544-2703, a stately bed & breakfast run by friendly people. Restaurants nearby. Moderate.

Don K Ranch, 2677 S. Siloam Road, 81005, ☎ 719/784-6600. Expensive. Lodge rooms and cottages. Pool, whirlpool, dude ranch activities.

CRIPPLE CREEK

Built around the turn of the century, the **Imperial Hotel**, 123 N. 3rd St., Cripple Creek, CO 80813, ☎ 719/689-2922, has seen its share of boom and bust days. Thankfully, the hotel is enjoying a renaissance of sorts and has recently received a much-needed sprucing up to go with its bustling casino. Moderate.

TRINIDAD

The **Bluehouse** bed and breakfast, ☎ 719/846-4507, offers comfortable accommodations and great food.

Best Western Country Club Inn, 900 W. Adams St., Trinidad, 81082, ☎ 719 846-2271, offers the usual amenities, plus an exercise room, meeting space and mountain views. Moderate.

VICINITY OF WALSENBURG

Echo Canyon Ranch, PO Box 328, La Veta, 81055, ☎ 800/341-6603. Horseback riding is the main draw for this resort. Moderate.

Great Sand Dunes Country Club & Inn, Zapata Ranch, 5303 Highway 150, Mosca, 81146, ☎ 719/378-2356. Featuring historic log buildings, an 18-hole golf course and an excellent restaurant. Deluxe.

Conejos River Guest Ranch, 25390 Highway 17, Antonito, 81120, ☎ 719/376-2464. Horseback riding, hiking and fishing available at your doorstep. Accommodations in lodge rooms or rustic cabins. Moderate.

Restaurants

COLORADO SPRINGS

The **Flying W Ranch**, just west of Colorado Springs, features an old Western town. At suppertime you eat Western chow and take in a Wild West show and musical. Reservations required. ☎ 719/598-4000. Open June to September. Moderate.

A special evening calls for special measures. Impress that certain someone with a meal at the **Penrose Room** in the Broadmoor Hotel, ☎ 719/634-7711. Panoramic views to accompany your Caesar salad, fresh fish and wild game entrées. Expensive.

Old Chicago, 4110 N. Academy, ☎ 719/536-0633, bakes up pizzas as you like 'em – big or small, meaty or vegetarian. Plus, a sinful number of beers and ales are available on tap or by the bottle. Moderate.

For a sandwich, appetizers and some good cheer, the younger crowd likes to hang at **Meadow Muffins**, 2432 W. Colorado Avenue, ☎ 719/633-0583. Moderate.

DelPhiniums Café, 1245 Canon Street, Guffey, ☎ 719/689-7766, east of Cripple Creek and south of the town of Hartsell, is worth the detour. Inventive pastas, sandwiches and main dishes change regularly depending on what's fresh. Sunday brunch is exceptional. Moderate-expensive.

The Village Inn, 217 E. Pikes Peak Avenue in the center of Colorado Springs, ☎ 719/598-4560, is located in an old church. This restaurant serves consistently decent food from a varied menu. Cocktail lounge. Moderate.

Silver Kettle Family Restaurant, 1605 N. Union Boulevard, ☎ 719/630-3565. Open 6AM-8PM. Homey. Inexpensive.

Old Country Buffet, 7665 S. Academy, ☎ 719/933-9923. Vast amounts of food in cozy setting. Senior discount. Inexpensive.

Camping

COLORADO SPRINGS

Colorado Springs offers the most abundant camping opportunities of this region by far. Listed below are a few facilities that you should try.

Garden of the Gods Campground, 3704 W. Colorado Avenue, 80904, ☎ 719/475-9450. Being so close to Garden of the Gods, this site is usually crowded. If you can get a spot, amenities such as a heated pool, playground and sightseeing tours await you. For a fee you can also attend pancake breakfasts on Sundays and ice cream socials. Open April-October.

Diamond Campground, US Highway 24, then a half-mile north of Woodland Park on Colorado Highway 67, ☎ 719/687-9684. Eighteen acres of pine forest. Each site has fireplace grill and picnic table. There is a separate tent area.

WALSENBURG

Country Host Motel and Campground, south on I-25 to Exit 52, ☎ 719/738-3800. Not very private. Situated next to a 17-unit motel.

San Luis Valley & Central Colorado

San Luis, Crestone, Alamosa & Crested Butte

The San Luis Valley is a study in contrasts, evident in the 7,000-foot elevation gain from the low-lying valley floor to 14,345-foot Blanca Peak. The Great Sand Dunes are reminiscent of the Sahara Desert. Fourteen-thousand-foot peaks, the spire-like Crestone Needle and its neighbor Crestone Peak, pride of the Sangre de Cristo ("Blood of Christ") Range, are the natural landmarks for the valley's eastern boundary. At the northern end of the area are the Valley View Hot Springs which harness some of the steaming water that pours from the ground. The western border of the valley incorporates the low-lying La Garita hills and the vast reaches of the Rio Grande National Forest.

The arid valley sits atop an aquifer that is the lifeblood to this agricultural region and perhaps a key to some of its mystery.

From the New Age energy center of Crestone to the steeped Catholic tradition of San Luis, men and women have sought spiritual inspiration here for centuries. The valley riches probably first drew human habitation long before Spaniard Don Diego de Vargas claimed the land in 1694.

After the Mexican war, when land grants enticed settlers to move here, the population finally began to grow. The land had previously been occupied by the Ute Indians and, before them, by the Mayans.

The valley provides the headwaters to the Rio Grande River. Early settlers built canals to access these waters, which would nourish their crops and farmland. Potatoes have flourished in this arid soil since the 1870s; carrots also thrive in this climate.

Across the flat valley from spud capitol center and commercial center Saguache, loom the town of Crestone and the myriad spiritual retreat centers – from Buddhist to Christian and Nation of Islam. They gather separately, but harmoniously, in the "Baca" development south of

Crestone. Some believe there are thousands of sacred sites in these lands, with powers that can be harnessed or at least utilized. Not surprisingly, there's a staunch devotion to protect this land and the underground aquifer that remains the San Luis Valley's lifeblood. Meditations are conducted where the water meets the mountains.

One certainly can't deny the physical power of this place: the magnet-like draw of the Crestone Needle; the pale glow of looming Mount Blanca. Is it any wonder that otherworldly sightings such as UFOs are not uncommon?

Getting Around

Alamosa is 210 miles from Denver via Highway 285 or Interstate 25 to Highway 160 (at Walsenburg). Durango is 150 miles west of Alamosa via Highway 160. Greyhound/Trailways buses provide service from the east and west; United Express operates through the Alamosa Municipal Airport.

Touring

The light on **Great Sand Dunes National Monument**, 11500 Highway 150, Mosca, 81146, ☎ 719/378-2357, at dawn or dusk creates one-of-a-kind shadows and colors. There are 55 square miles of dunes, some taller than ski slopes. The largest sand dunes in North America seem misplaced here upon first viewing, but their evolution makes perfect sense. They were probably created by a combination of wind and time and were molded over the past 15,000 years by displaced particles from the Rio Grande River that met the great barrier of the Sangre De Cristo mountains.

The dunes appear to be a mirage against the big peaks, rising 700 feet from the base of the Sangre de Cristos. The winds continue to affect the shapes of the sculptured, sometimes spooky sand dunes. Yet the formations actually keep some of their shape because they stay relatively moist from groundwater and the region's plentiful snow.

The Great Sand Dunes National Monument visitors center provides plenty of helpful information in explaining these land forms. Located near the monument's south entrance, the center is open daily throughout the year, except Christmas.

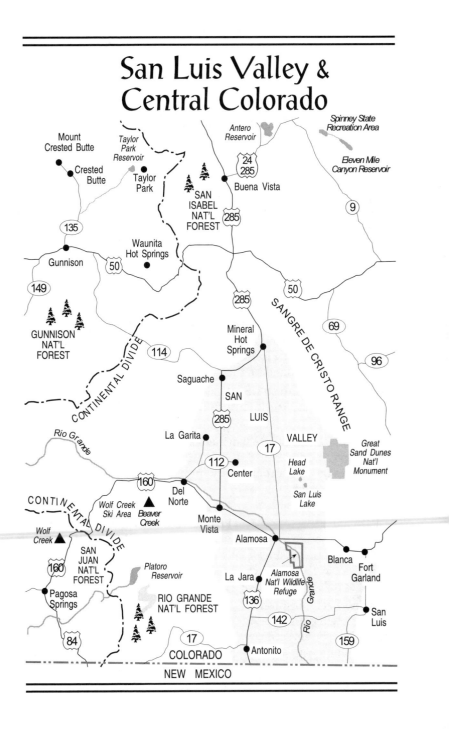

South of the dunes and visible from many different points is Blanca Peak, considered to be among the four sacred mountains of the Navajo. In fact, the original name for this section of mountains was "Range of White Light." Private landowners make access to Blanca tough if not impossible.

The San Luis Valley opens up at Alamosa, which emerged as the region's commercial supply center when railroad tracks were laid in the late 1800s. West of here are the pleasant towns of **Monte Vista** and **Del Norte** and the ski area **Wolf Creek.**

More sleepy agricultural towns exist quietly in the valley south of Alamosa, including Conejos, site of **Our Lady of Guadalupe Church,** ☎ 719/376-5985, the oldest church in Colorado. The Gothic structure was built by the first Spanish settlers to the area. Nearby is Antonito, gateway to the Cumbres and Toltec Scenic Railroad.

West of La Jara via Route 15 is the **Hot Creek State Wildlife Area.** A basalt canyon is lush with birds and plants – just made for a short walk or visit.

The **Alamosa/Monte Vista National Wildlife Refuge,** ☎ 719/589-4021, is east of Alamosa and provides the chance to see eagles, cranes and other birds in their natural habitat. An auto tour, plus self-guided walking and bicycling tours, give an introduction to the refuge. Take US 160 east from Alamosa, then south on El Rancho Lane.

Continuing eastward on US 160 takes the visitor through **Blanca,** once a hub for Japanese truck farmers selling carrots, broccoli and cauliflower.

Fort Garland, where there's an interesting historical museum, is north of San Luis. Founded in 1851, **San Luis** is Colorado's oldest community. These days this community, proud of its Hispanic heritage, is best known for the Stations of the Cross statues that were created by sculptor Huberto Maestas.

Fr. Pat Valdez, pastor of Most Precious Blood Church, helped oversee the construction of the **Stations of the Cross shrine,** which unscrolls along a 1½-mile hillside; it culminates with Christ's crucifixion. The shrine is near the intersection of Highway 142 and Highway 159 in San Luis. ☎ 719/672-3355 or 719/672-3685.

Doubling back north on the Los Camionos Antiguos scenic byway towards the Sand Dunes, a detour to **Zapata Falls** is recommended. Zapata Falls offers scenic waterfalls plus great views of the valley.

No, you're not hallucinating. That really is an **alligator farm** rising like a mirage in the valley alongside the Highway. If you're interested in visiting such a place on your Colorado vacation, stop in to see the

100-or-so reptiles that live on Highway 17 north of Alamosa. ☎ 719/589-3032.

The humble town of **Center**, smack dab in the middle of the state, is the potato capital for Russet, the red Sangre variety, those delicious yellow Yukon Golds, as well as trendy little purple and mini-spuds.

Nearby is the sober town of **Saguache**, home of the state's sole remaining lead printing press. Locals tend to look at their brethren in Crestone as peculiar types. The Saguache/Crestone rivalry further emphasizes the many contrasts evident in the San Luis Valley.

While not a part of the San Luis Valley per se, the old mining town turned sports mecca of **Crested Butte** is a worthwhile detour. It's reached via Hwy. 135, about 35 miles north of Gunnison.

The still sleepy town's Victorian architecture has been left unadulterated, while outside the immediate downtown, development continues at a rapid pace.

Mount Crested Butte, on the northern end of town, is where you'll find the new-fangled condominiums (and one heckuva great ski/snowboard mountain). During the summer the ski area is a jumping-off place for mountain biking, hiking and even wildflower tours. Art galleries, a brilliant live theatre company and low-key community are some of Crested Butte's other calling cards.

FOR MORE INFORMATION

Alamosa Chamber of Commerce, 425 4th Street, Alamosa, CO 81101, ☎ 719/589-3681.

Crested Butte Chamber of Commerce, PO Box 1288, Crested Butte, CO 81224.

Crested Butte Online, http://www.cbinteractive.com.

Crested Butte General Information, ☎ 800/545-4505.

Crested Butte Lodging & Reservations, ☎ 800-215-2226.

San Luis Valley Information Center, ☎ 719/852-0660 or 800/835-7254.

San Luis Visitor Center, ☎ 719/672-3355.

Adventures

On Foot

The **South Colony Lakes area** (beneath Crestone Needle, on the east side of Sangres), is the gateway to some of the steep trails that access the Sangre de Cristo range, including the route to Hermit Pass. Take North Crestone Creek road a few miles to the campground terminus. Willow Creek and Cottonwood Creek are other access points from the Crestone area.

There are a handful of marked trails along the **Great Sand Dunes** but most hikers just take off and wander the dunes. The tallest dunes reach nearly 700 feet high, so be prepared with good hiking shoes (don't attempt these climbs with bare feet) and plenty of water.

Those prepared for a wilderness excursion can set out on a seven-mile hike to Mosca Pass, which starts near the Sand Dunes visitor center. The trail traces an old Ute Indian route to the 9,740-foot summit into the Sangre de Cristo wilderness.

During the fall, aspen viewing is recommended in the **South San Juan Wilderness Area** of the Rio Grande National Forest. Take US 285 south to Antonito, then west on SR 17, following the Conejos River to Forest Road 250, where you turn north.

Climbing is popular on the precipitous 14,000-foot peaks above Crestone and in Penitente Canyon near La Garita.

In Crested Butte, trails set out into the **Maroon Bells/Snowmass Wilderness** from the vicinity of Gothic and Schofield Pass. Short day hikes into the alpine meadows are one option. Or, those seeking a longer experience can hike the 13 miles over spectacular East Maroon Pass on into Aspen.

Wildlife walks are also favored on **Mount Crested Butte**, especially during the peak flower season of mid-July into August.

On Wheels

Medano Primitive Road is a four-wheel-drive road that begins in the Sand Dunes. It travels north, slicing through the Sangre de Cristo

Mountains, to Medano Pass and the Rio Grande National Forest. The pass permits great views of the Sand Dunes.

Two-hour jeep tours of the Great Sand Dunes are offered through **Great Sand Dunes Oasis**, ☎ 719/378-2222.

Jeeps and other rugged four-wheel-drive vehicles may be used to traverse the rough road past Gothic over Schofield Pass and into the old mining town of Marble.

Cyclists can pedal five miles up Forest Road 660 to reach **La Ventana** ("the window") **Natural Arch**, a wonder of nature that was carved by thousands of years of weathering. The rock outcropping is 20 feet high by 20 feet wide.

From Del Norte head northeast on Highway 112 for 2½ miles. Turn at the La Garita Ranch sign and follow that road for five miles. Continue north to the forest road, which will be on the left side of the road. Follow the road until it dead ends at La Ventana Ranch.

The area surrounding **Zapata Falls** is also ripe for biking.

On Horseback

Goodnight Training Stables, PO Box 265, Crestone, 81131, ☎ 719/256-4009, has trail riding and a teaching facility.

On Water

The **Rio Grande River** offers oodles of fishing opportunities. Gold medal quality fishing is available between South Fork and Del Norte. The **Conejos River** in the Rio Grande National Forest, via FR 250, 20 miles west of Antonito, is said to have excellent fly-fishing.

Contact the **San Luis Valley Office of the Colorado Division of Wildlife**, 722 South Rd. 1E, Monte Vista, 81144, ☎ 719/852-4783.

Don't be shy: **Valley View Hot Springs**, PO Box 175, Village Grove, 81155, ☎ 719/256-4315, is a bathing-suit-optional resort.

Soak in private or with a group, in the mineral hot springs pools that dot the hillside. Open weekdays only to non-members.

On Snow

Wolf Creek Pass Ski Area, Highway 160, Pagosa Springs, 81147, ☎ 970/264-5629, is the state's snow magnet, receiving more than 400 inches per year. There's plenty of room for intermediates to make nice big turns. Wolf Creek offers a great learning area as well. On powder days, take your snorkel – the snow gets that deep!

There are plenty of places to cross-country ski between **La Manga and Cumbres passes** which can be accessed via Highway 17 south of Antonito. Those looking for a quiet getaway should be forewarned that snowmobilers like to share the area.

No matter what the season, skiers and snowboarders bring their old equipment and hike up the ever-shifting Sand Dunes for some fun. No lift ticket required.

Eco-Travel & Cultural Excursions

The country's longest, highest narrow-gauge railroad, the **Cumbres and Toltec Scenic Railroad**, PO Box 668, Antonito, 81120, ☎ 719/376-5483, chugs from Antonito, Colorado over 10,000-foot Cumbres Pass to Chama, New Mexico, through lush lands along the Los Pios River. The Denver and Rio Grande railroad line was originally laid to serve the mining operations in southern Colorado. Service was stopped after the mines shut down, but a community effort around 1970 to rebuild the tracks resulted in its reopening.

The Cumbres and Toltec Scenic Railroad operates from Memorial Day weekend through early October. Trips go to either Osier (the half-way lunch spot) or to Chama. The Chama trips require a bus return to Antonito.

Where to Stay & Eat

Accommodations

Club Crested Butte Club, Victorian Hotel & Spa, Drawer 309 Crested Butte, 81224, ☎ 800-815-CLUB, 970-349-6655, Fax 970-349-

7580. Victorian charm, complete health spa, each of seven rooms individually decorated with antiques, gas log fireplace in each room, complimentary breakfast. Moderate-expensive.

Cristiana Guesthaus, Bed & Breakfast, 621 Maroon Ave., P.O. Box 427, Crested Butte, 81224, ☎ 970-349-5326, 800-824-7899, Fax 970-349-1962. A European-style lodge in the National Historic District, with 21 rooms. Individually furnished with comforters or quilts, pine furniture, rocking chairs. All rooms have private baths. Moderate.

Great Sand Dunes Country Club and Inn, Zapata Ranch, 5303 Highway 150, Mosca, 81146, ☎ 719/378-2356 offers lodging in a setting that can't be beat. Moderate to expensive.

The Inn At Crested Butte, P.O. Box 2619, 510 Whiterock Ave., Crested Butte, 81224, ☎ 970-349-1225, 800-949-4828 (reservations only), Fax 970-349-1825. Constructed in 1993, the Inn features 17 non-smoking rooms with spectacular views of the surrounding mountains, each with a private bath, pine bed, armoire and down comforters. Moderate.

Sacred Earth B&B, 10 Baca Grant Way, Crestone, 81131, ☎ 719-256-4010. Moderate.

Wild Iris Inn Bed & Breakfast at La Garita Creek Ranch, 38145 Road E-39, Del Norte, 81132, ☎ 719/754-2533, has trout streams and outdoor pool, sauna, hot tub and tennis court. Moderate.

Valley View Hot Springs, PO Box 175, Villa Grove, 81155, ☎ 719/256-4315 has small cabins, dorm rooms and tent and RV sites. Inexpensive.

Restaurants

Le Bosquet, 201 Elk Ave., Crested Butte, ☎ 349-5808. Unique French cuisine, wild game, fresh seafood.

Casey's At The Manor Lodge, 650 Gothic Road, Mt. Crested Butte, ☎ 349-5365. Steak, seafood, pizza, chicken, paste, banquets, meal plans .

Common Grounds coffeehouse, 152 W. Silver Avenue, Crestone, ☎ 719/256-4288, is where you'll find great veggie cuisine, latté and desserts. Inexpensive-moderate.

Karolina's Kitchen, 127 Elk Ave., Crested Butte, ☎ 349-6765. Affordable home-style cooking in historic downtown.

Road Kill Café, 115 S. Alder, Crestone, ☎ 719/256-4975, has not only innovative eats but it's the place to tune in and find the local spiritual community (cards and flyers line the walls). Inexpensive.

Soupcon, 127 Elk Ave., Crested Butte, ☎ 349-5448. Innovative French cuisine served in an intimate cabin setting.

Swiss Chalet, 621 Gothic Road, Mt. Crested Butte, ☎ 349-5917. Swiss and German food, raclette and fondue.

Camping

Pinon Flats Campground has 88 sites within the Sand Dunes National Monument. Great Sand Dunes Oasis Campground and RV Park, Mosca, 81146, ☎ 719/589-9460.

San Luis Lakes State Park, PO Box 175, Mosca, 81146, ☎ 719/378-2020 has 51 sites, electric hookups and a shower building. Located eight miles from Colorado Highway 17 on 6 Mile Road north of Mosca.

For information about Rio Grande Forest Campgrounds, Buffalo Pass, Luders Creek, Storm King, Poso and Stone Celler, ☎ 719/655-2547.

FOR MORE INFORMATION

Sangre de Cristo Chamber of Commerce, PO Box 9, San Luis, CO 81152, ☎ 719/672-3355.

Alamosa Chamber of Commerce, Cole Park, Alamosa, CO 81101, ☎ 719/589-3681.

The following books shed light on aspects of the area not covered here and may be of interest:

The Smithsonian Guides to Natural America: The Southern Rockies. Smithsonian Books, Washington D.C. (Random House).

Guide to the Colorado Mountains. The Colorado Mountain Club, with Robert M. Ormes, edited by Randy Jacobs (Cordillera Press).

US Highway 40

Winter Park, Estes Park, Rocky Mountain National Park, Steamboat Springs

The state that brings you Aspen, Vail, Beaver Creek and Telluride is renowned for its skiing and snowboarding. Justly so. Colorado has a greater number of ski resorts and areas than almost any other US state or Canadian province. In all, you can ski at two dozen places that vary in size from giants like the Aspen complex to rustic alpine areas like Loveland Basin. Non-skiers find activities at the Colorado resorts as well.

Winter Park's history is interesting enough. A few hardy Denverites had already skied in the region by 1920. Winter Park, then "West Portal," consisted of saw mills and railroad shanties. A tunnel construction shack would serve as warming house to skiers who sought their thrills in forest glades and on logging roads. They climbed the Winter Park hills under their own steam, all the while dreaming of real trails. The dream became a reality in the mid-1930s when several ski clubs laid out better runs.

Denver's manager of Parks and Improvements was among the first to see the Winter Park potential. He appropriated the funds for a first ski tow, a T-bar of sorts, built with staves from old whiskey barrels. In March 1937, the Denver official told an astonished Colorado audience, "We'll create a winter playground unequalled in the world!"

Winter Park's official dedication took place on January 28, 1940. A band played. A ticket for the half-mile lift cost $1.50 for students.

By 1947, Winter Park had three T-bar lifts and four rope tows. The area made good progress during the early fifties. Soon there were numerous chairlifts. During the winter of 1960 Winter Park actually sold

US Highway 40

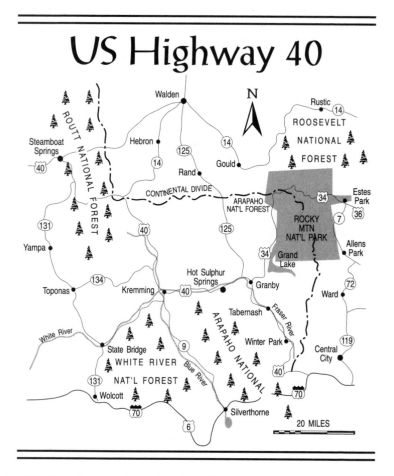

90,000 lift tickets. In 1964, it sold 158,000; in 1974, over a third of a million. In due time, the lift capacity doubled.

Keep in mind that the resorts offer summer programs, too. Highway 40 has two important ski resorts with enough to please hotshots, intermediates, and physically challenged skiers, as well as snow-boarders.

Getting Around

Reaching the hot destinations in this region means driving Highway 40. From Denver, use I-25 North to I-70 West. Follow signs to Highway 40 North past Georgetown.

Winter Park, the first destination in this route, is only a 1¼-hour drive northwest of Denver. To reach it, take I-70 west to Exit 232. Then use curvy Highway 40 over Berthoud Pass to Winter Park. **Silver Creek**, another ski area, is just 17 miles north of Winter Park on Highway 40. **Granby** is only a short jaunt along the Highway from there.

While **Steamboat Springs**, a booming mega-resort area, is the most outlying destination in this Colorado region, it is easy to reach in around 2½ hours from Winter Park by continuing along this north-westerly route.

When weather permits, Winter Park can be the easiest resort to reach from Denver. In a blizzard, the route over Berthoud Pass is best avoided; take the ski train.

If you stay on Highway 40, going through Granby and Kremmling, the views will reward you no matter what the season.

A little out of the way is **Estes Park**. One way to get here is to take Highway 40 through Granby to Highway 34. For many travelers Estes Park access is easier from Denver via Colorado 36.

Winter Park is lively in summer as well. The resort promotes flower walks and all kinds of hikes. At the same time, suspension bikes are for rent on 45 miles of bike trails with lift access. Moreover, the area's location is perfect for a drive to Steamboat Springs or, if you have less time, a trip to Granby where you can leave Highway 40 and depart to the scenic Grand Lake and eventually over the West's highest road to Estes Park.

Touring

Winter Park

The ski passions show up in Winter Park (☎ 970/726-5514). The mountain is constantly polished by a motorized army of snowcats, graders, rollers, and packers. On Saturday or Sunday noon, the major runs are usually pretty crowded. On holidays, thousands of Denverites come here by car, in chartered buses and via special weekend ski trains from Denver's historic Union Station. The distance from Denver is only 67 miles.

Consider Winter Park's skiing facilities. Most of the 10,800-foot mountain unrolls pleasantly for skiers who appreciate Winter Park's well-groomed terrain. The crews manning the many chairlifts are patient and you can ask them to slow down the machinery if necessary. Speedier skiers will appreciate the great number of rapid quads.

The addition of Parseann Bowl has rounded out the ski area's offerings – joining the moguls of Mary Jane, classic cruisers like Cranmer and the quiet, long trails of Vasquez Ridge.

A long awaited base area will finally bloom under the direction of Houston/Aspen Gerald Hines, completing the missing component in the Winter Park resort experience.

FOR MORE INFORMATION

Winter Park & Fraser Valley Visitor Information, ☎ 970/726-4118.

Estes Park

Estes Park, offers all kinds of action possibilities. A Swiss aerial tram, alpine slides for summer tobogganing, long hikes, easy or serious rock climbing, or the conquest of "Fourteeners" on non-dangerous trails are available. History buffs will want to know about an adventurer named Joel Estes who discovered the beautiful Estes area in 1860. After him came the British visitor Lord Dunraven, who attempted to establish a private preserve here. F.O. Stanley of the steamer fame came next. Thanks to him, Estes Park has a luxury hotel.

Today, Estes is a modern and well-equipped mountain city that serves the traveler well.

Most people begin their visit at the **visitors' center** on the south edge of town, at the intersection of Highways 34, 36, and 7. The large staff keeps the center open seven days a week in summer, with reduced hours in winter. It's here that you'll learn about the town's sightseeing tours. The center also offers a complete reservation service for over 100 regional accommodations and campgrounds.

Estes is an ideal place to rent horses and ride into the high country.

Estes Park connects with the 412-square-mile **Rocky Mountain National Park**. Only 70 miles from Denver, there are several roads to Estes Park, but the most spectacular threads its way through Big Thompson Canyon, site of a tragic 1976 flood.

The high point to everyone's visit at Rocky Mountain is a trip over **Trail Ridge Road**. Snaking its way over the mountains, it offers an 11-mile stretch above timberline, a chance to eat lunch in a café 12,000 feet above sea level, and a crossing of the Continental Divide.

Experts have counted some 200 species of wildlife in the Rocky Mountain National Park. More than 400 miles of trails, many of them gentle, others challenging, provide hikes to beautiful alpine mountain lakes surrounded by snow-capped peaks.

At the west end of the park is **Grand Lake**, another resort village set among stands of tall pines, and **Shadow Mountain Recreation Area**, 29 square miles of lakes and forest with many opportunities for boating, fishing and camping.

The sleepy village of Grand Lake is a popular area with many summer homes. The namesake lake, Colorado's largest natural body of water, and nearby Shadow Mountain Recreation Area have the nation's highest chartered yacht club, situated at two miles above sea level. Each summer, the group sponsors regattas and other boating events.

Grand Lake gets busy in July and August. Winters are quiet. You see some cross-country skiers on the frozen lake and at the **Grand Lake Ski Touring Area**, Box 590, Grand Lake, 80447, which is quite steep in places. On winter weekends the peace and quiet is shattered by snowmobilers, who have their own trails. Rentals are available. Wise visitors come to Grand Lake during the week instead of on weekends.

FOR MORE INFORMATION

Grand Lake Chamber of Commerce PO Box 57, Grand Lake, CO 80447, ☎ 970/627-3402.

Rocky Mountain National Park

No visitor to this part of Colorado should miss Rocky Mountain National Park. Its 300,000 acres are filled by stunning mountain views and, thanks to the Park Service, remain largely in their natural state.

Park Rangers exact a small daily fee to enter their domain. If you plan to visit other parks, it will pay off to buy a Golden Eagle Passport. It's good for your car and its occupants during the entire year. Travelers over 62 years old may ask for a Golden Age Passport.

Please note that the Rocky Mountain National Park has become so popular during recent years that every day several thousand cars stream through each of the entrances; the summer visitor count runs into the millions. Park your car at Bear Lake to get away from the motorists. A better bet for privacy is to head into the backcountry.

Hiking trails are well marked in the park. A popular hike suitable for only the hardiest walkers, and best accomplished with a push-off about 4 AM, is the conquest of Long's Peak, at 14,256 feet. Some 300 well-marked trails, many passing through meadows filled with wild-flowers, attract numerous hikers to the park.

The **visitors' center** a mile south of the Beaver Meadows entrance has a museum that interprets the history of the park. You can get park literature and maps or listen to talks about the natural wonders surrounding you. A half-mile, self-guiding nature trail starts here. Nature studies, lectures and tours are conducted by park rangers.

A Colorado fishing license entitles you to angle for trout in the park's many lakes. Since hunting is forbidden here, all forms of wildlife abound. Herds of elk and deer browse the high plains and slopes near the top of Trail Ridge Road during the summer. Above the treeline in the tundra area, you might encounter the yellowbelly marmot and the tiny pica. Beavers are also easy to observe.

You may actually be able to catch sight of some bighorn sheep, the elusive symbol of Rocky Mountain National Park. The bighorns can spot objects up to a kilometer or two away. They are exceptionally sure-footed. Look for them in the distance as they cling to precipitous slopes.

Above 9,000 feet or so, you wander among forests of Englemann spruce, subalpine fir, and limber pine.

Steamboat Springs

Some two hours west of Granby on Highway 40, giant Steamboat Springs caters to vacationers throughout the year. Steamboat has massive mountains, with a great number of lifts, a prestigious ski school and all kinds of accommodations in and around a community that sticks to its Western image – jeans, Stetsons, cowboy boots and all. The skiers' hostelries pack some surprises and cross-country enthusiasts, not just the downhill crowd, enjoy Steamboat immensely.

The resort organizes many public events all winter long, including its famous **Winter Carnival** and aptly named **Spring Stampede**. If you happen to be there in mid-January, you'll be treated to a unique Rockies' spectacle. They call it the **Cowboy Downhill**, no less, and it features Pro Rodeo winners and dozens of other rodeo stars, some of whom are trading saddles for skis for the first time. It's horse riders on a slalom course.

Steamboat, a.k.a. "Ski Town, USA," is closer to Denver (153 miles) than Aspen (205 miles). From the Winter Park ski area, the drive is less than three hours over good roads via Rabbit Ears Pass to Steamboat. Commuter flights arrive from Denver or direct from certain cities to Hayden Airport, 28 miles from the ski mountains. It's possible that the closer-to-town, more conveniently located Steamboat Springs airport will reopen to commercial traffic in the near future.

HISTORY

In 1865, three trappers wandered through the Yampa Valley, amazed by its many mineral springs. One bubbling spring made "chugging riverboat sounds" and, if the story is true, Steamboat Springs received its name right then and there. The area was being homesteaded as far back as 1875; some of the settlers were Scandinavians who soared down these snowy Colorado hills on long boards. High leaps from knolls were not uncommon either.

Skis, snowshoes and toboggans became a necessity when snow masses buried Steamboat's hinterland. In summer, the Yampa Valley lived from cattle ranching and farming. Before 1900, some temporary inhabitants – like Butch Cassidy and his desperados – also made their living here, but by means of guns.

After the turn of the century, the Moffat Railroad brought prosperity to the area. Before long, most everyone skied and jumped from the tip of a giant hill before many other Americans thought of such things. Some of the biggest jumps were built during the twenties. For years, Steamboat youngsters learned to ski, gratis, in kindergarten, through high school, and in the local college. Men with first names like Alf, Ansten, Lars, or Ragnar showed off their telemark turns and Steamboat's jumpers and racers – immigrants as well as natives – showed the world what they were made of. In those days Steamboat produced more Olympians than other Colorado communities.

Some of the local ex-racers and ex-jumpers eventually ran the Steamboat Ski School, helped lay out the trails and rented equipment to the visiting ski tourists. The Mount Werner ski area opened officially in 1962, drawing customers from Colorado and the adjacent states. Still, Steamboat's success as a resort remained modest at best for years.

In 1969, the image of a sleepy Western hamlet changed. Steamboat caught the interest of the Dallas-based LTV financial colossus. One of its subsidiaries, LTV Recreation Development, Inc., bought up Mount Werner and the Steamboat ski facilities. The deal included the existing lifts and buildings, plus 400 acres of prime land surrounding the mountain slopes. Another 1,100 acres were later added to the parcel, all of which eventually made Steamboat an important American vacation resort. The Texas owners ordered the Swiss Bell Gondola and put up the massive Village Inn, which earned the local nickname of "Dallas Palace," for its popularity with visiting Texans. They leveled a good many aspen groves, and built the new village known as "Dallas North."

Thanks to additional ski area expansion, and the reliable snow conditions, Steamboat progressed at a rate that astonished many. Reservations can be difficult to secure during Christmas, New Years, and Easter vacations, making this a good area to avoid during peak season.

Summers here guarantee you an adrenaline rush. The breaking in of wild horses, the barrel racing on horseback, the gallop through forest clearings are all exciting. Climbers have attacked the rock faces of Rabbit Ears Pass. And, of course, you can reach the Mount Werner summits in style by gondola and then test your leg muscles against the long downhill walks or ski runs through knee-high meadows or on logging roads.

FOR MORE INFORMATION

Rocky Mountain National Park, ☎ 970/586-2371.

Colorado Division of Wildlife, 6060 Broadway, Denver, CO 80216, ☎ 303/297-1192.

Colorado State Parks, 1313 Sherman Street, Rm. 618, Denver, CO 80203, ☎ 303/866-3437, provides information on camping and boating in state parks and recreation areas.

National Forests in Colorado: US Forest Service, Box 25127, Lakewood, CO 80225, ☎ 303/236-9431.

National Parks and Monuments in Colorado: National Park Service, Rocky Mountain Region, 12795 West Alameda Parkway, Lakewood, CO 80225, ☎ 303/969-2000.

Contact the following for lists of outfitters serving the area:

Colorado Department of Regulatory Agencies, 1560 Broadway, #1340, Denver, CO 80202, ☎ 303/894-7778.

Colorado Outfitters Association, PO Box 44021, Aurora, CO, 80041, ☎ 303/368-4731. Call or write for a list of guides and outfitters. Or visit online at www.onlinecol.com/sd/coa/035.htm.

Adventures

On Foot

WINTER PARK

To reach **Columbine Lake Trail**, take the Devil's Thumb Road turnoff from Highway 40. Follow the signs to Meadow Creek Reservoir, where the trailhead begins. This is a moderate hike that terminates at a serene mountain lake. Approximately five miles.

Byers Lake beckons the more ambitious hiker to its 12,804-foot summit. Take County Road 73 from Fraser to its trailhead.

Winter Park Resort, PO Box 36, Winter Park, 80482, ☎ 970/726-5514 or 800/453-2525. For hiking, mountain biking, or sightseeing on Winter Park Mountain, a seven-minute lift ride here delivers you to the 10,700-foot level through Labor Day, and weekends through September. The Alpine Slide is a scream of a good time.

ROCKY MOUNTAIN NATIONAL PARK

Hiking in Rocky Mountain National Park, you are almost certain to be rewarded with stunning vistas, some of Colorado's most spectacular scenery, and rare encounters with nature, such as a bugling elk. Some of Rocky Mountain National Park's easier hikes are up to the area's striking waterfalls. One of these, **Adams Falls**, can be accessed from Tunnel Road, east of the town of Grand Lake. This easy hike is only a half-mile from start to finish. **Cascade Falls**, on the other hand, is a slightly more ambitious walk. This trail measures approximately three miles and also terminates at a cool, crystal clear falls. You can catch this trail at the north Inlet Trailhead on Tunnel Road.

One moderately difficult but sure-to-please hike is the **Onahu Creek/Green Mountain Loop**. This trail is among the Park's finest for mountain scenery and critter spying. The trail takes you through moose and elk habitat among marshes and forests. To reach this pure delight, start at the Onahu Trailhead on Highway 34 north of Kawuneeche Visitor's Center. Approximately seven miles long.

Rock Climbing

The National Park Service has authorized the **Rocky Mountain Climbing and Guide Service** of Estes Park to conduct climbs and hiking trips within the park.

The park offers classes for various heights and difficulties. If you haven't climbed before, the instruction will give you a foundation to be a safe climber. If you have climbed before, this is a great opportunity to polish your skill.

Call ☎ 970/586-5758 for more information.

STEAMBOAT SPRINGS

Miles of trails criss-cross the aspen stands and conifer forest in **Routt National Forest**. To be precise, there are 30 marked hiking trails in the Yampa Valley, one for every age and ability. Heartier souls might go in for the multi-day backpacking trip along the 10,000-foot-high **Wyoming Trail** on the Continental Divide.

If you have only a few hours, instead of days, one jewel is the one-hour jaunt to **Fish Creek Falls**. You will be awed as you come up the trail. Water plunges 283 feet from a rocky mountainside, thundering into a crystal pool. What's more, you'll enjoy the miles of footpaths that meander around the area. Take advantage of the vistas. This is an ideal spot for brown-bagging.

On Wheels

WINTER PARK

Mountain Biking

If you ask the locals, they'll eagerly tell you that the Winter Park area can't be beat for mountain biking. In fact, the local paper probably mentions that the Fraser Valley has been dubbed "Mountainbike Capital, USA."

The Fraser Valley, including Winter Park, Fraser and Tabernash, boasts some 600 miles of fat-tire trails, of which 250 miles are single-track trails. Another interesting aspect of the area is the 45 miles of lift-accessed trails within Winter Park Resort itself.

A beginning rider might be interested in pedaling along the Fraser River on the **Fraser River Trail**. This wide, flat trail meanders alongside the river from Winter Park to the town of Fraser. It represents the perfect opportunity to stretch your legs on an afternoon.

More experienced riders can seek their thrills on **Mountain Goat Trail**. Actually within Winter Park, the Mountain Goat challenges riders with technical sections like creek crossings and switchbacks.

Those of you with stamina might like to pedal your way to the top. The trail, **Roof of the Rockies**, takes riders up to the summit of the 11,200-foot Mary Jane Mountain. This trail guarantees drop-dead views.

Corona Pass is one of the moderate-to-difficult rides. It follows along the path of the first railroad in the county and accesses Forest Service Road 49, which climbs to the top of the Continental Divide. The trail is south of Winter Park along Highway 40.

Riders will be pleased to know that **Zephyr Express**, one of Winter Park's high-speed chairlifts, will whisk you and your bike to 45 miles of trails that wind down Winter Park Mountain. ☎ 800/453-2525. Rentals and tours are available at the resort.

Rail Trips

For some 60 years Denverites have supported the rail trip to Winter Park. It starts at Denver's Union Station and ends on the ski slopes. The first such train ran in 1936. In the meantime, skiers welcome the reliable schedule, departing on weekends at 7:30AM and returning to Denver at 6:15PM. The two-hour adventure covers 56 miles, travels through 29 tunnels and climbs almost 4,000 feet.

For more information contact the **Ski Train**, c/o Ansco, 555 15th Street, Denver, 80202, ☎ 303/298-1000.

On Water

WINTER PARK

River trips starting from Winter Park require at least a small drive downstream from the source of the Colorado River and the true beginning of water adventures. Trips also head to Clear Creek, the Arkansas and North Platte Rivers.

Lake Granby, Grand Lake and Shadow Mountain Lake comprise the bodies of water known collectively as "Grand Lake." This is the largest natural lake in Colorado, the deepest, too, and home to Kokanee, brown, rainbow and lake trout, salmon and mackinaw.

Granby is the largest and also a mecca for fishermen. Motorboats and sailboats explore the nooks and crannies of Grand Lake during the short summer season. The truly brave windsurf the cold waters.

The well-established, Winter Park-based Mad Adventures outfit organizes rafting trips of various types on the nearby Clear Creek, or full summer days on the Arkansas River. Buffet meals are included. For more information contact **Mad Adventures**, PO Box 650, Winter Park, 80482, ☎ 800/451-4844.

At the Western edge of Rocky Mountain National Park, the headwaters for the Colorado River amass before beginning their thousand-mile-plus journey downstream to the Gulf of California. Three bracingly cold water lakes – Grand Lake, Lake Granby and Shadow Mountain Reservoir – host motorized, sail and hand-powered boaters. The truly brave may chose to windsurf on the reservoir. **Trail Ridge Marina**, 12634 Hwy. 34, Grand Lake, 80482, offers reliable boat rentals, ☎ 970/627-3586.

Raven Adventure Trips, PO Box 108, Granby, 80446, ☎ 800/332-3381, offers river trips both mild and wild on rafts and duckies.

ESTES PARK

Even the most avid of anglers will want to cast attention towards Estes Park.

For fly-fishing, the Colorado River cannot be faulted. Have your frying pan sizzling because the fish thrive in the chilly waters here. Indeed, the Colorado has been named a Gold Medal Trout Stream because of the high number of trout over 14 inches pulled from its waters.

Perhaps you are looking for more of a sure thing. **Trout Heaven**, PO Box 1629, Estes Park, 80517, ☎ 970/586-5525, may just be your ticket. This fishery farm does not require a license to hook their 10-28-inch rainbow trout. Besides, you pay only for what you catch. And, as an added bonus, the proprietors will clean and pack your catch on ice.

STEAMBOAT SPRINGS

The Steamboat area offers a multitude of watersports, from gentle river floats to churning whitewater rafting, from light sailing to challenging sailboarding, and everything in between.

Anglers will love **Steamboat Lake**, north on County Road 129. This most scenic fishing hole allows fly, lure and bait fishing.

Kayakers should try the **Yampa** and **Elk Rivers**. **Adventures Wild**, 8th St. and Lincoln Avenue, ☎ 800/825-3989, can help you arrange trips by the hour or by the day.

The Strawberry Park Hot Springs, ☎ 970/879-0342, may be just what the doctor ordered after a day of high adventure. Soak away the tensions on the slope in natural, backcountry pools. Cabins are also available for rent.

On the way to Steamboat Springs from Winter Park, via Highway 40, is the rustic **Hot Sulphur Springs Mineral Baths**, Hot Sulphur Springs, 80451, ☎ 970/725-3306. Steaming waters of 110-120°, where the Ute Indians once took refuge, surge into the mineral pools. Management has been spotty in the past, so call first. Located in Middle Park at an elevation of 7,660 feet.

On Horseback

ESTES PARK

A favorite way to enjoy this park and surrounding country is on horseback. Estes Park calls itself "the horse capital of Colorado" and rental stables exist en masse. Horses can be leased by the hour or day; you can ride with a guide or on your own. Horses with guides are available inside the park's east entrance.

Two stables are close to Estes Park. **Elkhorn Lodge Stables**, ☎ 970/586-5225, is at 650 W. Elkhorn Road, Estes Park, 80517. **Sombrero Ranch Stables**, ☎ 970/586-4577, is at 1895 Big Thompson Road, Estes Park, 80517.

DUDE RANCHES

The concept actually started in the 19th century when cattle barons began to set aside a few rooms for their invited guests and later for paying ones. As the idea spread through the West, the "dudes" told their friends about their experience. In time, more and more people were attracted by the home-like atmosphere. The dude ranch became a success.

Guests can still rely on well-cooked meals with lots of beef, served family-style. The long tables allow you to get acquainted with other people.

You can dress in jeans or other casual wear for this kind of vacation. Bring flannel shirts and a sweater; dude ranches require no elegant clothes, ever. The ride itself will be more comfortable if you come with some kind of boots and a windbreaker in case of rain.

Colorado's four dozen dude ranches emphasize horseback riding, but some ranches also feature swimming pools and tennis courts. Fishing in mountain streams is popular, too.

Some of these places are working cattle ranches where visitors become part-time cowhands. You can generally expect comfortable cabins, cookouts, and horseback riding aplenty – from a guided beginner's ride to breakfast rides, steak fries at night to six-day pack trips through the wilderness. Colorado's dude ranches are getting more popular, so reservations should be made as far in advance as possible, never less than two months ahead.

The owners of some ranches have pleased and entertained their guests for three decades. At one establishment, couples showed up on their first trip together and returned 25 years later for their wedding anniversary. There is a warm feeling about these vacation centers, hiding out there in natural surroundings, nestling deeply in forests, straddling mountain tops, overlooking rivers that rush and splash all night. Dude ranch lodges are usually built of the pine or spruce woods and the stone and rock of the region. Your window will surely look out upon pretty scenes.

In general, dude ranch horses are easy-going critters. You'll learn how to make them go left or right in one quick lesson. Besides, a guide always comes along, making sure that everything goes well.

FOR MORE INFORMATION

Latigo Ranch, Box 237, Kremmling, 80459, ☎ 800/227-9655. It's especially lovely here during the quiet winter months, when cross-country skiing opportunities abound.

Lazy H Guest Ranch, PO Box 248, Allenspark, CO 80510, ☎ 800/578-3598.

Drowsy Water Ranch, PO Box 147A, Granby, CO 80446, ☎ 800/845-2292 or 303/725-3456.

Aspen Canyon Ranch, 13206 County Road #3, Star Route, Parshall, CO 80468, ☎ 800/321-1357.

Bar Lazy J Guest Ranch, Box ND, Parshall, CO 80468, ☎ 303/725-3437.

To find out what's available throughout the state, contact **Colorado Dude and Guest Ranch Association**, PO Box 300, Tabernash, CO 80478, ☎ 970/887-3128.

Among the most deluxe and well-run guest ranches found anywhere are three area properties. Two are near Steamboat Springs, Vista Verde Guest Ranch, and the Home Ranch. One is in Granby, the C-Lazy-U. These properties are described elsewhere in the text and are each worthy of a separate trip, or repeated visits.

On Snow

ESTES PARK

Once home to the now-defunct Hidden Valley ski area, Rocky Mountain National Park these days hosts only Nordic and telemark skiers and snowshoers content to glide along on their own (rather than using chairlifts). Ski and snowshoe routes follow the well-trod hiking trails of summer, including the Bear Lake and Fern Lake Trailheads on the eastern end of the park.

WINTER PARK

The Winter Park region abounds with free cross-country ski trails, along with a major cross-country center. Make a note of **The Devil's**

Thumb Ranch, west of Fraser and a mere 20-minute drive from Winter Park. It excels in terrain, trail management, scenery and general atmosphere. The ranch trail network measures 40 miles (67 kms). The rental shop is excellent, too. ☎ 970/726-8155.

Adjacent to Winter Park, the **Corona Pass Road** (directly off Highway 40) is perfect for the average Nordic skier. No fee. **Beaver Village**, the first-rate condo complex, connects with the Idlewild trails, as well as having its own free trails.

STEAMBOAT SPRINGS

The **Steamboat Ski Area** consists of Storm Peak, Sunshine Peak, Thunderhead Peak and Christie Peak.

Storm Peak is favored for its trails, bump runs and powder fields. Buddy's Run, a long intermediate cruiser, is one of the best intermediate level trails in Colorado. The top of Storm Peak provides access to the "Tourtes," a series of three very steep chutes, to Big Meadow and to Sunshine Peak.

Sunshine Peak is your key to Steamboat's famous gladed tree runs, Shadows and Twilight. The variety of terrain available on Sunshine ranges from easy, spirited cruising on trails surrounding Sunshine Lift to bone-crunching mogul runs on Priest Creek and Sundown. Beginners revel in Sunshine Bowl. Intermediates can hone techniques on Two O'Clock and Three O'Clock before making the lunch run to elegant Ragnar's or picnicking on "The Beach" at Rendezvous Saddle.

From **Thunderhead**, the top of the Silver Bullet Gondola, a number of ego-building runs connect the average skier with the valley.

Steamboat is one of the most versatile ski resorts. It provides lessons for every type of skier, caters to telemark skiers, and arranges special three-hour lessons for snowboarders. More adventure is generated by backcountry skiing. For additional information, contact **Steamboat**, 2305 Mount Werner Circle, 80487, ☎ 970/879-6111 (ski area), 800/922-2722, or **Steamboat Springs Chamber Resort Association**, PO Box 774408, Steamboat Springs, 80477, ☎ 800/922-2722.

Much alpine action is to be found at **Howelsen Hill**. The Hill was the site of Carl Howelsen's 119-foot jump at Steamboat's first Winter Carnival back in 1914.

Today, it attracts world-class skiers from far and wide. Howelsen Hill now has five different ski jumps that are used for Olympic-level qualifying meets and training. The hill is serviced by a poma lift and rope tow for those daring enough to brave it. Howelsen is deceptively steep. For visitors who can't get enough skiing/boarding during the day, the slopes are open most evenings, so bundle up.

After you've had your fill of swooshing down the slopes on skis in the fashion of Howelsen, "The flying Norseman," himself. You might want to try your hand at whizzing down the mountain in a sled.

Howelsen Hill has a 4,800-foot bobsled run – one of the few in the country open to the public. And what a thrill it is. The heavily padded sleds do not require steering. All that's left for you is to sit back, hang on, and enjoy the ride

At the Mount Werner ski area itself, the **Steamboat Touring Center**, PO Box 772297, Steamboat Springs, 80477, ☎ 970/879-8180, is recommended. And 25 miles from Steamboat, the **Vista Verde Ranch**, Box 65, Steamboat Springs, 80477, enjoys an isolation which is ideal for cross-country skiing. ☎ 970/879-3858.

In the Air

ESTES PARK

The Estes Park Aerial Tramway, west on US 34 to Moraine Park Road, carries passengers through the air to the 8,896-foot summit of Prospect Mountain for an unmatched look at the community and surrounding mountains. It's a short ride and operates from mid-May through September.

STEAMBOAT SPRINGS

To truly get the lay of the land, take to the skies and get a bird's eye view of Steamboat's stunning snow-capped peaks, daring downhill runs and quaint town.

A few area balloon operators can help you earn your wings. Keep in mind it is best to have a reservation.

Aerosports Balloonists, PO Box 881891, 80488, ☎ 970/879-RIDE (7433).

Balloons Over Steamboat, The Village at Steamboat Resorts, Pine Grove Circle, 80488, ☎ 970/879-3298.

Where to Stay & Eat

Accommodations

WINTER PARK

The best slopeside lodging is found at the **Iron Horse Resort Retreat,** ☎ 970/726-8851. Units are spacious and offer a view of mountains. Soak in the large hot tub and enjoy the other on-site amenities, which include a good restaurant and conference center. Deluxe.

Beaver Village, Beaver Village Drive, ☎ 800/824-8438. Large, clean condos. Sound-proofed walls, handsome stone fireplaces. Friendly management. Expensive.

Meadow Ridge Condominiums, ☎ 800/551-9943. Ten minutes west of Winter Park on a hillside overlooking the Fraser Valley. Remote and idyllic. Good for large families, groups or honeymooners. Swimming pool. Tennis courts. Free shuttles to skiing. Expensive.

Alpine Vacations, PO Box 3123, 80482, ☎ 800/551-9943. Condos in many Winter Park locations. Moderate.

Aspen Canyon Ranch, 13206 County Road #3, Star Route, Parshall, 80468, ☎ 800/321-1357. Moderate.

Alpen Rose Bed & Breakfast, 244 Forest Trail, 80482, ☎ 800/531-1373. Moderate.

Engelmann Pines Bed & Breakfast, PO Box 1305, 80482, ☎ 800/992-9512. Moderate.

Arapahoe Ski Lodge, Highway 40, 80482, ☎ 970/726-8222, is a cozy alpine-style lodge located downtown. Heated swimming pool, spa and restaurant. Moderate.

ESTES PARK

Stanley Hotel, 333 Wonderview Avenue, 80517, ☎ 970/586-3371. Handsome, historic hotel with Victorian rooms and a fine ambiance. Large solar-heated outdoor pool. Restaurants, theater. This was the setting for the Stanley Kubrick-Jack Nicholson movie, *The Shining.* Moderate-expensive.

Inn at Estes, 1701 Big Thompson Avenue, 80517, ☎ 970/586-5363. On Highway 34. Overlooks lake, with three heated pools, playground, pleasant rooms. Moderate.

Holiday Inn, 101 S. Vrain Highway, 80517, ☎ 970/586-2332. At Highways 36 and CO 7. Large rooms, Olympic indoor pool, and game area. Restaurant and bar on premises. Favored by conventions.

Ponderosa Lodge, 1820 Fall River Road, 80517, ☎ 970/586-4233. Year-round. Family-owned and friendly. Fishing, playground, picnic tables. Moderate.

Aspen Lodge and Guest Ranch, Long's Peak Route A, 80517, ☎ 970/586-4241. Situated in an aspen grove, with lake, riding, square dancing, hiking, pool, hot tub, fishing. Lodge and cottages. Open all year. Conferences. Expensive.

Wind River Ranch, PO Box 3410D, 80517, ☎ 800/523-4212. Expensive.

The Anniversary Inn Bed & Breakfast, 1060 Mary's Lake Road, 80517, ☎ 970/586-6200. Expensive.

The Baldpate Inn, 4900 Highway 7, 80517, ☎ 970/586-6151. Moderate.

GRAND LAKE & GRANBY

The big piney **Grand Lake Lodge**, PO Box 569, Grand Lake, 80447, ☎ 970/627-3967 is a landmark in this small mountain town, perched overlooking Grand Lake and Shadow Mountain Lake. Cabins in the woods offer welcome getaways and the lodge, with its big fireplace, is a great place to gather. Located north of town on Highway 34. Open summers only.

Monte Lodge, Box 105, US Highway 40, Granby, 80446, ☎ 970/887-3348. TV, heated pool, playground, pets limited. Café and cocktail lounge. A Best Western chain member. Expensive.

Daven Haven Lodge, Grand Lake, 80447, a quarter-mile south on Main Street, ☎ 970/627-8144. Small summer complex on Grand Lake. Boats, waterskiing, mini-golf, shuffleboard, badminton, heated pool. Cocktail lounge. Restaurant. Moderate.

Driftwood Lodge, Box 609, on US 34, ☎ 970/627-3654. Three miles south of town. Open all year. Many amenities. Overlooks lake, with tables and grills furnished for picnicking. Moderate.

C LAZY U

This is a highly regarded year-round dude ranch in Granby with a sauna, two bars, a masseuse, championship tennis courts, indoor racquetball, skeet shooting, guided cross-country skiing, and golf. This 180-horse ranch is the only such establishment to consistently earn a top Mobil Award or the AAA's Five Diamonds. For good reasons, too. Cocktail hour with hors d'oeuvres takes place at the most elegant lounge in this part of the Rockies, where original oil paintings grace the walls. There is silver service dining under chandeliers and, on occasion, a pianist plays light music.

The atmosphere is congenial. The food is outstanding. Vintage wines flow.

The C Lazy U, 90 miles west of Denver, pampers its guests. A ranch hand carries your luggage and leads you to plush accommodations. You get a personal horse for your stay, and you and your group set out into a quiet, slightly remote, truly relaxing 5,000 acres of mountains and hillsides, forests and rivers, ponds and lookout points.

Apart from breakfast cookouts, there are daytime excursions of between one and three hours, some of them meant for novices. Hardier riders are often in the saddle for six hours or longer as they travel into the high country. At night, "steak fry cookouts" are popular. Complimentary riding lessons are offered for those who need a helping hand.

You can make a C Lazy U vacation as active or as lazy as you wish. You could, for instance, sit all day around the award-winning swimming pool, or test the waters of the huge whirlpool facilities. You could play table tennis on several tables which are hand-polished every day. You could hike with a guide, alone, or with that special someone in the fresh mountain air, far away from the city. C Lazy U can arrange rafting, golfing, and tennis lessons. A jogging track is on the grounds.

Pond, lake and stream fishing will satisfy discriminating anglers. Beautiful Willow Creek runs through the Ranch for nearly 1½ miles. Professional guides lead you to secret beaver ponds and crystal-clear mountain streams.

In December, events are playing ice hockey, skating and tubing. At the Nordic shop, 100 pairs of cross-country skis, boots and poles await the lucky folks.

Just who comes to a dude ranch like the C Lazy U? You could meet up with some of the top Country Western stars, especially those from Tennessee and other Southern states. Reason: The South gets hot in summer while the Rocky Mountain West remains cool. Lately, Japanese, Arabian and wealthy South Americans have been spotted here, too. European visitors nowadays go in for

Colorado's Wild West; Germans often travel fully equipped in riding outfits bought at Western-style stores in Munich or Frankfurt. Because of the privacy and laid-back style, movie celebrities often use the C Lazy U as a retreat. That idea also works for honeymooners.

If you ask beforehand, your host's van will be at the Granby airport to meet your private plane. The C Lazy U will also pick you up from the train in Granby. Limousine service from the Denver airport can be arranged. Keep in mind that rates at C Lazy U are plush, to say the least.

Contact C Lazy U, PO Box 379, Granby, ☎ 970/887-3344.

STEAMBOAT SPRINGS

Sheraton Steamboat, at the gondola, ☎ 800/848-8878. Ideal location for skiers, saunas, heated pool, restaurants. Convention facilities. Expensive.

Rabbit Ears Motel, 201 Lincoln, ☎ 970/879-1150. Clean motel on Steamboat's Main Street; refrigerators and microwaves in rooms. Moderate.

The Home Ranch, Box 8221, Clark, 80428, ☎ 303/879-9044. Home Ranch is a peaceful, upscale, chuck-it-all mountain retreat, complete with horses, miles of trails, a hot tub on the deck of your private cabin, and other goodies. These include fresh chocolate chip cookies in your cabin, and a wood stove that has been carefully stuffed with kindling. The food is top-notch, not cowboy gray. Terrific cross-country skiing in winter. Expensive.

Vista Verde Ranch, Box 465, 80477, ☎ 303/879-3858. Open June 1-September 30, and December 15-March 15. Exceptionally peaceful. Remote. Well-run and accommodating. Moderate to expensive.

The Log Cabin Bed & Breakfast, 47890 County Road 129, 80487, ☎ 970/879-5837. Moderate.

Steamboat Valley Guest House, 1245 Crawford Avenue, 80477, ☎ 800/530-3866. Moderate.

A former church turned guest house, the **Steamboat Bed & Breakfast**, 442 Pine Street, 80477, is roomy, friendly and has a resident cat. Within walking distance of all of downtown's activities and the mountain shuttles. Inexpensive.

Restaurants

WINTER PARK

The Last Waltz Restaurant, PO Box 181, 80482, ☎ 970/726-4877. Mexican favorites. Moderate.

The Chalet Lucerne Restaurant, ☎ 970/726-5402. Interesting continental fare, with some American items. Chef-owned. Good open wines. Friendly. Closed Mondays. Moderate.

GRAND LAKE

Red Fox, Grand Lake, ☎ 970/627-9404. Continental restaurant. Dinner only. Deluxe to expensive.

Chuck Hole Café. 1119 Grand Avenue, ☎ 970/627-3509. Home cooking. Locally popular. Inexpensive.

ESTES PARK

Aspen's Restaurant, at Holiday Inn. Pleasantly lighted. Variety of dishes. Outstanding salad bar. Moderate.

Nicky's, 1½ miles from downtown on US 34, ☎ 970/586-5376. Locally popular beef restaurant. Year-round. Moderate-expensive.

Stanley Hotel. 333 Wonderview Ave., ☎ 970/586-3371. Charming and elegant. Good management. Expensive.

Old Plantation. 128 E. Elkhorn, ☎ 970/586-2800. Yankee pot roast, baked chicken, rainbow trout. Summer and fall only. Moderate.

The Other Side Restaurant. In National Park Village, Highway 34, ☎ 970/586-2171. Handsome restaurant overlooking lake. Great variety of foods. Coffee shop. Bar. Moderate.

STEAMBOAT SPRINGS

Ore House, 1465 Pine Grove Road, ☎ 970/879-1190. Expensive.

Mazzola's, between town and mountain on Highway 40, ☎ 970/879-2405. Lunch and dinner. Italian. Moderate.

Dos Amigos, Ski Time Square, ☎ 970/879-4270, Mexican and more. Moderate.

Camping

ESTES PARK

Camping is permitted in many wilderness areas. Obtain a permit from any ranger station within the park. There are several roadside campgrounds, which tend to fill up early each day during the summer. Informative campfire programs are conducted by ranger-naturalists at major campgrounds, along with guided nature walks. Bring warm clothing. This region can get cold at night.

Moraine Park Campground (elevation 8,200 feet). One mile west of Moraine Park Visitor Center off Bear Lake Road. 256 campsites. Flush-type comfort stations, fireplaces, running water, picnic tables.

Glacier Basin Campground (elevation 8,500 feet). Nine miles west of Estes Park on Bear Lake Road. 185 sites. Facilities similar to Moraine Park. Spectacular views.

Aspenglen (elevation 8,230 feet). Five miles west of Estes Park on the Fall River Road (US 34). 110 campsites. Similar to Moraine Park.

Endovalley (elevation 8,650 feet). Nine miles west of Estes Park on the Old Fall River Road at the extreme west end of Horseshoe Park. 75 campsites. Tents only. Same facilities as others, except that comfort stations are of pit privy type.

Longs Peak (elevation 9,500 feet). Eleven miles south of Estes Park and one mile west of South St. Vrain Highway. 35 campsites. Located at foot of Longs Peak Trail. Popular with those who plan to climb Long's Peak. (Full day required.)

Wild Basin Campground (elevation 8,400 feet). Seventeen miles south of Estes Park, and 2½ miles west of South St. Vrain Highway. One campsite. Facilities include pit privy comfort station, picnic tables and fireplaces. Situated at the start of Wild Basin trail system.

FOR MORE INFORMATION

Rocky Mountain National Park, Estes Park, CO 80517; Backcountry Office, ☎ 970/586-1242.

STEAMBOAT SPRINGS

Routt National Forest

Routt National Forest offers ample camping opportunities amid striking vistas. Among the choices:

Dry Lake. At 8,000 feet, this site might just take your breath away. This is a no-fee campground. Only eight sites, so arrive early. Seven miles from town, up Buffalo Pass Road.

Hahns Peak Lake. This 26-site campground is one of the most popular in the whole forest. Sites have tables, fireplace grates, vault toilets and dumpsters. Thirty-three miles north of Steamboat.

WINTER PARK

Just five miles from Winter Park, on Highway 40, the **Robbers Roost Campground** offers 11 sites. Also on Highway 40 is the **Sitzmark Cabins & RV Park**, Box 65, Winter Park, 80482, ☎ 970 726-5453, which features a rustic RV park and housekeeping cabins.

FOR MORE INFORMATION

USFS Hahn's Peak District Ranger Office, ☎ 970/879-1870.

I-70 West

The Continental Divide & Ski Areas

Of all the Highways leading west from Denver to and over the Continental Divide, Interstate 70 is the busiest and scenically the most impressive. The steady climb from mile-high Denver to Idaho Springs (elevation: 7,524) to Georgetown (elevation: 8,512) to the Eisenhower Tunnel once required enormous efforts from road engineers and workmen.

The roads are now smooth and efficient across the Divide to the Colorado ski resorts. Here's a vast landscape that once saw huge herds of buffaloes; Kiowa, Cheyenne, and Sioux Indians rode at breakneck pace across these mountains. There were the trappers and traders, the map-making surveyors and the artists, all facing the summer sun and the winter blizzards. Explorers like Pike, Fremont, and Long trekked across this high country; in 1855, an Englishman named Lord George Gore and his large retinue hunted antelope, deer and elk near what is now the Vail resort. Transportation across Loveland Pass and other heights posed tremendous barriers for migrants.

The West's high gold and silver finds sped up construction all over the Colorado territory. But the steep terrain and the need for many switchback curves devoured the builder's funds. Some made fortunes with toll roads across these mountains. Business could be brisk in the Rockies. Marshall Sprague, a Western mining authority, described the hustle and bustle of 1878 when thousands streamed across the Divide to Leadville. The road was "jammed with wagons, stages, buggies, carts. There were men pushing wheelbarrows, men riding animals, men and dogs driving herds of cattle, sheep, pigs and goats."

Most of the area's stage coach traffic would slow down in winter. Travel across the Continental Divide's High Line Road was always fraught with hazards. A stage coach with 10-15 coach passengers required plenty of patience. The six-horse teams would get stuck in the snow to their bellies, and it was not unusual for the sleighs to topple over, catapulting their human cargo into a soft snowbank. The teamsters wore long overcoats and burlap sacks to keep warm. In summer, the stage line promised "No walking, no dust, no danger." But storms and rains could rut roads over the Divide. Things could get so bad that drivers had to put planks across the washed-out or potholed road sections. Between present-day Dillon and Georgetown, some stages had to turn back altogether.

At the end of the 19th century, the rails had been laid in many high places, too, and trains ran along hair-raising mountain shelves. Thanks to mining riches, there was frequent discussion about an "Atlantic-Pacific" tunnel to be built with convict labor through the Divide. Nothing came of it, but a unique idea was hatched by W.A.H. Loveland, who'd built the original High Line Road, and after whom Colorado's Loveland Pass was eventually named.

The financier wanted to build a railroad across this mountainous hurdle. Loveland had organized the Colorado Central Railroad, and one of his tracks ran from Denver to Georgetown, some miles short of the pass. An extension to Utah and the Pacific seemed attainable. But Loveland's scheme faced obstacles. Trouble began when the residents of a mountain hamlet mobbed the Chinese railroad laborers. The Chinese crew fled in terror. Other workers found the laying of rails – and the climate – too rough, and many of them quit. Besides, there was the problem of ferrying the tracks across the inhospitable Continental Divide. The resourceful W.A.H. Loveland planned to haul the rails over the ridges by cable. Eventually, his money petered out, and the project was abandoned. But the Union Pacific trains were running across the Divide in Wyoming and other states. By 1885, the Canadian Pacific spanned the Rockies to the north. Today a perfectly engineered Interstate Highway curves smoothly to the elevations, then down to the rich mountain communities.

You can drive through the time-saving Eisenhower Tunnel – the highest in the world – or, snowstorms permitting, opt for Loveland Pass and rejoin I-70 in Summit County, meaning Dillon or Keystone.

Getting Around

HIGH MOUNTAIN DRIVING

For the first-timer, some driving advice is in order. It's not as difficult as you may think. The Highways through the Colorado Rockies, especially the Interstates, are excellent roads and well-maintained in bad weather.

Every turn on the Highway, every crest of a hill, opens up new breathtaking vistas that make driving I-70 West a stimulating experience.

If you've never driven in Colorado before, here's some helpful information for your trip to this mountain wonderland.

◻ **Steep Grades** – Any passenger car in good condition will have no trouble on major Colorado Highways, which never have a grade of more than 6%. Only certain little-used dirt roads are so steep that jeep or truck travel is recommended.

◻ **Rocks On Road** – Especially during the spring melting season there may be an occasional rock that rolls down from a mountain slope onto the Highway. At the worst spots the Highway department erects signs warning motorists to watch for rocks on the road. The Highways are patrolled regularly and the debris is removed in a short time.

◻ **Narrow Roads** – If you get into the mountain backcountry you'll find some roads so narrow that only one car can travel at a time. The motorist going uphill always has the right of way. Therefore the downhill driver should anticipate approaching traffic and hunt for turnouts whenever necessary.

◻ **Hairpin Curves** – On federal highways these are found only on mountain passes such as Loveland Pass. However, they are common on scenic second class mountain roads. Since some of these curves are blind you should hug your side of the road and travel slowly.

◻ **Down Grades** – You can use engine compression to slow your descent down mountain grades. Sometimes it is necessary to shift into a lower gear. But never coast downhill in neutral. This is both dangerous and illegal.

◻ **Tunnels** – You'll find a number of tunnels through the Rockies. Warning signs at the entrances will tell you to turn on your lights. Never stop in a tunnel.

◻ Lastly, slow down when visibility is poor.

Interstate 70 West
The Continental Divide & Its Ski Areas

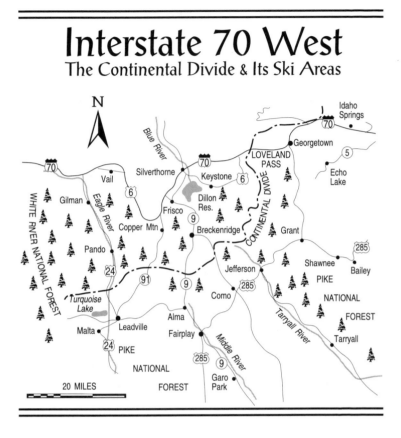

COPING WITH ALTITUDE

Most out-of-state visitors need a day or two to become accustomed to the altitude. Los Angeles, New York, and Dallas are at sea level. Colorado's resorts and lifts are at 8,000 to 12,000 feet. Some skiers may fly to Vail and immediately storm the slopes. They'll probably ski their initial runs with knees made of jello. And they'll tire more easily. A suddenly transplanted midwesterner or southerner may not sleep as well the first night in the high mountains. The ski patrol advises older people especially not to overdo it on the first day. According to the patrol, persons with chronic heart or lung problems should take it very easy at the higher elevations. Doctors claim that it takes a day to acclimatize yourself to each thousand feet of elevation.

Touring

Georgetown

Georgetown, in a cool dark valley near I-70, is the jumping-off point to the ski areas, especially Loveland Basin, which is a mere 20 driving minutes away. Ensconced between high Swiss-looking peaks at 8,500 feet, Georgetown serves skiers from the region with its numerous little après ski bars – especially on weekends. But even during the week the Clear Creek County and Summit County lift crews, instructors, patrolers, and customers make it a practice to congregate in Georgetown's red brick saloons.

The old mining community deserves some attention. The local Historical Society continues to restore various buildings, and a well preserved Main Street exudes an aura of last century's days of ore and riches. The Victoriana suits Georgetown's silversmiths and weavers, the antique shops, and dealers in rare gems and rock. Various handcrafted items, along with roasted chestnuts and other goods, come into their own each year on three weekends preceding Christmas. That's the time for Georgetown's rustic, uncommercial **Christmas Market**. Then try to visit the town during the evenings.

Most out-of-state skiers inspect the local landmarks such as the **Hotel de Paris**, now a small museum, still with its Tiffany fixtures, its lace curtains and hand-carved furniture. **The Maxwell House** and the restored **Hamil House** are other examples of the Victorian style that makes Georgetown's old homes so attractive. Even the newer edifices, like the local fire department, adhere to this style of architecture.

This historic community does well in summer and fall. The shops are busy; the historic houses attract lots of people. Cyclists unload their bikes here and pedal up the strenuously steep Guanella Pass to Grant. Various hikes take off from the same rugged, curvy road. On the edge of Georgetown, meanwhile, there are lake fishing possibilities.

FOR MORE INFORMATION

Georgetown Chamber of Commerce, ☎ 800/472-8230.

Loveland Basin

Loveland Basin is a treat at daybreak. The Continental Divide is a dark blue silhouette that slowly dissolves into angles and arches. Many visiting skiers from the Alps and countless Americans who appreciate stunning vistas along with their ski instruction come here to ski.

The mountains shine and glitter in the sun, reaching into the blue sky. This is one of the state's most attractive ski areas, drawing many Denverites on weekends. First of all, there is the location, a mere 60-70 minutes from downtown Denver. Loveland Basin sits directly under the pass, which you needn't cross, nor must you drive through the 11,000-foot-high Eisenhower Tunnel, where the traffic becomes bumper-to-bumper on weekends.

The winterscape topping Loveland Basin is something else. The ski area hugs the east slope of the 12,500-foot-high Continental Divide. Massive open snow fields are crowned by dramatic rock.

Snowboarding is a thrill at any age, and Loveland has just the teachers for those who have been skiing for years and would like to try something new. A couple of Loveland's snowboard instructors know what the transition takes; they've made it themselves. Call 303/571-5580.

The Ski Center shuts down in late spring. Since Loveland Basin doesn't operate any hotels nor does it offer condos, it is one of the few ski places that quits after the snow melts. The summery slopes are full of mountain flowers and footpaths beckon hikers. It takes stamina to reach the upper crests. When winter comes, the "Basin" is one of the first Colorado ski areas to open.

FOR MORE INFORMATION

Loveland Ski Areas, PO Box 899, Exit 216, I-70, Georgetown, 80444, ☎ 303/569-3203.

Georgetown Chamber of Commerce, ☎ 800/472-8230.

Keystone

The well-designed Keystone Resort, now owned by the same people who run Vail, is an easy 74 miles from the Colorado state capital. Car rental is unnecessary; you can get to Keystone by airport bus and then use the free shuttles that connect the scattered condos and hotels with the various lifts. The Keystone gondola is at the River Run Plaza. There are handsome base facilities: benches to buckle your boots, open-air barbecues, complimentary ski checking, and even free Kleenex to wipe a runny nose. The ride on the Skyway gondola brings skiers congenially close together; you sit knee-to-knee in Keystone's Swiss-built **Gondelbahn**. It rises in silence and never clicks when passing a girder. You travel smoothly upward for almost two miles through glades of healthy fir trees. The Skyway sails over the easy Bobtail run; you can survey other well-maintained trails like the Spring Dipper and Jackwhacker.

After an early ban on snowboarders, Keystone now embraces riders wholeheartedly and has built a snowboard park with amenities.

All kinds of eateries await you at the top. The view of Summit County is excellent, and on your downhill run over the popular Schoolmarm Trail you will notice a metal plaque that tells you the names of the peaks – Royal Mountain, Quandary Peak, Mount Guyot, among others. Keystone offers the longest daily – and nightly – operating hours of any Colorado ski resort: You can ski or take lessons from 8:30AM to 10PM.

Keystone Village has grown. You can ice skate on a large lake, play indoor tennis, or go sleigh riding.

FOR MORE INFORMATION

Keystone Resort, Highway 6, Keystone, CO 80435, ☎ 970/496-2316, 800/222-0188.

Arapahoe Basin

Arapahoe Basin is no longer owned by the same people who own Keystone. Throughout its ownership shifts, A-Basin has remained funky and wildly independent. This hotel-less area also has the longest ski season in Colorado.

The lifts here open up fantastic slopes for average skiers. "A-Basin's" two upper lifts give access to a treeless terrain, including the **Upper Lenawee** and the **Norway Mountain Face** runs. The variety in slopes extends from the super-expert **Palivacinni** (matched only in difficulty by Telluride's Plunge), to the lower part of the mountain, where there is plenty of easy stuff. A-Basin's April pleasures cannot be topped. In May, the old outdoor tables are filled with shirtless skiers soaking up the sun and picnickers and partiers enjoying their repast. A-Basin still attracts skiers in early summer.

"Stay in tune, Skiing is Great\When it's late, We're open till June," reads an amateur poem tacked to a lift shack.

At press time, Arapahoe Basin still shares phone service with Keystone, ☎ 970/496-2316.

Breckenridge

Of course, this area's history did not begin with miners; it was once the summer hunting grounds of the nomadic White River and Middle Park Utes.

The first white settlers arrived during the summer of 1859 and constructed a fortress-like camp along the banks of the Blue River. In January 1860, General George E. Spencer of Spencer & Co, a prospecting operation, gave the area the name Breckenridge in honor of then-Vice President John Cabell Breckenridge. Soon a boisterous mining town of 8,000 miners and fortune-seekers spread out, its residents living in log cabins, tents and shanties.

During the 100 years that followed, Breckenridge was the site of many gold and silver booms and busts. The last of the river dredges shut down in the 1940s, but the fortunes that were made during the mining heyday were impressive.

SUMMER & AUTUMN

Recreation comes with a capital R in this popular Colorado summer retreat some 86 miles southwest of Denver, but Breckenridge is higher, at 9,600 feet. Horseback excursions – some for three days – are just one of the ways to enjoy the outdoors here.

Thousands of peaceful mountain acres yield endless possibilities for hikers and backpackers. Some people set out to photograph the columbines and mariposas, Indian paintbrush and other mountain flowers. Anglers catch ample rainbow and brown brook trout just outside the lodge doors; the village overlooks good angling streams and lakes. Fishing tackle and licenses can be bought locally. Breckenridge is close to **Lake Dillon**, with its boating and sailing. In fall, the entire region serves hunters.

Visitors who want motorized recreation can rent a jeep for the day; special jeep trails lead to dozens of old ghost towns, to abandoned mining shafts and remote aquamarine lakes. As though all this were not enough, you also have a choice of Breckenridge's late-summer and early-fall events. An annual pack burro race is a hit with spectators, especially youngsters.

The accent is on The West. With its authentic Victorian architecture and designation as a National Historic District, several Breckenridge streets remain as they looked more than 135 years ago when hardy miners and settlers worked the hills and set a course for the future.

WINTER

Snow became the white gold when Breckenridge turned into a winter-sports mecca. In addition to a terrain exclusively for snowboarders, Breckenridge has 1,915 snowboardable acres. For the extreme snowboarder, it offers the above-timberline steeps and deeps of Peak 7, and the immense bowls on Peak 8. Peak 9 has long, groomed runs for carving the perfect snowboard turn and Peak 10 offers the challenge of bumps and trees. Moreover, snowboarders' lift tickets are also good at Arapahoe Basin and Keystone.

For those who wish to hone their snowboarding skills, Breckenridge has special lessons available for every level, from the first-time boarder to expert carvers.

An aerial view of Breckenridge's four interconnected mountains shows the scope of the resort's 1,915 acres of terrain, crowned by the massive expanses of above-timberline bowls that provide steep skiing. Breckenridge, Summit County's largest ski area, has six skiing bowls, four of which are served by the Peak 9 T-Bar. The Peak 7 Bowl and Imperial Bowl are accessed by hiking from the top of the Peak 8 T-Bar.

FOR MORE INFORMATION

Breckenridge Resort Chamber, 311 South Ridge Street, PO Box 1909, Breckenridge, CO 80424, ☎ 970/453-2913.

Breckenridge Ski Resort, PO Box 1058, Breckenridge, CO 80424, ☎ 970/453-5000.

Copper Mountain

Copper Mountain is all-American, with wide open spaces between the condos. You can pit your physique against long descents and steep faces, or ease down the intermediate runs. The area is famous for its separate facilities for expert and adventurous skiers; intermediates have their own runs. Wherever you are on Copper Mountain, you can see I-70.

The Copper Mountain ski terrain swoops from a base elevation of 9,600 feet to summits at 12,050 feet; there are runs suited for all skiing skills and every type of skier.

For people to whom the overall ambiance is less important than outstanding cross-country trails, the **Copper Mountain Ski Touring Center** is just right. Copper provides some 18 scenic miles of touring. Both guides and lessons are available and you can rent gear here, too. The terrain is great for the average skier; moreover, the trails steer away from the downhill melée. Copper Mountain is 75 miles west of Denver on I-70. Lots of Denverites ski here. Unlike Vail or Aspen, Copper gets no celebrities.

FOR MORE INFORMATION

Copper Mountain Resort, PO Box 3001, Copper Mountain, CO 80443, ☎ 970/968-2882.

Leadville

If you're in Copper Mountain and have some time to spare, you might drive south for about an hour on Colorado SR 91 to the historic town of Leadville. The old brick buildings here are just like those in Georgetown or even in Aspen. But, rather than being filled with trendy shops, they are probably vacant. Leadville, like other Colorado mining centers, grew enormously rich. The gold and silver sagas yielded fascinating stories like those of H.A.W. Tabor and his second wife "Baby Doe," whose lives later inspired an opera. Later, when the mining boom played out, the town suffered and still reels from recent mine closures.

The National Mining Hall of Fame and Museum, PO Box 981, Leadville, 80461, ☎ 719/486-1229, showcases many mining achievements. The murals and many more samples will be of interest to history buffs. Open all year; inquire about hours, which can change. While Leadville itself has no major ski area, summer action includes one of the most demanding competitions. The Boom Days Burro Races cover 21 miles of mountain terrain, including a high-speed ascent to the Mesquito Pass and back again. The athletes run; the burroes run. Riding is not permitted. It's a rugged event!

FOR MORE INFORMATION

Chamber of Commerce, 116 E. 9th St., Leadville, CO 80461, ☎ 800/933-3901.

Vail

The year-round resort of Vail is 100 miles west of Denver, reachable by I-70; in fact, the Highway zips right through this internationally famous mecca.

Vail is America's answer to European four-season resorts, a masterpiece of planning, a super-combination of skiing, lodging, shopping, a genuine "total resort." From the start Vail was cosmopolitan, innovative and idea-rich, polite and policed, fashion-conscious, the ideal place for people-watching.

This winter sports town has handsome people, attractive hotels, the widest ski bowls, and the most extravagant array of lifts. They practically invented the high-speed quad here. Vail's mayor likes to tell how his ski town differs from the average city. "We don't have the prejudices and problems of the metropolis. We have no strikes. We don't see a hostile face; smog is unknown. People come here to escape from all of those things, and revitalize themselves."

Others who come here criticize the community for its strict fashion consciousness, artificiality and an almost codified sense of well-to-do unreality.

Oil and stock market tycoons, Senators and Congressmen, US government cabinet members, models, and "Playmates" ski these slopes along with well-to-do Texans. There is a movie theater and supermarket. Shops sell imported $4,000 fur coats, French champagnes, Swiss watches, Irish linen and fine Danish cheeses. You'll find an almost-complete village. Vail is the most expensive place in Colorado.

HISTORY

Vail's founders never anticipated a success of such magnitude. Although thousands of mountain troopers and skiers passed through the valley during the 1940s and 50s, none of them saw the potential of Vail Mountain, since the best slopes were out of sight above the Highway. But Peter Seibert, an ex-10th Mountain Man and a ski racer, knew a lot about ski areas; he spent two years hiking, climbing and skiing all over the Rockies to look for the ideal resort location. One day in 1957 he scaled the Vail summit with a local prospector who lived in the valley. Upon seeing the bowls, glades, and open slopes, Seibert knew he'd found the perfect site.

Seibert and some friends invested their savings. But more money was needed. Unfortunately, at that time Denver's conservative bankers wouldn't gamble on a large new ski area, with Aspen already doing well. All the same, Seibert kept looking for partners. He turned to Michigan, Missouri, Wisconsin, Texas, and other states. He bought a snow cat and brought visitors to his magic mountain. He showed films of his powder bowls all over the country. He invited prospective investors to ski with him. One day, he finally hit pay dirt. A Michigan oilman/skier recognized the potential and found other wealthy backers who spread Seibert's gospel. They raised $5 million, formed Vail Associates, successfully tapped the Small Business Administration and the no-longer-reluctant Denver bankers. Then they sold real estate to precisely the people who had shaken their heads the hardest.

During the summer of 1962, the bulldozers started to dig in. A Milwaukee architect had drawn up the plans and now supervised the frantic building activity.

When the dust settled, there stood the first lodges, apartments, malls, homes and lifts of Vail. Seibert then chose the right people to help him publicize and manage the booming resort.

FOR MORE INFORMATION

Vail Valley Tourism & Convention Bureau, ☎ 970/476-1000
Vail Central Reservations, ☎ 800/525-3875

Adventures

On Foot

GEORGETOWN

Standing in pure majesty just 10 miles from Georgetown are **Grays** and **Torreys Peaks.**

At 14,270 and 14,267 feet respectively, these famed "Fourteeners" beckon hikers to don boots and conquer them.

The hike becomes all the more inviting once you realize that you're up and down the two mountains in one outing. From the summit of Grays it is not difficult to traverse the half-mile ridge to Torreys.

The views are unequaled and hikers should not be surprised to see a sure-footed bighorn sheep surveying the terrain from high atop a rocky precipice. Bring a camera.

KEYSTONE

The 13,207-foot **Argentine Pass** once connected old mines in Summit County and Georgetown. Now this 2.3-mile rocky trail is steep and at times very narrow – a challenge even for hikers with stamina.

At the summit, though, you'll be rewarded with eagle-eye views of Georgetown and Mount Evans.

To reach the trailhead from Keystone, head approximately five miles southeast on Montezuma Road. Turn left onto Peru Circle Road. Park at Shoe Basin Mine.

With Llamas

Thanks to these animals, Keystone visitors can enjoy a four-hour trek from the summit of Keystone Mountain to North Peak. The llamas carry the picnic lunches. Longer llama treks can be arranged. For more information contact **Keystone Resort/Arapahoe Basin**, PO Box 38, 80435, ☎ 303/468-2316.

COPPER MOUNTAIN

Copper Mountain's Nature Center is the starting point for US Forest Service guided nature hikes. Offered twice each day, weather permitting, these complimentary guided hikes provide an in-depth look at the surrounding environment. Each hike is rated easy to moderate, and Forest Service naturalists are available to provide information or answer any questions on Copper Mountain's flora and fauna.

After exploring the mountain, ride the American Eagle chairlift or hike down one of many trails leading to Copper Mountain's base village.

High altitude tennis training sessions are designed to take advantage of the cool, thin air in an effort to sharpen competitive skills and increase speed. These sessions are offered on weekends throughout the summer and include a total of 10 hours of instruction, video analysis and access to additional facilities in the club. The Strokes and Strategies class runs on a weekly basis and is open to tennis players of all ability levels. Sessions for both singles and doubles play are available.

In addition to tennis instruction, the **Copper Mountain Racquet and Athletic Club** offers a full serve pro shop. Services available include racquet, court shoe and ball machine rentals, racquet demos, racquet stringing and more. The pro shop also sells high altitude tennis balls, accessories and brand name tennis racquets.

LEADVILLE

Well-conditioned adventurers won't want to miss a chance to hike Colorado's highest mountain, **Mount Elbert** (14,433 feet). Depending on time and abilities, hikers can choose one of the mountain's two main trails:

North Mount Elbert Trail is a 4½-mile hike to the summit. Go west on Highway 24 for two miles to Highway 300. Continue west on Highway 300 for one mile and turn south on Forest Road 110. Continue to Halfmoon Campground. Park here.

South Mount Elbert Trail is not as crowded. This is a six-mile hike to the summit. The trailhead is near Lakeview Campground.

Ironically, a longer hike can be found at **Mount Massive**, even though this mountain is smaller (by 12 feet) than Mount Elbert. This trail requires you to be in good shape because of a 4,500-foot elevation gain.

The trail begins above Halfmoon Campground. Expect to spend a full day on this journey.

VAIL

The Vail planners loved the outdoors. They also realized that not everyone skis. Guests had to be able to walk as well. Thus the **Vail Trail**, which rises and falls, straightens and curves all the way from the Westin Hotel to the Antlers condos, the Lodge at Vail, past the library and east toward the Vail Manor, then uphill toward Vail Pass. The trail is kept snow-free all winter and is a delight in summer. For a shorter walk, ask directions to the **Betty Ford Alpine Gardens**. The location is easy to find; just follow the lovely Gore Creek to the Gerald Ford Park, and you'll come upon the public gardens at 8,200 feet, reputedly the highest public alpine gardens in the world. The dedication took place in August 1989, with the former First Lady in attendance.

Come summertime, a profusion of crocus, heather, forsythia, wild roses and perennials of all kinds greet the visitor.

There is no charge to visit the Betty Ford Alpine Gardens. Donations, however, are accepted. For details, write to **Vail Alpine Garden**, 183 Gore Creek Drive, 81657.

Shrine Ridge is an easy hike that can be accomplished in two to three hours. You climb through open meadows with abundant wildflowers, then up the steepest part of the trail to the 12,000-foot summit. While atop the mountain, look for "Lord Gore," a man-shaped rock to the northwest.

To reach this spot, take I-70 to Vail Pass, Exit 190. Proceed on road #709 to Shrine Pass Summit. Turn left here and drive to Shrine Mountain Inn, where you can park.

Missouri Lakes. Hikers are sometimes discouraged by evidence of a water project at the start of this trail. However, after the first mile, the trail cuts into the plush wilderness. Rustic log bridges help you cross Missouri Creek on your way to the crystal clear lakes. Anticipate a walk of approximately five hours if you go all the way to the lake within Holy Cross Wilderness.

To get to Missouri Lakes, take I-70, Exit 171, to Highway 24. Drive south to Homestake Road #703. Turn right. Turn right again onto #704 and travel to a T in the road. The trailhead is on the left.

You can rent hiking boots at the Vail or Beaver Creek **Merrell Hiking Centers**. Call Vail Associates for more information, ☎ 970/476-5601.

If you plan on more advanced, more remote or simply longer Vail area adventures, contact the **Paragon Guides**, Box 130, 81658, ☎ 970/926-5299. This adventure and guide outfit can satisfy your needs in llama trekking, backpacking, and backcountry skiing. Trips last from three days to a couple of weeks. Also bear in mind that **Antlers at Vail**, Lions Head, ☎ 970/476-2471, will give you advice regarding long hikes, rock climbing, river rafting, and other action sports. "We're recreation advice specialists," says Bert Farin, one of the managers.

On Wheels

GEORGETOWN

You can take a giant step backward in time and board the old **Colorado and Southern narrow-gauge train** that runs the four miles between Georgetown and Silver Plume. The line was a main supply route a hundred years ago. Now, visitors can make the 45-minute loop – so called because the track runs over and under itself repeatedly – on great bridges rising 600 feet above the valley floor. The train stops at the Lebanon Mine for tours of the shaft and an adjoining museum. The trains run from Memorial Day through September. For more info, contact **Georgetown Loop Railroad**, ☎ 970/670-1686.

BRECKENRIDGE

An intermediate biker might consider the 10-mile trip to the summit of **Boreas Pass**, an 1800s railroad bed for the Denver South Park and Pacific Railroad Companies.

Here views over the quaint town of Breckenridge and vistas of Tenmile Range are superb. What's more, a short history lesson awaits riders at Baker's Tank, a well-restored 100-year-old tank that stored water for locomotives making the run. From Breckenridge, drive south on Highway 9 and watch for the sign.

Kodi Bikes, a Breckenridge outfit, offers both bike rentals and guided tours of the Arapahoe National Forest. For information, contact ☎ 800/468-3031, Bell Tower Mall, 80424.

COPPER MOUNTAIN

As is the case with many ski areas, Copper Mountain has free chairlifts that will transport you and your bicycle up the mountain.

American Eagle is Copper's high-speed quad that will allow you to access high mountain trails.

LEADVILLE

Trails in Leadville are no more difficult than in other mountain towns. The difference is that the high altitude (Leadville's elevation tops 10,000 feet) makes you think the hills are steeper and the inclines longer.

A nice easy ride goes from downtown to Turquoise Lake. Follow the six-mile route around the shoreline.

The more ambitious cyclist can then head up another seven miles on Forest Service Road 105 to Hagerman Pass.

For supported trips, check in with **Sawatch Naturalists & Guides**, 817 Harrison Ave., Leadville, ☎ 719/486-2797.

VAIL

The easiest way to find ample mountain biking is to visit the **Vail Valley** or **White River National Forest**. Here, numerous trails offer whatever you're looking for.

To reach **White River National Forest**, where 4,000 acres of alpine terrain await you, hop on Vail's Gondola or Vista Bahn express. There are miles of professionally designed trails.

Vail Associates is also a valuable mountain biking resource. They rent bikes and conduct guided tours.

Mountain bikers will not want to miss the trail maps put out by **Vail** and **Beaver Creek Resorts**. These maps will show you all the hotspots to bike within the resorts themselves. What's more, because the maps are put together using familiar ski symbols – black diamond or blue square – you will be able to locate a level that will suit you.

Scenic jeep tours offer an opportunity to see the backcountry. Three-hour tours journey through panoramic vistas on Red and White Mountain or Benchmark Mountain. Gourmet lunch and dinner tours are among the choices.

On Horseback

BRECKENRIDGE

The Eagle's Nest Equestrian Center, ☎ 719/468-0677, has 1,000 acres alongside national forest lands, where you can roam on horseback. Hourly or full-day rides for all ages. Breakfast, lunch and dinner rides too. From I-70 Silverthorne/Dillon Exit, go north on Highway 9.

On Water

GEORGETOWN

The lakes here are crowded in summer, except for **Silver Dollar Lake.** This out-of-the-way lake has decent fishing. From Georgetown, go 8½ miles south on Guanel Pass Road. Turn right at Silver Dollar Lake sign.

KEYSTONE

Keystone's own little lake is picturesque enough; it serves skaters and ice hockey players in winter. Come spring, the ice melts and by summer you see people in rowboats, while others stroll around the lake. Umbrellas are unfurled by the restaurants, gardeners hasten to take care of the flowers, and you think you're in the Alps.

BRECKENRIDGE

The **Blue River** offers exciting whitewater trips, while the **Colorado River** is for gentle family floats. Both can be arranged through **Kodi,** Bell Tower Mall, 80424, ☎ 970/453-2194. Other rafting entrepreneurs:

Performance Tours, 110 Ski Hill Roard, 80424, ☎ 800/328-RAFT (7238).

The Adventure Company, 101 Ski Hill Road, 80424, ☎ 970/453-0747.

Breckenridge Whitewater Rafting, 849 N. Summit Boulevard, Frisco, 80443, ☎ 970/668-5323, 800/247-RAFT (7238).

Colorado River Runs, Inc., Star Route Box 32, Bond, 80423, ☎ 800/826-1081.

LEADVILLE

Turquoise Lake, three miles west of Leadville via 6th St. and Turquoise Lake Road, is renowned for its trout fishing. Because of its accessibility and spectacular setting, the lake suffers from overuse in summer. Better to try nearby **Twin Lakes Reservoir**, near the junction of Highway 24 and 82, for rainbow and cutthroat trout or mackinaw.

VAIL

Vail is near three very popular rafting rivers: the **Colorado**, the **Eagle** and the **Arkansas**. There are numerous entrepreneurs who will provide trips, along with plenty of fishing guides.

Gore Creek Fly-fisherman, Inc. is at 183 Gore Creek Drive, 81658, ☎ 970/476-3296.

Guided fishing is offered through the **Nova Guides** – half-day or full-day. Fish the Colorado, Roaring Fork and Eagle rivers, as well as lakes and streams in the White River National Forest. Use a fly or spinner, according to your preference. Equipment and instruction provided, if needed. Catch and release only. ☎ 970/949-4232.

On Snow

VAIL

Cross-Country Skiing

☞ A freebie in posh Vail? Surprise, surprise! Because the local Recreation Department runs the **Vail Nordic Center**, you can cross-country ski for free. The terrain is nearly flat, with the gentlest undulations, as might be expected because you are on a golf course (park free behind the golf clubhouse). While you ski, the view is of the jagged Gore Range, which looks like the Swiss Alps. The trails lead east and west under the villas, townhouses and palaces of Vail.

The Vail Nordic Center offers plenty of cross-country rental skis plus pricey lessons by first-rate instructors.

Vail now has so many vast alpine slopes and wide boulevards, so many downhill trails angling in all directions and spread across several mountains, that you will still be discovering new areas even after a month of exploration on skis. Many visitors feel most exalted and tuned-in to these mountains when they ski the vast Vail bowls. Their number remains unparalleled in the Rockies, a veritable orgy of slopes. The best known are the **China Bowl** and the **Teacup, Siberia** and **Mongolia Bowls**.

VAIL STATISTICS

ELEVATION

Base elevation: 8,200 feet or 2,500 meters.

Mid-Vail elevation: 10,200 feet or 3,110 meters.

Summit elevation: 11,450 feet or 3,491 meters.

Vertical drop: 3,250 feet or 975 meters.

TRAILS

Total trails: 120 named trails.

Total developed trails: 3,787 acres.

Total permit area: 12,500 acres.

Longest run: 4½ miles – Flapjack to Riva Ridge.

Expanse: Seven miles from Cascade lift on the West to the Mongolia Bowl surface lift to the East.

Vail is the largest single ski mountain complex in North America and offers more than twice as much skiable terrain as any other ski area in Colorado.

For more information contact, **Vail Associates, Inc.,** PO Box 7, 81658, ☎ 970/476-5601.

Snowboarding

Vail and Beaver Creek mountains offer terrain for all types of snowboarders, including alpine snowboarders and freestylers.

It puts snowboarders to the test with amusements such as the traditional-shaped halfpipe, a cobra, a double roll and a teaching area. Vail's park is below Chair 6 on Ruder's Run on Golden Peak. Beaver

Creek Mountain also has a designated snowboard park, **Boarder Beach**, in Rose Bowl at the top of C-Prime and Stone Creek.

Backcountry Skiing

For a slightly off-the-beaten-path ski experience, try Vail's backcountry hut-to-hut skiing. The 10th Mountain Division Hut Association was formed in 1980 to build a backcountry ski hut system in the mountains of Colorado between Aspen, Leadville and Vail.

Now, you can reserve the huts for a fee as a takeoff for day adventures or to ski from hut to hut. These shelters are within White River and San Isabel national forests so stun ning vistas are guaranteed. This trip won't be for everyone, however; the Forest Service advises that the trails require skiers to have at least intermediate ability. The Hut Association also requires that someone in each group be proficient in backcountry skills such as avalanche awareness and compass reading.

Huts sleep 16 and include woodburning stoves, propane burners, cooking and eating utensils, kitchen supplies, mattresses and pillows.

For information, call the **Hut Association, ☎** 970/925-5775.

Where To Stay & Eat

Accommodations

GEORGETOWN

Georgetown Motor Inn, Exit 228 off I-70, ☎ 303/569-3201. Thirty-two-room motel. Café. Moderate.

Kip on the Creek Inn, PO Box 754, 1205 Rose Sreet, 80444, ☎ 800/821-6545. Moderate.

KEYSTONE

Keystone Lodge has 152 rooms in the center of Keystone Village. Quality facilities and services, along with a lakeside location, make this elegant hotel an award winner. Daily maid service, turndown service, valet parking, ski check, room service, and 24-hour-a-day front desk and concierge service. Work out at the fitness center, play indoor tennis, head into the backcountry, ice skate or take a dip in the heated swimming pool. Two restaurants and two cocktail lounges. Box 38, 80435, ☎ 800/222-0188. Deluxe.

Ski Tip Lodge. A historic 1880s stagecoach stop and Colorado's first ski lodge serving Arapahoe Basin in the 1940s, this rustic yet charming bed and breakfast nestled in the pines offers four-course meals inside a cozy dining room. Guests enjoy dessert, coffee and aperitifs in armchairs before a crackling fire. For overnight guests, Ski Tip packages lodging with two meals per day, including a hearty skier breakfast and dinner. At mid-day, cross-country skiers and other visitors can refuel with light yet power-packed lunches and salads, homemade breads and soups fresh from the kitchen. Expensive.

Keystone Resort/Arapahoe Basin, PO Box 38, 80435, ☎ 970/453-3210.

BRECKENRIDGE

Allaire Timbers Inn, 9511 Highway 9, South Main Street, Breckenridge, 80424, ☎ 970/453-7530. Moderate.

MC2 Mountain Condominium Management Company, PO Box 462, Dillon, 80435, ☎ 800/525-3682. Moderate to expensive.

Breckenridge Mountain Lodge, 600 S. Ridge Street, PO Box 468, Breckenridge, 80424, ☎ 970/453-2333. Cozy, rustic. Expensive.

Refurbished to its Victorian glory, the **Delaware Hotel**, 700 Harrison Ave., Leadville, ☎ 719/486-1418, features private baths and is close to downtown attractions. Breakfast is included in the tab. Moderate.

COPPER MOUNTAIN

Copper Mountain Lodging Services, PO Box 3117, Copper Mountain, 80443, ☎ 800/458-8386. All price ranges.

VAIL

The Lodge & Spa at Cordillera, in Edwards, 81632, close to Vail, ☎ 800/877-3529, offers more sports and adventure than most first-class resorts in Colorado. While staying at this remote European castle-like lodge in winter, guests can join Alaskan dog-sled rides, rent contemporary snowshoes and join a professional snowshoe guide. Take lessons in cross-country skiing and skating (equipment is for rent), train for cross-country races, or get free bus service to nearby Beaver Creek for downhill skiing. In summer, the Lodge & Spa at Cordillera features guided flower hikes, mountain biking, golfing on an 18-hole course, and swimming in an Olympic pool. Use the whirlpools or the genuine Finnish sauna, work out on Stairmasters or Lifecycles in a large gym and weight room, then get pampered with massages, body wraps, or facials at the prestigious spa. All this plus 360° mountain views, fly-fishing, tennis, and seclusion on 3,600 wilderness acres. This retreat has superb accommodations for 84 persons, along with two restaurants. A lively, luxurious place for a moneyed clientele. Deluxe.

The Westin's 322 rooms and suites are bright, with mountain and creek views and large closets. Guests will also welcome the Westin's Athletic Club, with indoor squash and racquetball courts, running track and spacious weight rooms. In fact, the hotel even has its own chairlift that ties in with Vail's other uphill transportation. 1300 Westhaven Drive, 81657. ☎ 970/476-7400. Deluxe.

Beginning skiers might consider staying at the plush **Manor Vail**, directly under the beginner's area Golden Peak lifts. A sojourn at Manor Vail allows you to use the Lord Gore Club's facilities, such as gyms and elaborate saunas. The condominium units come in various sizes and styles, including some with kitchens. 595 E. Vail Valley Drive, 81657. ☎ 970/476-5651. Expensive.

The **Holiday Inn** differs from its namesakes elsewhere because of the distinct ski lodge features; you can avail yourself of the ski storage area, a shuttle to the lifts, a skier's sauna, guaranteed après ski entertainment, and intimate dining in booths. This Holiday Inn's rooms don't conform with other members of the chain; the decor is ritzy Old West, with guns, satins, wallpapers and other touches. 13 Vail Road, 81657. ☎ 970/476-5631. Expensive.

Antlers at Vail occupies a lucky spot, just three walking minutes from Lions Head gondola and near many shops and cafés. Antlers offers some of Vail's best-furnished and most deluxe condos (including large ones for groups). All of the 70 units – even those for two people – come with fireplaces, Jacuzzis, and modern kitchens that will beat Vail's generally high restaurant prices. Reserve your pricey Antlers accommodations many months before your arrival. (ABC's Peter Jennings didn't and was turned down; no room that day.) 680 W. Lionshead Place, 81657. ☎ 800/843-8245.

7W Guest Ranch, 3412 County Road 151, Gypsum, 81637, ☎ 800/524-1286. 9,000 feet elevation. Open during summer and winter only. Moderate to expensive.

Black Bear Inn of Vail, 2405 Elliott Road, 81657, ☎ 970/476-1304. Expensive.

Restaurants

GEORGETOWN

The Renaissance, 1025 Rose Street, ☎ 303/569-3336. Northern Italian cuisine prepared by Europeans. Expensive to very expensive.

KEYSTONE

The Snake River Saloon, Highway 6, ☎ 970/468-2788. Serves lunch and dinner in an atmosphere recalling the rich, plush era of the 1880s. A complete menu features exclusive recipes, plus superb steaks and seafood. Keystone's "in place" for the locals. Moderate-expensive.

BRECKENRIDGE

The Blue Spruce Inn, Dillon. Across from the Summit County Library, Frisco, ☎ 970/468-2968. Open seven evenings a week. No reservations. Fireside lounge, warm cozy atmosphere, delicious steaks and seafood. Expensive.

LEADVILLE

The locals look to **Casa Blanca,** 118 E. 2nd St., Leadville, ☎ 719/486-9969, when they want to eat authentic and reasonably priced Mexican food. A bit off-the-beaten-track, so it's usually missed by the tourist crowd. Inexpensive.

Slightly more upscale is **Callaways,** ☎ 719/486-1239, in the Delaware Hotel, which features salads, pastas, steaks and plenty of specials.

VAIL

Gasthof Gramshammer. Austrian menu. Tyrolean atmosphere. Antlers Room features rack of venison, elk steak and children's plates, all at high prices. Outdoor café. Open all year. ☎ 970/824-5737. Very expensive.

Sweet Basil, 193 E. Gore Creek Drive, 81657, ☎ 970/476-3696, has homemade soups and desserts, innovative pasta dishes and the most consistently excellent food you'll find in Vail. Serving lunch and dinner. Expensive.

The Left Bank, at the Sitzmark Inn, dates back to 1970. It is one of Vail's entries in the realm of French cooking. They feature delicate escargots or a hearty French onion soup, along with other appetizers. *Beaucoup de dollars* buy the rest of your authentic French meal. Try the elk or ask for coq au vin. Fine desserts, too. Wines. The owner is French and returns to France every August. Dinner is often sold out, despite the prices. Reservations. Very expensive.

Camping

BRECKENRIDGE

Arapahoe National Forest

Camping sites aplenty, but they fill up early. **Blue River Campground**, nine miles north of Silverthorne on Highway 9, is worth a try.

LEADVILLE

Baby Doe. Fifty sites adjacent to Turquoise Lake. Two miles west on County Road 37, 2½ miles west on County Road 4, then 2¼ miles north on County Road 9C.

Father Dyer. 26 sites. 2½ miles west on County Road 37, 2½ miles west on County Road 4, then 2¼ miles north on County Road 9C. ☎ 719/488-0752.

VAIL

White River National Forest

Gore Creek. 17 sites. From East Vail, take Exit 180 onto Highway 6. Head east two miles.

Aspen Ski Country

More than a century ago, silver prospectors braved the wilderness of the Roaring Fork River, long a favorite hunting ground of the Ute Indians, to discover one of the richest silver lodes in the world. They came from Leadville, the second largest city in Colorado at the time, crossing the 13,000-foot Independence Pass on snowshoes. Thirteen hardy sourdoughs endured the rough winter of 1879 to protect their claims. They called their tent community Ute City. But as more miners arrived in the spring, the name was changed to Aspen, a tribute to the graceful trees prevalent in the valley.

By 1890, thousands of fortune seekers had arrived in Aspen to stake their claims. Aspen's silver mines produced nearly a quarter of a billion dollars, including the largest silver nugget ever found. It weighed over a ton and was 93% pure. The 14 daily trains were not enough and the ore, awaiting shipment, was stacked in the streets like high gray snow drifts. In 1890, there were 12,000 inhabitants in Aspen, six newspapers, three schools, 10 churches, a modern hospital, an opera house, 70 bars, first-class hotels and a flourishing brothel district.

Aspen's fortunes fell with the end of the silver standard in 1893. Many of the larger mines shut down. As mining declined, the local economy became more dependent upon ranching and farming. By the 1930s, Aspen's population had shrunk to approximately 700 people. But by the mid-1930s, a new group of pioneers came to the Roaring Fork Valley in search of the ideal location for a ski resort. They even hired a famous Swiss avalanche expert, Andre Roch. A group of investors constructed a lodge with plans to build a complete resort. But, following the outbreak of World War II, their plans had to be cancelled.

Meanwhile, skiing in the Roaring Fork Valley was actually spurred on by the presence of the Army's 10th Mountain Division, training in nearby Leadville. Many of the soldiers would go over to Aspen to ski on weekends. Several of those early 10th Mountain troopers came to Aspen and began buying up mining claims and surface rights with the idea of building a ski area. Chicago industrialist Walter Paepcke supported the resort plan. Paepcke, chairman of Container Corporation of America, was interested in the community's prospects as a summertime cultural haven, but he also recognized the skiing potential.

In 1945, Paepcke and other investors created the Aspen Skiing Corporation. One year later, the resort was officially opened, and in 1950 Aspen held America's first World Alpine Ski Championships.

Walter Paepcke became interested in Aspen for his planned Institute for Humanistic Studies, primarily a cultural, educational and rest center for business executives. Paepcke died in 1960, but not before he had translated his idea into fact. The town now attracts artists, musicians, sportsmen, statesmen and writers of international fame. An important music festival takes place here every summer.

As a ski complex, Aspen is unsurpassed. Its four lift-serviced areas – Aspen Mountain, Buttermilk Mountain, The Snowmass, Aspen Highlands – encompass 160 miles of ski trails reachable by dozens of lifts that can hoist 25,000 skiers an hour. The areas are all within quick driving range and kept in shape by a fantastic array of slope-conditioning machines, plus an army of patrolmen and summer crews. Because of the high investment, lift rates are steep.

Getting Around

Aspen is some 210 miles from Denver – a long drive. And in winter, of course, the drive is tricky. But there are many alternatives to driving. If you prefer taking to the skies, major airlines connect from Denver International Airport to Aspen's own airport. Additionally, some airlines will fly to Grand Junction, where you can arrange for ground transportation to Aspen. Eagle County Airport, a 90-minute drive, is another option.

Amtrak also provides transport to the area. This scenic trip takes passengers to Glenwood Springs.

For those ready, willing and able to make the drive, take I-70 to Glenwood. Then take CO 82 into Aspen. Expect the drive to be between four and five hours. A slightly shorter route is over Independence Pass, although this closes frequently in winter due to snow; the other route is more reliable. The drive is delightful in summer.

Aspen Ski Country

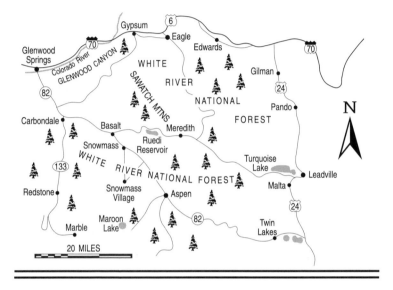

Touring

Aspen

Some ski resorts consist of a few condos and a ski hill. By contrast, Aspen has many ski areas and Aspen itself is a town. At one core area you find a handsome pedestrian mall with flower boxes and benches. Aspen's red Old West brick buildings and the Victorian gingerbread homes are periodically restored. The antique cherry wood bars shine, as do the new Tiffany lamps and the stained glass windows. Green plants grace many Aspen stores and cafés. Aspen outranks most North American ski resorts when it comes to the sheer number and variety of restaurants and nightlife possibilities. There are 100-plus spots to dine. Aspen has bistros, bars, saloons, pubs, subterranean dives, cafeterias, cafés, pastry shops, coffee houses, and several internationally famous restaurants. A cosmopolitan town, Aspen appeals to skiers and nonskiers, couples or families. Several hundred shops invite browsers; amusements and sports of every kind beckon.

In summer, Aspen holds an important music festival, as well as conferences.

Negatives? Traffic is heavy. Parking in town has improved, thanks to the installation of a European-style parking system. Christmas is the busiest time and spring break the second hardest time to secure reservations. Otherwise, local lodges, hotels and condos typically have ample space.

Prices during the ski season have risen to formidable heights at even the most unremarkable motels. And, while direct air connections from Denver via feeder airlines are available, you pay top dollar for the 35-minute flight to Aspen.

To be sure, Aspen is an important four-season resort. The area offers adventurous activities. Or you can sit in the European-style cafés and pastry shops, sun yourself on the balconies and terraces of Aspen's motels, or swim in any one of 50 pools. You can never quite get through all of the restaurants.

At night you can watch torchlight ski descents, foreign movies, and ski movies. The ski school gives downhill racing lessons; never forget that the US's first big-time downhills were held on these slopes.

FOR MORE INFORMATION

Aspen Chamber Resort Association, ☎ 970/925-1940.

Aspen Skiing Company has information and trail maps on all four area mountains, ☎ 970/925-1220.

Snowmass Village

Snowmass Village is eight miles from the town of Aspen. Turn left just before you get to the airport. The Owl Creek Road or the Brush Creek Road from Glenwood Springs will get you there. This is spacious country; it seems to expand the closer you get to your destination. Hills are tufted by willows, scrub oak and, higher up, spruce. You'll see several working ranches. Weathered sheep pens, barns, and corrals give way to a long-forgotten schoolhouse. You see far-away ski trails flowing through the Snowmass Village woods.

The day after Snowmass was opened, a great skier wanted to give it a shot. He told everyone how ridiculously easy the skiing would be. But the four-mile-long trail, slicing through 8,500 acres, got to him. After the last 4,000 vertical feet of descent, he arrived quivering and exhausted.

The village is compact and intimate. Honey-colored windows beckon in the night. The buildings stand terrace-fashion, giving a feel of unity. To the west, you glimpse one of the ski lifts and the beginner's hill.

The village blends with the white meadows, the frozen creeks, the aspen trees. Houses blend with the flow of scenery. There is a sense of order. The hotels, for example, were placed at right angles to the slope, so that guests could have a good valley view from all balconies. Yet each building differs from the next. Colors were chosen with restraint. A soft green, an ochre, a russet, or a beige were fine, but bright blue or poster red were outlawed. Stained wood, regional stone, and rough stucco are okay, but artificial materials, like plastic, or nailed-on Tyrolean shutters are not. You won't see chain link fences, jutting television antennas, fake facades, gingerbread ornaments, decorated garage doors, or the flashing lights of commercial suburbia.

Snowmass skiing is famous for its ego-building runs. Crowds are unknown here.

Snowmass summers are a delight. The rocks are warm and the moss is dry; there is the promise of anemones, bluebells, gentian and Indian paintbrush. Hikers move upward through the meadows. In a nearby ranch building an arts and crafts school will be in session. Aspen's music festival is only 20 minutes away.

In summer Snowmass is a center for picnickers, kayakers, jeepsters and rockhounds. There is also a free weekly concert series on the ski hill.

The climbers are there, setting out for the Maroon Bells. Coiled ropes and other gear hang from them. Soon the fishermen arrive, resplendent with nets, tackles and flies. They're ready to angle rainbow trout from the many creeks. All summer, there are tenderfoot horseback riders, too. Pale city faces shielded by bold cowboy hats, they climb into the saddle and trot up the mountains. Then come the hunters, stalking deer in the timbered areas and in the mountain cirques.

FOR MORE INFORMATION

Snowmass Resort Association, ☎ 970/923-2000.

Aspen Mountain

Aspen Mountain is challenging to ski. The runs are steep and often narrow. Expert skiers race past you, inches away. Deep powder skiing is available. In 1948, the only way to Aspen's highest point was by single chairlift. The journey took almost an hour. On the new 13,000-foot-long *Silver Queen*, you can now be on the Sundeck in 13 minutes. The alpine views of shining Castle Peak, Cathedral Peak and Mount Hayden remain as spectacular as ever.

Actually, Aspen's powers-that-be resisted the gondola idea for many decades. The *Silver Queen* inauguration back in January 1987 was an important event, with much attention from the press. The *Silver Queen's* 165 cabins can transport 2,000 skiers per hour; the vertical rise is a steep 3,367 feet. During the uphill trip, you see the White River National Forest, the powder face of Bell Mountain and such historic runs as Spar Gulch and Ruthie's. With three people sitting back-to-back, Aspen's slick method of locomotion seems a little claustrophobic by contrast.

The trails are for the strong-legged and they satisfy the advanced skier. There are steep, tumultuous runs such as Walsh's, Silver Queen and the Ridge of Bell.

From town, the Aspen Mountain lifts hoist you at a steep angle; the chairs whirring upward over forest spurs and logger's cattracks, over deep ravines and gorges. From the lodges you can see just a small portion – perhaps one tenth – of the entire 11,212-foot peak.

FOR MORE INFORMATION

Aspen Skiing Company, Box 1248, Aspen, CO 81612, ☎ 970/925-1220.

Buttermilk & Aspen Highlands

The third Aspen ski area is Aspen Highlands, known as the "balanced mountain." Here's a winter playground for every category of skier. The vast mountain allows an escape from others. For instance, you can travel all the way to the 11,800-foot top; it matches Aspen's altitude record, besides offering an unforgettable descent down a narrow, knife-like ridge. The Highlands' wide boulevards exhilarate; the many lifts criss-cross and link cleverly, and you'll seldom stand in line.

Buttermilk got its name from a local farmer who liked the drink. With 3,800 feet of vertical descent, the area has a long vertical drop indeed. Numerous chairlifts can trans port you to a versatile mixture of beginner, intermediate and expert terrain, encompassing more than 50 miles of trails.

Buttermilk provides Aspen's easiest skiing. The hills here are gentle – ideal for the lower, intermediate and novice skier or snowboarder.

Buttermilk's undulating terrain caters to older skiers as well. Even the non-athletic can have a ball on these tame slopes. Two cafeterias – one on the summit, facing spectacular Pyramid Peak, and one at the bottom – are for people who want to rest (it has deck chairs al fresco). On the other side of the same area, a few trails appeal to hardier types.

FOR MORE INFORMATION

Aspen Skiing Company, Box 1248, Aspen, CO 81612, ☎ 970/925-1220.

Glenwood Springs

CO 82 continues from Aspen to Glenwood Springs, 42 miles northwest. It sits in the White River National Forest, a 2½-hour drive from Denver. Glenwood's two million acres are renowned for all manner of open-air sports. The attractions include the Flat Tops Wilderness, a huge 117,800-acre plateau north of Glenwood Springs and Rifle, which extends into three counties.

Glenwood became known for its hot springs mineral baths, which are open all year. In the 1880s, silver baron Walter Devereaux decided to convert the springs, which had been used by the Utes, to a health resort for the rich. He built the two-block-long swimming pool for the guests of the posh adjacent hotel. By the early 1900s, so many wealthy and famous people came to the spa that a rail siding was installed beside the hotel for private railroad cars. Teddy Roosevelt made Glenwood his "summer White House" in 1901 while bear hunting in the nearby hills.

The mineral baths and vapor caves are open to visitors, with trained personnel to guide and supervise. Locals say the water is a quick cure for visitors' aching muscles and stiff joints after hiking the nearby wilderness or skiing Aspen's slopes.

FOR MORE INFORMATION

Glenwood Springs Chamber of Commerce, 900 Grand Avenue, Glenwood Springs, CO 81601, ☎ 970/945-6589.

Glenwood Hot Springs Pool, 401 N. River Street, Glenwood Springs, CO 81601, ☎ 970/945-7131.

Adventures

On Foot

ASPEN

West of Aspen along Maroon Creek, hikers will discover the often-photographed Maroon Bells peaks. A glacial lake lies at the foot of the jagged, snow-capped mountain giants, the Bells. The area is part of the **Maroon Bells/Snowmass Wilderness**, with its many hiking trails.

Day-trippers will want to venture to **Crater Lake** or hike the five miles to splendid **Willow Lake**. Those prepared for an overnight excursion may meander throughout the Maroon Bells/Snowmass Wilderness to **Snowmass Lake**. Side routes to **Capitol Lake** and **Avalanche Creek** near Redstone are also highly recommended.

Other new trails include the following:

Midway Pass trail starts at the Lost Man parking lot, about 12 miles east of Aspen, via Highway 82. The trail is steep at the start but after eight switchbacks it finally mellows into meadows and woods. The summit ponds, about 2½ miles from the trailhead, are a good place for a break or to eat lunch.

Rio Grande Trail is an easy, flat path that starts below the post office in Aspen and sidles along the Roaring Fork River. The paved trail continues for 1½ miles, after which the path becomes dirt. Continue the seven miles to Woody Creek or return back to Aspen.

The **Cathedral Lake** trail takes hikers through dense forest to a beautiful subalpine lake just below Electric Pass. Allow at least two hours each way for this route, which is best completed early in the day (there's a reason why the adjacent pass is called "Electric"). Find the trail head near the end of Castle Creek Road, approximately 11 miles from downtown Aspen.

SNOWMASS VILLAGE

In Snowmass Village, the spectacular **Rim Trail** starts behind the Mountain View employee housing complex and skirts the ridge separating the village and the exclusive area known as Wildcat. A quick ascent provides big rewards, including views of the Maroon/Snowmass Wilderness.

GLENWOOD SPRINGS

Here are better than average hiking possibilities. Begin with the hike to **Hanging Lake**, off I-70 approximately nine miles east of downtown Glenwood. The climb is steep but brief, with scenic rewards of a small waterfall and creeks. Hanging Lake gives you a dramatic view of Glenwood Canyon and other hikes.

Boy Scout Trail. Go up to the end of 8th Street to the dead end. There is a parking area on the left. Follow signs up the trail. The trail is maintained for the first mile. It takes you to the rim of Glenwood Canyon. Spectacular views. Bring water – it's high and dry. 1½ mile hike; allow 45 minutes.

On Horseback

ASPEN

Some of the state's, and certainly Aspen's, most scenic group rides can be joined at the T-Lazy 7, a longtime working ranch. **T Lazy 7 The Ranch**, 3129 Maroon Creek Road, 81612, ☎ 970/925-4614.

SNOWMASS VILLAGE

Also try **Brush Creek Outfitters,** 1020 Brush Creek Road, 81615, ☎ 970/923-4252.

For multiple day excursions into the wilderness, try **Snowmass Falls Outfitters,** 11500 Snowmass Creek Road, ☎ 970/923-6343.

For rides near Redstone, check out **Chair Mountain Stables,** Redstone, ☎ 970/963-1232.

On Wheels

ASPEN

One of Aspen's most beautiful mountain bike rides is the jaunt to **Maroon Lake**. This 18-mile round-trip ride is on paved roads. At the end of the road, prepare to see Maroon Bells in all its stunning glory. Take Highway 82 out of Aspen for one mile. Turn left at the Aspen Highlands sign. Begin your ride on Maroon Lake Road.

Pearl Pass is a much more difficult ride, which leads into Crested Butte, via dirt trails and a little bushwacking. Head up Castle Creek Road and bear right past Ashcroft until the road turns to trail. Only for experienced mountain bikers, equipped with good maps and supplies.

Smuggler Mountain trail is the gateway to the Hunter Creek wilderness, which is chock-full of single-track trails through the aspen groves. Start on the barren hillside northeast of town and pedal up the 800-foot vertical rise. From there, choices abound around Hunter Creek and Warren Lakes.

The recently completed **Aspen to Basalt bike trail** is a real boon for riders of all abilities. The 18-mile-trek is a gentle downhill ride as it winds through the towns of Woody Creek and Old Snowmass. Those unwilling to pedal back "up-valley" are offered the option of riding a bus home (they'll transport your bike for a small fee).

GLENWOOD

Even though mountain bikes are prohibited in the White River National Forest, there are still many two-wheeler possibilities.

For starters, the canyon trail along the Colorado River in **Glenwood Canyon** is open year-round.

For a short trip, pedal the five scenic miles from downtown **Glenwood to Grizzly Creek**. Or continue to **Hanging Lake** trailhead. The more ambitious can ride the entire canyon – about 18 miles one way – to the eastern portal, also known as Dotsero. Start early because the winds build in the afternoon, making the ride back west challenging.

CARBONDALE TO REDSTONE

One favorite tradition of locals in the Roaring Fork and Crystal River valleys is to mount a bike on Sunday morning and pedal the 19 gradual miles from Carbondale to Redstone along Highway 133. The route (which is well traveled, so go early) passes farms and ranches as it hugs the aptly named Crystal River. After about 14 miles, the rider comes upon Avalanche Ranch, a wonderful country antique store and guest cottages.

Another five miles south is the town of Redstone. Ride down Redstone Blvd. past the tasteful gift shops, small hotels, the church and artist's studio. The cyclist's destination is finally here – the **Redstone Inn**, 82 Redstone Blvd., Redstone, 81623, ☎ 963-2526, for Sunday brunch. Reservations are recommended.

On Water

GLENWOOD

The much-acclaimed **Hot Springs Pool** is a unique attraction for any season: an open-air swimming pool over two city blocks long, possibly the largest in the world. Loaded with minerals and steaming water, some pool areas are hotter than others. Diving boards, a waterslide, lawns, deck chairs, and outdoor lunches make this a delight.

Not far from the pool are **Vapor Caves**, where visitors soak in the luxury of warm steam or enjoy massage and other special services.

For more info, contact **Hot Springs Pool**, PO-D Box 308, 81601, ☎ 970/945-6571.

Glenwood Rafting

Glenwood Springs' location at the confluence of the Roaring Fork, and Colorado rivers make it the state's most popular river rafting center. Guides are everywhere with trips of all lengths and difficulties.

Whitewater Rafting and Rentals offers guided and guide-yourself river trips on the Colorado and Roaring Fork rivers. Rentals available for overnight trips. Late May through early September. Economy rates. I-70 Exit 114 (West Glenwood on the Colorado River). ☎ 970/945-8477.

White Water Rapids Transit Authority. Half-day, full-day, overnight, and twilight trips on the Colorado. 319 6th Street, Glenwood Springs, 81601, ☎ 970/945-6225.

Blazing Paddles, Snowmass Mall, Snowmass Village, 81615, ☎ 970/923-4544 is a veteran guide service offering trips on the Roaring Fork, Colorado and Arkansas rivers, plus overnight trips on the Gunnison.

For windsurfing, water skiing and picnicking, head to **Ruedi Reservoir**, 18 miles east of Basalt on Frypan River Road. Boardsailing headquarters is Freeman Mesa about half-way down the lake. There is also a small "yacht club" launch area.

On Snow

ASPEN

The four local mountains, Aspen, Aspen Highlands, Snowmass Ski Area and Buttermilk, which encompass more than 4,000 acres of skiing and snowboarding terrain, are all owned and operated by the **Aspen Skiing Co.**, PO Box 1248, 81612. ☎ 970/925-1220. One lift ticket is good at all four resorts.

Take the free bus to Snowmass and do some Alaskan-style **dogsledding** at Krabloonik. It's an expensive but exciting proposition. The same area serves hikers in summer and fall. ☎ 970/923-3953.

Cross-country skiing is better than average in the Aspen area. One good place to start cross-country skiing is at the **Aspen Cross-Country Center**, just off Highway 82 between Aspen and Buttermilk. Trails on the nearby golf course link up with the free Nordic Council trail system. Rentals and instruction are available; ☎ 970/925-2145.

The **Snowmass Lodge & Club Touring Center** is just off the golf course in Snowmass, and also connects with the trail system. You'll find a full rental shop, plus snacks and hot drinks. ☎ 970/923-5600.

Ashcroft Ski Touring offers rentals, rolling terrain with tracks for both diagonal-stride skiing and skating, and the Pine Creek Cookhouse. ☎ 970/925-1971.

Glenwood Springs has its own respectable ski area in **Sunlight Mountain Resort**, Glenwood Springs, ☎ 970 945-7491, about 12 miles southwest of town. Three chairlifts serve 38 runs and the new steep expanse called Sunlight Extreme. Ticket prices are always among the lowest in the state and the area remains a friendly alternative to the giants.

In the Air

ASPEN

The **Aspen Paragliding School** offers a three-day course of instruction in paragliding technique and equipment. All classes are held on Eagle Hill right above Tiehack Café. For information, call ☎ 970/925-7625. And on Aspen Mountain, you can paraglide with an experienced APA certified pilot from near the summit of the mountain. Scheduled on a daily basis. No experience necessary.

Operating out of Aspen and Glenwood Springs is **DBS Air Inc.**, ☎ 970 945-8808, a helicopter charter and rental service serving the Roaring Fork Valley, Denver and beyond.

For scenic flights or special charters, contact Kirk Lawrence at **Snowmass Aviation**, Pitkin County Airport, Aspen, ☎ 970 923-2229.

Eco-Travel & Cultural Excursions

ASPEN

Don't miss Aspen's summer culture. Inquire about the **International Design Conference, Aspen Music Festival, Ballet/Aspen Summer Dance Festival, Aspen Art Museum, Aspen Community Theatre, Aspen Writers' Conference, Aspen FilmFest, Aspen Theatre Company, Snowmass/Aspen Repertory Theater, Anderson Ranch,** and over 30 other art galleries.

FOR MORE INFORMATION

Aspen Resort Association, 303 E. Main Street, Aspen, CO 81611, ☎ 970/925-1940.

Aspen Central Reservations, 700 S. Aspen, Aspen, CO 81611, ☎ 970/925-9000.

Where To Stay & Eat

Accommodations

ASPEN

The Aspen region's horn of plenty extends to the accommodations, with a bed to everyone's taste, from a super-duper rental condominium (sleeping a large family or retinue), to the free-spending vacationer's quality room in a ski lodge to the busy little Victorian house where a budget skier or student can sleep well for $60 a night. There are some ex-rooming houses with baths down the hall, motor hotels, log cabins, apartments, houses, a converted country club, guest ranches, and even a Holiday Inn. The ski traveler's choice will depend on the airline package, on the pocketbook, or on where he/she wants to ski. Please note that the four Aspen ski areas are well linked by free transportation.

The Little Nell is Aspen Mountain's ski-in/ski-out hotel, at the base of the mountain. This elegant, European-style facility offers the personalized service and ameni ties of a grand hotel, including a swimming pool, hot tub, and fitness center. Luxury accommodations are found in 92 rooms, including 13 suites. Courtesy van service and a parking garage are also available. The Little Nell is an AAA Five Diamond award recipient and a member of the exclusive Relais and Chateaux Association. 675 Durant Avenue, 81611, ☎ 970/920-4600. Deluxe.

The Ritz Carlton, Aspen is at the base of Aspen Mountain, between the Silver Queen Gondola and Lift 1A. The 257-room resort provides all-day dining in The Terrace Restaurant and après ski in the Lobby

Lounge with live musical performances. Additional al fresco dining is provided in the Courtyard during the summer months. The hotel has an extensive fitness center with indoor/outdoor whirlpools and an outdoor heated pool. Superior accommodations, including 28 suites and 40 Ritz-Carlton Club rooms with a private concierge. Courtesy ski shuttle. Parking garage. Four-Star, Four Diamond hotel. 315 E. Dean Street, 81611, ☎ 970/920-3300. Deluxe.

Aspen's T Lazy 7 Ski Ranch is on Maroon Lake Road, four miles from Aspen. Here, you will not be disturbed. Cabins come with kitchens, snack bars, and baths. Bar, heated pool, around which the grass is always green thanks to infrared heat lamps. Cook your own breakfast or have it ranch-style. Free shuttle to your ski area. Informal. Ideal for Highlands skiing. ☎ 970/925-7254. Expensive.

If you must be near Aspen Mountain, you might consider **The Fasching Haus**, a condominium complex not far from the Little Nell lifts. One to three bedrooms available, private fireplaces. 747 Galena Street, 81611, ☎ 970/321-7025. Expensive.

The Aspen Square Condos are in the same vicinity, with balconies, the availability of studio flats, maid service, elevator, underground parking, and many nearby shops. 617 E. Cooper Street, 81611, ☎ 800/862-7736. Expensive.

The Hotel Jerome has been in the center of things since 1889, when it was built for the rich miners and their ladies. Much of the Victorian era – beds, couches, night stands, bathtubs, the large lobby, staircases, and a three-story bar – have survived, even after several renovations. Most rooms are small and come with a TV. A good summer choice when the large pool is opened and coffee is served in the garden. Reserve far in advance. 330 E. Main Street, 81611, ☎ 970/920-1000. Deluxe.

Boomerang Lodge waits nearby, offering a skier's gathering place, with a look at the mountain, or at the ski bunny beside the fireplace. Nice modern rooms, with soft, piped-in music. Heated outdoor pool, hot (185°) sauna. 500 W. Hopkins, 81865, ☎ 970/925-3416. Expensive.

SNOWMASS VILLAGE

For visitors who like the layout of Snowmass Village and don't intend to budge from there except to ski the superb terrain, there's no point in commuting to Aspen. The sturdy, warm, prosperous-looking accommodations found in Snowmass provide everything you could wish for.

The Silvertree Hotel is the largest, with oversized, well-furnished bedchambers, many fireplaces, sauna and pool. 100 Elbert Lane, 81865, ☎ 970/923-3520. Moderate-expensive.

The Snowmass Mountain Chalet is the smallest lodge, but a homey one. Full breakfasts and family-style dinners on Sunday nights here. 115 Daly Lane, 81615, ☎ 970/923-3900. Moderate.

For condominiums, check out the **Top of the Village**, 855 Carriage Way, 81615, ☎ 970/923-3673. Expensive-deluxe.

The Fryingpan River Ranch, 32042 Fryingpan Road, Meredith, 81642, ☎ 970/927-3570. 8,800 feet. Open May 28 through October 29. Deluxe accommodations in a rustic setting. Moderate-expensive.

FOR MORE INFORMATION

Aspen Chamber Resort Association, 425 Rio Grande Place, Aspen, CO 81611, ☎ 303/925-1940.

GLENWOOD SPRINGS

Hotel Colorado, 526 Pine Street, 81601, ☎ 800/945-6511. Handsome restored 120-room hotel with suites, convention facilities, health spa. Elegant. Near the famous Glenwood Pool. Moderate to expensive.

Holiday Inn, 51359 US 6, 81601, ☎ 970/945-8551. Two miles west at I-70 Exit. Chain member with heated pool, saunas. Restaurant, bar, entertainment, dancing. Car needed. Expensive.

The Historic Redstone Inn. Open all year. Dining room (breakfast, lunch, dinner, Sunday buffet), lounge, stables. An elegant old inn in a historic mining town. In the Crystal River Valley, on CO 133, 25 miles from Glenwood Springs. Excellent ski touring, fishing, horseback riding, hiking. ☎ 970/963-2526. Moderate-expensive.

Restaurants

ASPEN

Aspen has dozens of restaurants, and they're much better than you'd expect in a town of 5,000 inhabitants – especially a Western town, where you mostly get steaks, roast beef, or fried chicken. The joy of Aspen is that you can eat Spanish, Italian, German, Chinese, Swiss, Austrian, French haute cuisine or simple French food. Explore a different country every night.

There is no space to describe all of Aspen's restaurants, so we'll limit coverage to a few special places.

The Crystal Palace turns into a lively operatic stage each night. Excerpts from Broadway shows are sung with gusto and expertise. You can watch the well-rehearsed doings amid Victorian decor, or you can listen at a table. Prix fixe dinner, simple menu, and unique ambiance. 300 E. Hyman Avenue, ☎ 970/925-1455. Expensive.

The **Red Onion** flanks one of Aspen's malls. This restaurant is an Aspen institution; the portals in its red brick exterior already attracted notables who arrived for the FIS World Championships back in 1950. The accent is on Mexican food. Excellent liquor. Fine for lunch, too. The walnut bar dates back to 1892. This restaurant stays open seven days a week. 420 E. Cooper Street, ☎ 970/925-9043. Moderate.

Across from the Red Onion, the classic **Guido's Swiss Inn** is hard to overlook because of its authentic Swiss chalet architecture. The operators are Swiss and, while they're less friendly than Guido and Trudi Meyer, the original owners, you'll still find good schnitzel and other veal dishes, fondues made of Swiss cheeses, and fine pastries. Comfy bar. 403 S. Galena, ☎ 970/925-7222. Very expensive.

Chart House. Steaks and crab. Fabulous salad bar. Excellent value. 219 E. Durant Avenue, ☎ 970/925-3525. Moderate to expensive.

The beautiful **Little Nell Hotel** also offers fine dining. The chef prepares unusual American fare such as Texas caribou and wild boar ham with mushrooms, roast salmon with tomato chutney, or fruitwood-smoked duck and ginger-plum mustard. Reservations recommended. 675 E. Durant Avenue, 81611, ☎ 970/920-4600. Expensive.

The best Mexican food in town can be found at **La Cocina**, 308 E. Hopkins Avenue, 81612, ☎ 970/925-9714. Go early to avoid the crowds and when the owner tells you it will be a 20-minute wait, get ready to down some margaritas in the interim. Moderate.

SNOWMASS VILLAGE

In Snowmass Village, Butch Darden reigns supreme with his "down East" inflected menu that features lobster, shrimp and other fresh catches. **Butch's Lobster Bar**, Timberline Lodge, Snowmass Village, 81615, ☎ 970/923-4004. Expensive.

FOR MORE INFORMATION

Aspen Chamber Resort Association, 425 Rio Grande Place, Aspen, CO 81611, ☎ 800/262-7736.

GLENWOOD SPRINGS

Restaurant Sopris, five miles south towards Aspen on Highway 82. American and European cuisine. Wide choice of appetizers and wines. Steak Diane, Wiener schnitzel, variety of steaks, Swiss spaghetti and Chateaubriand. ☎ 970/945-7771. Expensive.

Good, hearty south-of-the-border menu items can be found at **Dos Hombres** restaurant, 51783 US Highway 6 & 24, ☎ 970/928-0490. Inexpensive.

Families and couples in search of well-priced Italian food and pizzas check in to the **Italian Underground**, 715 Grand Avenue, ☎ 970/945-6422. Moderate.

FOR MORE INFORMATION

Glenwood Springs Central Reservations at ☎ 800/221-0098, or write to **Glenwood Springs Chamber Resort Association**, 1102 Grand Avenue, Glenwood Springs, CO 81601.

Camping

ASPEN

Difficult Campground offers the closest camping to Aspen, just three miles east of town via Highway 82. Fee sites, hiking trail. **US Forest Service**, 806 W. Hallam Street, Aspen, ☎ 970/925-3445.

Weller Campground. 11 sites. Six miles southeast on SR 82, a quarter-mile south on FR 15104. Adjacent to Roaring Fork River. Two miles farther on Highway 82 is the equally accessible Lincoln Creek Campground. **US Forest Service**, 806 W. Hallam Street, Aspen, ☎ 970/925-3445.

Avalanche Creek, five miles south of Redstone, has a rustic campground and access to excellent hiking trails.

BRB Crystal River Resort, Highway 133, Redstone, has 22 RV sites and 30 tent sites and is open May 15 through the end of October.

GLENWOOD SPRINGS

Deep Lake. Twenty-one sites. 16¾ miles east on US 6 and 24, two miles north on CR 301, then 26½ miles northwest on FR 600. **US Forest Service**, 900 Grand Avenue, Glenwood Springs, ☎ 970/945-2521.

The Hideout. Cabins and campground. Amenities include hot showers, firewood and ice. Two miles south of Glenwood on Road 117 (Sunlight Ski Road). ☎ 970/945-5621.

Rock Gardens Campground. On the Colorado River in Glenwood Canyon. Two miles east of Glenwood at Exit 119 on I-70. ☎ 970/945-6737.

Central Western Colorado

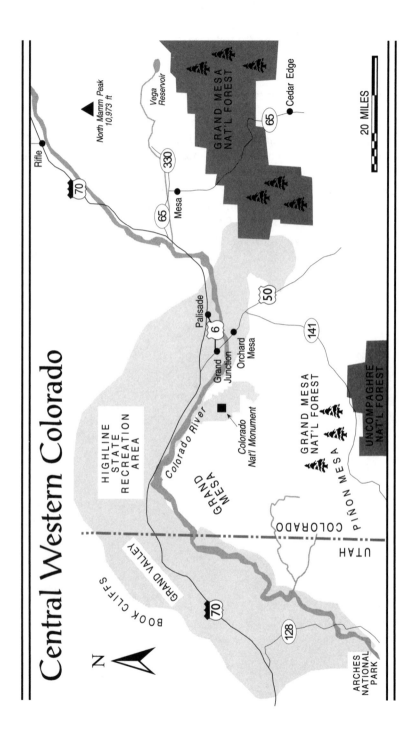

N

20 MILES

BOOK CLIFFS

GRAND VALLEY

HIGHLINE STATE RECREATION AREA

Colorado River

GRAND MESA

Colorado Nat'l Monument

UTAH

COLORADO

PIÑON MESA

GRAND MESA NAT'L FOREST

UNCOMPAHGRE NAT'L FOREST

ARCHES NATIONAL PARK

70

128

141

50

Grand Junction

Orchard Mesa

6

Palisade

Rifle

70

65

Mesa

330

North Mamm Peak
10,973 ft

Vega Reservoir

GRAND MESA NAT'L FOREST

65

Cedar Edge

Central West Colorado

Grand Junction, Grand Mesa & Palisade

Geography & History

The far western reaches of Colorado represent the final curtain call for the Rocky Mountain topography as the territory evolves, slowly but surely, into the desert landscape. The rugged country that even dinosaurs could not tame now commemorates the now-extinct beasts' existence with digs, displays and research into their demise.

Vast expanses of wild, rugged, roan-colored hills make up this country. The bustling city of Grand Junction – so named for the confluence of two rivers – is the gateway to the wilderness and Utah's rugged terrain.

Just east of Junction is Palisade, a valley lush with peaches and pears that abuts the 50-mile-wide flat-topped Grand Mesa bursting with recreational activities.

To the west of Grand Junction is Colorado National Monument, a place to find sandstone canyons that were carved into the Uncompahgre Plateau.

To the north are the Book Cliffs and eventually Dinosaur National Monument.

East of here, on the edge of the Rockies is the cattle country of Meeker and Craig. In the same region is the energy-producing city of Rangely. A real estate firm in northwestern Colorado hawked property as "real land for real people."

Grand Mesa and much of the Grand Valley is said to have been the peaceful home of the Ute Indians until the US Government started moving the Utes out of their claimed environment. They were supplanted by farmers and ranchers whose fortunes were aided by the institution of railroad service by the Denver & Rio Grande in 1887.

There have been many financial ups and downs since then. The region was helped, then ultimately hurt, by the pullout of oil shale, in the early 1980s. Agriculture, too, has had its deviations due to weather. But the ever-resilient people of western Colorado have survived the storms and are banking on tourism to offer a stable future.

Getting Around

Walker Field Airport is served by United Express, Sky West, the Delta Connection, the new Air 21. Sometimes other seasonal carriers serve this airport that rarely suffers weather-related delays. 2828 Walker Field Drive, ☎ 970/244-9100.

Amtrak trains stop in Grand Junction, arriving from Denver and Salt Lake City. For schedules call ☎ 800/878-7245.

Greyhound/Trailways serves Rifle and Grand Junction daily from Denver. ☎ 970/625-3980.

Touring

Grand Junction

In late May each year, tomorrow's stars of baseball come to Grand Junction for the Junior College World Series. Locals still recall fondly the year Kirby Puckett knocked a couple of balls out of the stadium at **Mesa College**.

Dinosaur Valley, 362 Main Street, ☎ 970/241-9210, has re-created dinosaurs in scary proportions. An on-site laboratory has scientists working on recent finds. The new **Children's Museum** in Fruita has also recently opened.

Colorado National Monument, Fruita, 81521, ☎ 970/858-3617, comprising more than 20,000 acres between Fruita and Grand Junction. It's where canyons dip to more than 1,000 feet. There are plenty of jumping-off places to explore the land.

Rim Rock Drive is the serpentine road that winds around the sandstone monoliths were dedicated as a national monument by President Taft in 1911. Reach the west entrance of the monument via I-70 to

Fruita. **Colorado National Monument Visitor Center, ☎** 970/858-3617.

Wineries

Swallow this: Since 1990, the number of licensed Colorado wineries has increased by more than 200%. Why the boom? The consumer demand is incredible. The wineries open their doors to the public for the **Colorado Mountain Winefest** in mid-September.

Orchard Mesa is the heart of the state's burgeoning wine industry because of its abundant sunshine, warm days and cool nights. **Grand River Vineyards,** at Exit 42 off I-70, offers Bordeaux-styled blends as their specialty. ☎ 800/264-7696.

Carlson Vineyards is at 461 35 Road, Palisade, ☎ 970/464-5554. Parker and Mary Carlson started wine-making as a hobby. Parker is a true character and so are his wines like "Gewurzasaurus" and "Sipasaurus" that recall some of the beasts that used to roam this area. The Carlsons appear to enjoy entertaining visitors in their farmhouse complex on lush East Orchard Mesa.

While in the area, also visit **Colorado Cellars,** the state's oldest wine-maker, ☎ 800/848-2812.

Grand Mesa

Don't drink and drive if you're planning on taking the 78-mile **Grand Mesa Scenic & Historic Byway** (driving the road sober is tough enough). Start at Highway 65, 23 miles east of Grand Junction via I-70. Drive through Plateau Canyon to the town of Mesa, past the Powderhorn Ski Area and onto the Grand Mesa. There, you have the option of driving on wild and woolly Land's End Road, which switchbacks its way back to Grand Junction and its terminus with Highway 14, about 15 miles south of the city.

Or, continue on the Grand Mesa Scenic & Historic Byway to Cedaredge, another bucolic agricultural area. Head back to Grand Junction via Highway 65, Highway 92 or north at Delta on Highway 50.

Grand Mesa National Forest boasts 300 lakes and reservoirs. The Colorado and Gunnison Rivers on either side of Grand Mesa probably helped shape the landform. At an average elevation of 10,000 feet, hundreds of lakes, forests, and meadows attract wildlife to its conifer-covered mountainsides. **Grand Mesa Visitor Center,** ☎ 970/856-6961.

Adventures

On Foot

On the Colorado National Monument, the **Alcove Nature Trail** is suited to all abilities, while Monument Canyon Trail dives deep into the rock and requires a half-day minimum excursion.

Rattlesnake Canyon offers a large concentration of rock arches. But its access through the monument and Glade Park is difficult. Maps are available from the BLM.

Hike as long or short as you please on the **Crag Crest National Recreation Trail.** It's 10 miles, with viewpoints up to 11,000 feet elevation and steep drop-offs on both sides. The trailhead is near Island Lake on Grand Mesa.

On Wheels

For a touring ride, it's hard to beat **Rim Rock Drive**, which climbs 2,300 feet in a 35-mile loop around Colorado National Monument. A shorter ride of 10 miles begins at the visitor's center and continues to Artist's Point.

The **Kokopelli Trail** is 128 miles of slickrock and canyons between Loma and Moab, Utah. Sections range from mellow roads to meandering single-track trails. The route is named in honor of the flute-playing Native American figure, Kokopelli. For maps and information write to the **Colorado Plateau Mountain Bike Trail Association**, PO Box 4602, Grand Junction, 81502, ☎ 970/241-9561.

Well-suited to grape growing, Grand Valley is also good for cyclists. Every year the 25-mile **Bacchus Tour** meanders through the gentle hills and rolling meadows of downtown Palisade and Orchard Mesa. It takes place during the wine festival. Call **Bicycle Outfitters,** ☎ 970/245-2699, for information.

Bike rentals and maps are available through the **Bike Peddler**, 710 N. 1st Street, Grand Junction, 81502, ☎ 970/243-5602.

Scenic Byways, PO Box 2972, Grand Junction, 81502, ☎ 970/243-9337, offers day trips, tours and weekend packages for mountain and road bikers.

On Water

The Colorado River is calm through Grand Junction but it becomes lively downriver from Loma at Horsethief Canyon. The black-walled Westwater Canyon, just next door in Utah, boasts the Skull Rapid and Room of Doom as part of its wicked ride. Permits are required to run Westwater, which is best in fall. Contact **Rimrock Adventures**, PO Box 608, Fruita, 81521, ☎ 970/858-9555, for trips on the Colorado, or **Adventure Bound River Expeditions**, ☎ 800/423-4668, for trips into Westwater, Desolation and Canyonlands.

FISHING

Grand Mesa's lakes are stocked by the Division of Wildlife with rainbow, brook and cutthroat trout. Ice fishing is popular in the winter on the Mesa but dress warmly.

On Horseback

Mount Garfield Stables, 747 35 3/10 Road, Palisade, 81526, ☎ 970/464-0246, offers hourly and daily horseback rides. Also available: horse boarding, lessons and training.

On Snow

Powderhorn Ski Area, PO Box 370, Mesa, 81643, ☎ 970/268-5700, is a pleasant surprise this close to a medium-sized city (35 miles from Grand Junction via I-70 and Highway 65). Steeper than you'd expect, Powderhorn also has good bump runs. Still, half of its slopes are ranked for intermediates. *Bill's Run* is the longest trail on the mountain, a favorite of skiers and snowboarders of all abilities.

The **Powderhorn Nordic Center** also grooms about a dozen kilometers of trails.

Grand Mesa cross-country trails are plentiful near the shuttered Land's End Road, favored by snowmobilers.

Nordic trails are maintained along Highway 65.

Where to Stay & Eat

Accommodations

Cabins with kitchens are spacious and well-equipped at **Grand Mesa Lodge**, PO Box 49, Cedaredge, 81413, ☎ 970/856-3250, perched near Island Lake. Pets are permitted. Moderate.

The **Alexander Lake Lodge**, PO Box 93, Cedaredge, 81413, ☎ 970/856-6700, has cabins, some with kitchens. Moderate.

Grand Junction Hilton, 743 Horizon Drive, Grand Junction, 81506, ☎ 970/241-8888, offers 264 large rooms, meeting facilities, a heated pool and Jacuzzi, tennis courts and a gym. Expensive.

True to its name, **Gate House Bed & Breakfast,** 2502 N. First Street, Grand Junction, 81501, ☎ 970/242-6105, once stood in the shadow of the Redstone Castle. Since its 1945 relocation – completed stone by stone – it has been turned into a guest house well-known for delicious breakfast repasts. Moderate to expensive.

Restaurants

The **Winery**, 642 Main Street, Grand Junction, ☎ 970/242-4100, is a comfortable restaurant for special occasions or just a good night out. Predictable beef and fish entrées accompanied by a salad bar and the perfect wines make a good meal. Expensive.

Slice O Life Bakery, 105 W. 3rd Street, Palisade, 81526, ☎ 970/464-0577, uses whole grains and local fruits in its specialties. Inexpensive.

Camping

Saddlehorn Campground in Colorado National Monument has 81 sites. Backcountry camping is allowed within the monument borders. ☎ 970/858-3617.

Island Acres State Park, Box B, Palisade, 81525, ☎ 970/464-0548, is 15 miles east of Grand Junction. Thirty-two tent and RV sites are available.

Grand Mesa is blessed with more than a dozen campgrounds offering 250-plus sites. Reserve by calling ☎ 1-800-283-CAMP.

The BLM manages the **Book Cliffs** area north of Grand Junction. ☎ 970/856-6961.

Northwest Colorado

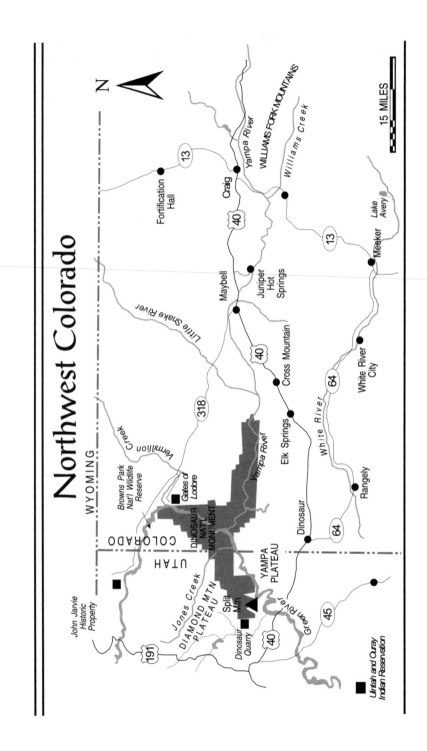

N

WYOMING

COLORADO

UTAH

Fortification Hall

13

Craig

Yampa River

WILLIAMS FORK MOUNTAINS

Williams Creek

40

Maybell

Juniper Hot Springs

13

Meeker

Lake Avery

Little Snake River

318

Cross Mountain

40

White River

64

White River City

Vermillion Creek

Browns Park Nat'l Wildlife Reserve

Gates of Lodore

Elk Springs

Yampa River

Dinosaur

DINOSAUR NAT'L MONUMENT

64

Rangely

John Jarvie Historic Property

191

Jones Creek

DIAMOND MTN PLATEAU

YAMPA PLATEAU

Split Mtn

Green River

Dinosaur Quarry

40

45

Uintah and Ouray Indian Reservation

15 MILES

Northwest Colorado

Meeker & Dinosaur Country

Geography & History

Meeker and Rio Blanco County mark the transition between the
expansive rangelands abutting the Colorado/Utah border and the
high alpine tundra of the Flat Tops Wilderness Area. People here
still earn a living in the cattle and sheep-herding fields.

Meeker was the site of the infamous Meeker Massacre in 1879, when
long-simmering tensions erupted after Native Americans wouldn't conform to the white man's ways. The Utes fought bravely, but they ultimately lost the war and were forced westward to less friendly lands in
Utah and extreme southwestern Colorado. A marker on Highway 64
shows the site of the massacre. Each year for the Fourth of July the town
reenacts the Meeker Massacre in a melodrama with dozens of Indians,
white men and frightened families, horses and dogs. It's all part of the
Range Call Fourth of July Celebration. ☎ 970/878-5510.

Dogs really do work the land here. In the **Meeker Sheep Dog Trials**,
handlers and canine companions show sheep where to go. In honor
of *Babe*, they have started a division for pigs. The wacky event is held
in September, which is also when hunters flock here in search of big
game like elk and deer. In the extreme northwestern corner of the state,
Dinosaur National Monument attracts visitors throughout the year.

Touring

UINTA MOUNTAINS

The area is populated by small, friendly towns, whose residents still
work the land, an anomaly in modern-day western Colorado. The

earliest inhabitants of the Uinta Mountains on the border of Utah were probably the Ute Indians. The mountains have gained a sort of notoriety for their east-west heading, unusual but not unique in the lower 48 states.

At the eastern end of the region, the **Flat Tops Scenic Byway** starts in the White River Valley at Meeker and continues over Ripple Creek Pass en route to the tiny town of Yampa. Take Highway 13 north to CR 8 to begin the drive.

Irish Canyon, a slice of geologic history, is about 75 miles west of Craig via Route 318. The canyon road reveals quartz and limestone on the sheer walls and was thought to have been visited by the early Fremont people. A short nature trail leads visitors to Fremont petroglyphs that have been preserved through time.

Continue on Route 318 west of Irish Canyon to **Brown's Park National Wildlife Refuge.** Scenic, unspoiled Brown's Park is 25 miles east of Flaming Gorge Dam via Highway 191 and the maintained gravel road known as Clay Basin Creek dips for two miles into steep Jesse Ewing Canyon. There you'll find, in addition to one of the west's remaining remote outposts, the historic John Jarvie property. A cluster of Jarvie's century-old buildings remain, including a blacksmith shop, a stone house, and a corral built from hand-hewn railroad ties.

The Uinta Mountains (basins and landforms may be spelled Uintah) run from Brown's Park to the Kamas area east of Park City. It's an area of high mountains, alpine basins filled with more than 500 lakes, and thick stands of conifers.

FOR MORE INFORMATION

US Forest Service, Box 279, Manila, UT 84046, ☎ 801/784-3445.

The BLM administers the John Jarvie site. More information is available at ☎ 801/789-1362.

DINOSAUR NATIONAL MONUMENT

Many million years ago, a flash flood or other natural disaster trapped a dinosaur colony living near present-day Green River within the surrounding canyon walls. Earth and water conspired to entomb this pack of dinosaurs in a sandbar where they would have remained indefinitely had intrepid paleontologist Earl Douglass Ford not spotted eight tail bones of a brontosaurus sticking out of the earth during the summer of 1909. During the next 15 years, he excavated 1,000 tons of bones, most of which had been preserved in their pristine state.

About 17 miles east of Vernal, Utah, via Highway 40 and Highway 149, is the infamous quarry and an excellent museum, which hints at the domination these fascinating beasts had 150 million years ago. The quarry is where dinosaurs were actually entombed in their mud mausoleum and is where more than 1,600 bones were excavated from an ancient river bed. Past joins the present in a kind of surreal stone-age-meets-space-age experience. There are Brontosaurus bones, a reconstructed allosaurus and the hump-backed stegosaurus.

Woodrow Wilson established Dinosaur National Monument as an 80-acre preserve in 1915. In a 13-year period, more than 350 tons of bones were shipped to the Carnegie Museum in Pittsburgh.

This real-life Jurassic Park sits on the Colorado/Utah border in **Dinosaur National Monument**, Box 128, Jensen UT 84035, ☎ 801/789-2115 or 4545 Highway 40, Dinosaur, 81610. (Colorado's headquarters has no fossils at its visitor center.)

The park is diverse in many ways. It's the meeting place of desert, Great Plains and Uncompaghre cultures and has been occupied in one form or another by humans for more than 9,000 years. Dinosaur is biologically diverse, as well. The Yampa and Green rivers meet here and the water courses helped carve through these rugged canyon lands. It's a rough, tough land, with temperature extremes on either end and often sparse vegetation

Dinosaur is a good place to see a golden eagle or a peregrine falcon but visitors are usually enticed by the prospect of seeing all those bones. Although a week is necessary to see the park for all its worth, it is possible to gain the essence through only a day trip.

The monument's wild lands, including the confluence of the Green and Yampa rivers. were annexed to the park in 1938. They are best seen by river. Permits are required for boating either river in Dinosaur and they are doled out on a lottery basis. ☎ 970/374-2468 for an application.

Vehicular access to the park's scenery is available from both the Colorado and Utah sides. From Highway 40 in Colorado, six miles east of the town of Dinosaur, is monument headquarters and the visitor's center. That's the start of the road to **Harper's Corner**

In a few miles you'll pass **Plug Hat Butte** and **Blue Mountain**. The road continues to weave towards the monument, straddling the Utah/Colorado state line en route to Harper's Corner.

At the Canyon Overlook and picnic area is the rugged country of the **Green and Yampa rivers,** which twist and wind through goosenecks. Those interested in geology will see examples of Uintah quartzite and Weber sandstone. Continue to the trail's end and take the hiking path to enjoy views of the Green River. To the north is **Wild Mountain,** which well-describes the area and the nearby fabled rapids of the Gates of Lodore.

Echo Park Campground and a 13-mile side trip on the unimproved road to Echo Park is reachable from the Harper's Corner scenic drive. The Echo Park Road plunges deep into the monument's heart and features prehistoric rock art and views of the Green and Yampa river confluence, as well as landmark Steamboat Rock. Between the historic Chew Ranch and Echo Park are the Pool Creek petroglyphs, which, strangely enough, are very different from the park's other petroglyphs. The Whispering Cave may also be seen from this route.

The **Gates of Lodore,** accessible from Highway 318 west of Maybell, CO, is tough to get to but worth the effort. Considered one of the most beautiful stretches of the Green River, its red canyon walls are sprinkled with lodgepole pine and fir trees. Lodore Canyon is packed with churning rapids boasting names like Hell's Half Mile and Disaster Falls. Take the short trail to the overlook and watch the river run.

That same Highway 318 will take you across the Green River on a swinging bridge where the waterbirds from the National Wildlife Refuge can be viewed.

The **Yampa Bench Road** is 25 miles one-way and impassable when wet. It sidles alongside the Yampa River offering views of the twisting river before it meets up with the Green. The road can be accessed from Echo Park off Highway 14 at Elk Springs in Colorado.

Visits which commence in Utah should originate at the quarry. Turn left at the junction and head toward **Split Mountain,** a popular put-in place for river runners. Along the way is a marker telling the story of the Green River Valley. At the Split Mountain Campground turn left and drive down to the river. Near the boat ramp is a John Wesley Powell Memorial marker.

Tour of the Tilted Rocks is the name of the self-narrated 22-mile round-trip drive. Pictographs and prairie dogs, Split Mountain, and the Elephant Toes Butte may be spotted from the paved road. Pick up a copy of the Tour of the Tilted Rocks brochure at the Visitor's Center for more information about the tour.

A side journey to **Josie Morris' cabin** in the Cub Creek Valley is well worth the effort. The remains of Josie's homestead, behind Split Mountain, demonstrate her self-sufficient and industrious nature.

Runoff and springs brought her water. A chicken coop and fruit orchard provided her food. Morris' cattle were kept in natural corrals, the steep box canyons with near-vertical walls. More visited these days than in Josie's heyday, the area still exudes an aura of calmness.

There are other options from the Utah entrance. **Island Park Road to Rainbow Park** meanders past colorful badlands and follows on the other side of Split Mountain, so-named because of its division by the Green River. At **McKee Spring** are some of the park's best petroglyphs. Huge, human-like figures are etched into the sandstone cliffs. To reach the Island Park Road, follow Brush Creek Road five miles towards Vernal after leaving the Monument, then 16 miles northeast.

Pets must be leashed and carefully monitored for heat prostration and dehydration. In this deceptively harsh climate extreme winter days can hit 40° below when cold settles into the basin, and in July temperatures can reach 104°. Oddly enough, most visitors choose to come in the heat of summer, rather than waiting for better weather that accompanies the wildflowers of spring or the fall colors.

FOR MORE INFORMATION

Grand Junction Tourist Information Bureau, 759 Horizon Drive, Grand Junction, CO 81506, ☎ 800/265-6723.

The Grand Junction Ranger District Office, 764 Horizon Drive, Grand Junction, CO 81506, ☎ 970/242-8211.

Blanco Ranger District, 317 Market Street, Meeker, CO 81641, ☎ 970/878-4039.

Meeker Chamber of Commerce, PO Box 869, Meeker, CO 81641, ☎ 970/878-5510.

Dinosaur National Monument, 4545 Highway 40, Dinosaur, CO 81610, ☎ 970/374-2216.

National Park Service, Box 25287, Denver, CO 80225, ☎ 303/969-2000.

Bureau of Land Management, 2815 H Road, Grand Junction, CO 81506, ☎ 970/244-3000.

A good book on this remote area is *Colorado Cabins, Cottages & Lodges*. Rocky Mountain Vacation Publishing, Inc., Boulder, CO 80303.

Adventures

On Foot

The rolling hills of the Flat Tops Wilderness Area are ideal for hiking and mountain biking. Wildflower-filled meadows and hidden little lakes fill this beautiful area.

Mirror Lake is a 2½-mile intermediate trail. Access the trailhead via Trappers Lake Road. The **Trappers Lake Trail** climbs more than a dozen miles beyond Trappers Lake into the Flat Tops Wilderness. It's 49 miles from Meeker via Highway 13 and CR 8 to Trappers Lake Road. From there, travel another 10 miles to the lake.

HUNTING

Northwestern Colorado is renowned for its big-game hunting, including deer, elk and mountain lion. Meeker is the jumping-off point for safaris into the Piceance wilderness area and westward to the Flat Tops.

The Day Tripper, 801 E. Victory Way, Craig, 81625, ☎ 970/824-3620, supplies hunters with what they need.

On Wheels

The Day Tripper, 801 E. Victory Way, Craig, 81625, ☎ 970/824-3620, rents and sells mountain bikes and accessories.

On Water

This arid region has unusually rich water possibilities. The **White River** starts at Trappers Lake on its westward flow through Meeker and Rangely.

Kayakers are challenged by the double diamond waters of **Cross Mountain Gorge** and rafters explore the **Yampa River** at Deerlodge Park. Permits are required for individuals and groups. Contact **Dino-**

saur National Monument, 4545 Highway 40, Dinosaur, 81610, ☎ 970/374-2216. Commercial trips explore the depth and breadth of Dinosaur National Park in single and multi-day trips.

FISHING

The **Green River** in Utah is renowned for its trout population. Especially popular is the section of the Green River below Flaming Gorge Dam in Utah.

Outdoor Connections, 380 Tucker Street, Craig, 81625, ☎ 970/824-5510, has boat and canoe rentals and sales for fishing and boating trips. The company also provides a shuttle service.

The **Flat Tops Wilderness**, like Grand Mesa, has many high-altitude lakes and rivers. But the difference here is accessibility: Unlike easy-access Grand Mesa, foot or horseback are the allowable modes of transport into the wilderness areas.

Trapper's Lake is known for its special strain of trout, found only here.

Check in with **Dry Creek Anglers**, 115 Jefferson, Hayden, 81639, for fly-tying and rod-building supplies and instruction, plus current fishing conditions. Free fly-casting lessons on Saturday.

ON HORSEBACK

Trail rides and outfitting can be arranged through the Sleepy Cat Ranch (see below).

Where To Stay & Eat

Accommodations

Sleepy Cat Ranch, 16064 County Road 8, Meeker, 81641, ☎ 970/878-4413 has comfortable cabins and a homey atmosphere. Located 15 miles from Highway 13 and CR 8. Inexpensive.

Meeker Hotel, 560 Main Street, Meeker, 81641, ☎ 970/878-5062, keeps animal heads displayed in the lobby, kind of in the manner of an authentic Western hotel. Built around the turn of the century, the hotel offers private and semi-private rooms and suites. Inexpensive.

Holiday Inn, 300 S. Highway 13, Craig, 81625, ☎ 970/824-4000 is a motor inn one mile from downtown. Aside from the usual amenities, it features a lounge with entertainment. The hotel is welcoming after a day on the road, and the kid in all of us certainly appreciates the game room. Moderate.

Rusty Cannon Motel, 701 Taughenbaugh Boulevard, Rifle, ☎ 970/625-4004 is right off the highway and near the Colorado River. Laundry facilities. Inexpensive.

It's basic, but if you need to stop in Rangely, try the **Escalante Trail Motel**, 117 S. Grand Street, Rangely, 81647, ☎ 970/675-8461. Inexpensive.

Restaurants

For a side of beef or some other comfort food after a day in the wilderness, **Sleepy Cat Ranch**, 16064 County Road 8, Meeker, 81641, ☎ 970/878-4413. Big desserts, salad bar and good breakfasts are standard. Located 16 miles from Meeker via Highway 13 and CR 8. Moderate.

Trappers Lake Lodge, PO Box 1230, Meeker, 81641, ☎ 970/878-4288, also serves hearty meals. Moderate.

The Breeze Street Bakery, 572 Breeze Street, Craig, ☎ 970/824-8148 offers dishes made from scratch daily, plus fresh roasted coffee. Inexpensive.

Camping

South Fork Campground in the White River National Forest is recommended. Follow CR 8 along the White River to South Fork Road. The 17-site fee campground is another 12 miles on an unmaintained road.

Himes Peak Campground, off Trappers Lake Road, has nine sites.

Southwest Colorado

Durango, Telluride & Cortez

Colorado's southwestern corner encompasses a blending of cultures derived from at least two easily discernible sources. This much is known: Indians controlled the land for a very long time before white settlers arrived seeking gold and silver, or trailing herds of livestock shortly after the Civil War. Descendants of both are still here, doing things their own way and offering a rare chance in this modern world to experience a place where Indians and cowboys are the common folk. And you can add historic Hispanic flourishes along with modern civilization to the mix. You will also undoubtedly notice bulging car racks sporting mountain bikes, inflatable kayaks, skis or snowboards, as well as service directories touting herbal healers and body piercing, micro-breweries, bagel shops and espresso bars.

Geography & History

The area revels in its historic roots. The ancient Anasazi Indians left behind their cliff dwellings and mysteries 700 years ago at Mesa Verde National Park, Ute Mountain Tribal Park, and Hovenweep National Monument, among other sites. The white men who came seeking riches built ornate Victorian structures, as well as railroads to haul their precious ore, at the end of the last century. Fine examples of this architecture can be seen today in Durango, Silverton, Ouray and Telluride. And 200,000 tourists ride the famous Durango & Silverton Narrow Gauge Railroad every year between these two cities, the only line left from all the rail routes that once serviced the remote mountain communities.

The historically accurate train belches black smoke, and airborne cinders are likely to become tangled in your hair as you look out at spectacular forest views from open-air gondola cars. It follows exactly the same route that it did in 1891. The first 10 miles or so through Durango have changed a lot in the last century, but outside town the forests and wilderness are not much different than they were 100 or 1,000 years ago.

Southwest Colorado

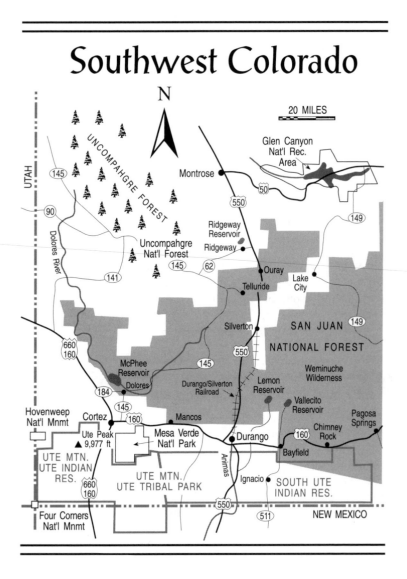

Durango's population of 14,000 makes it the big city in these parts. Cortez has a population of around 7,000, while Telluride boasts 1,400. Silverton, Ouray, Ridgway, Dolores, and Mancos measure populations in the hundreds only. These numbers are, however, on the rise. Some believe this is yet another regional boom and bust cycle, due to deflate as soon as newcomers experience a rough winter, realize there's not much of a job market, or dissipate their savings. Others insist growth is here to stay.

One thing is certain: These small, scattered communities are in an area of exceptional beauty. All resonate with history, while offering everything you need in the way of hospitality. You can find all sorts of services here, from campsites to top-notch resorts, from fast foods to fine dining. And these tenacious communities, far off the beaten path, are separated by epic hiking trails, mountain bike routes and ski slopes. There are rugged rivers to run or to fish for trout. Spruces, aspens, gambel oaks, and cottonwoods offer forest cover for deer, elk, and the occasional black bear; grizzlies are all gone, or so experts say. The howling of coyotes echoes through rocky, pastel-shaded canyons. Shimmering deserts are dappled with yucca, cacti, and pinyon. Ruins evoke mysteries – a clarion call for explorers.

The humbling geography bridges two terrains. The year-round snow-caps of the San Juan Mountains reach cloud heights surpassing 14,000 feet near Silverton, Ouray, and Telluride. Evergreen and aspen thickets extend from the barren treeline, cloaking the angular grades and packing the valleys of Lizard Head Wilderness near Telluride, Weminuche Wilderness near Silverton, as well as the adjacent Uncompaghre and San Juan National Forests.

The San Juan Forest is immense, covering nearly two million acres. It stretches from peak to peak across southwest Colorado, butting up against high desert in the south and west, near Indian land. Beyond the mountains the land is dry, dominated by sandstone, apparently inhospitable, yet with its own distinctive geological features. To the south lies New Mexico.

Along the western edge of the forest the Dolores River slices through this borderland, pouring out of the most rugged range in the Rockies. The San Juans seem to plunge abruptly rather than blend into the 130,000 square miles of the Colorado Plateau, a region distinguished by sensational natural forms, sage-scented bluffs, deep, vertical-walled canyons, and the wind whistling through elegantly sculpted sandstone created over millions of years. It's a powerful landscape and one in which man has always had to face challenges. Change is visible in epochal time. Adventure materializes routinely.

Southwest Colorado receives abundant sunshine, averaging 300 days of it each year. In the high country, snows average 300 inches yearly, which means that in a typical year water will gush from the mountains each spring as snows melt. No doubt this beneficence of nature attracted the nomadic Indian tribes who found this place around 1,500 years ago, evolving into the community-centered Anasazi, who were probably the earliest settlers here. They first lived in caves and holes dug in the ground, eventually mastering irrigation techniques for farming beans, corn, and squash. Agriculture preceded the building of primitive cities in protected canyons that feathered off from the fruitful mesas.

These stone and mortar neighborhoods have lasted a lot longer than their architects, a fact that continues to intrigue nearly a million visitors yearly to Mesa Verde National Park. Covering 52,000 acres, it contains the largest concentration of excavated Indian ruins in the American Southwest, although it is not even close to the largest ancient Indian site in southwest Colorado. That distinction belongs to the Ute Mountain Tribal Park. It surrounds Mesa Verde on three sides and covers 125,000 acres. And it's practically unknown. Only around 3,000 people visit the site each year.

Spanish settlers, who came through here briefly in the 1600s looking for gold, left mainly Hispanic names in and around today's San Juan Mountains. Durango was built on the banks of *El Rio de las Animas Perdidas*, "The River of Lost Souls," known today simply as the Animas. *Mesa Verde* means the "green table." Nearby are the towns of Cortez and Dolores. The names have outlasted the Spanish, who overlooked the gold and silver riches to be found here. Although modern Hispanic communities and influences continue to contribute to the cultural mix of southwestern Colorado, it is to a lesser extent than in neighboring areas, such as in nearby New Mexico.

Gold strikes in the 1870s precipitated the development that has extended to today. Miners and related fortune-seekers settled the snowy San Juans and the remote region was poised to soon rival Denver as the hub of the Rockies. Silverton was incorporated in 1874. Durango was founded by the Denver and Rio Grande Railroad in 1880. Cattle ranchers built Mancos in 1881. As millions of dollars in gold and silver were extracted from the region, boom towns attracted gunslingers employed to protect the haul, hookers intent on extracting their share, gamblers, and many others. Boisterous saloons prospered, along with business services catering to miners and cowhands. Silverton, Ouray, and Telluride were built to serve hard-rock miners. Indians were never far away. It was the Wild West. In many ways it still is.

The Western spirit remains. Add staggering natural beauty and, despite these busy times, liberty to play, and you can see how southwest Colorado has prevailed through boom and bust with an expansive sense of optimism. Scenic splendor and a sense of history are the most obvious attractions here. There are hundreds of miles of trails for you to hike, backpack, mountain bike, and ride on horseback, with more miles of rivers to raft, canoe, or kayak. There are hot springs to soothe your weary bones, and the fish are biting in lakes and streams. You can ski the steeps in Telluride, or more moderate terrain at Purgatory. Or you can explore the snowy backcountry. You can wander through ruins or soar above it all on a scenic glider flight. Under a night sky brimming with stars you can conjure visions of Indians and cowboys who knew a good place when they found it.

Getting Around

Southwestern Colorado is a long way from any major highways. There are only a few main roads, which essentially loop though forests, mountains, and deserts punctuated by towns every 20-50 miles. Durango offers the greatest variety of services, including the largest regional airport. It makes a good base for day trips in all directions. And since the Durango-Silverton narrow-gauge train is the biggest visitor attraction in town, our suggested route heads north to Silverton, tracing the route of the San Juan Skyway, starting on US 550, one of America's premier scenic drives. In order, the 232-mile loop road passes through Ouray, Ridgway, Telluride, Dolores, Cortez, Mancos, and Hesperus before heading back to Durango. Of course, we'll take a few detours along the way, tarrying at mountains, rivers, and canyonlands of the Southwest, which are clearly the major sightseeing attractions. But the hand of man has also created a number of sights that may enhance your knowledge and enjoyment of the surrounding natural environment, and perhaps help define the spirit of this place. We'll hit those special places, too, tracing roots that reach from the ancient Anasazi through the Wild West and mining eras – areas that are lovingly nourished to this day.

FOR MORE INFORMATION

Colorado Road Conditions: ☎ 303/639-1111.

Colorado Division of Wildlife, Central Regional Office, 606 Broadway, Denver, CO 80216, ☎ 303/296-1192. Information on fishing licenses and regulations throughout the state.

US Forest Service, PO Box 25127, 11177 West 8th Avenue, Lakewood, CO 80225, ☎ 303/236-9431. Information on travel, camping, hiking, and other activities in national forests.

US Bureau of Land Management, 2850 Youngfield Street, Lakewood, CO 80215, ☎ 303/236-2100. Information regarding recreation on BLM land.

National Park Service, PO Box 25287, Denver, CO 80225, ☎ 303/969-2000. Covers all aspects of travel within national parks, national monuments, and recreation areas.

Colorado Division of Parks and Outdoor Recreation, 1313 Sherman Street, Denver, CO 80203, ☎ 303/866-3437, offers information on state parks and recreation areas.

US Geological Survey, 1961 Stout Street, Denver, CO 80294, ☎ 303/844-4196. Provides topographical maps.

Colorado Outfitters Association, PO Box 32438, Aurora, CO 80041, ☎ 303/751-9274. Offers listings of backcountry outfitters.

Colorado Campground Association, 5101 Pennsylvania Avenue, Boulder, CO 80303, ☎ 303/499-9343. Offers details on private campgrounds.

Touring

Durango

Rural philosopher Will Rogers once characterized Durango as being "out of the way and glad of it." In some respects this is still the case today, although no place is that far out of it anymore, and Durango has been discovered by people from all over as a great place to visit and to live. A 1990s influx of new residents essentially tripled real estate values in only a few years and, along with tourism, has breathed great gusts of liveliness into the community. If you try to find a parking space in July on historic Main Avenue – still the center of commerce in this small city – you'll see that the secret is out.

Summer has always been the busiest time of year for Durango. The winters can be harsh, with snow and cold weather, though always leavened by plenty of sunshine. It's great for skiers, even though the local ski area is actually 25 miles north of town. The distinction makes Durango less of a resort community than a bastion of real life, a town for families and homey values, including inexpensive places to eat and stay, shady city parks, even a local drive-in movie where kids under 12 usually get in free.

In recent years, Indians, miners, ranchers, and cowboys have been joined by others who appreciate the diverse natural endowments of the area. You are equally likely to see fancy all-terrain vehicles toting bike racks or kayaks as you are to see ranchers in battered trucks hauling bales of hay, horses, or cattle. What they all share is an appreciation of the outdoors. The setting, nestled among red sandstone cliffs that frame the Animas River, which flows through town, is impressive. There are many turn-of-the-century Victorian structures, including complete national historic districts on commercial Main Avenue and residential Third Avenue. Both areas can be walked in an hour or so, or you can ride in a horse-drawn carriage. A new summer business that's also great for touring town is a pedicab service, featuring lightweight carriages pulled by serious bike riders.

The Durango & Silverton Narrow Gauge Railroad still chugs through town, tooting its horn and billowing smoke. Its authentically restored cars add to the sense of the Old West that lingers here and is carefully maintained by several historic hotels, honky-tonk saloons, Western melodrama performances, modern and traditional Indian and Western art galleries. There is even an in-town rodeo. Specifics on these attractions and many more are listed in detail throughout the rest of this chapter.

For the most part, simply wandering around the historic downtown business district on Main Avenue, from Fifth to 12th streets, will lead you to the best local architecture, shopping, and dining. The area has all the elements of a real main street, including the train station, a hardware store and a Woolworth's. Notable among the various shops are numerous western and Indian art galleries (for information contact the **Durango Gallery Association**, PO Box 3816, Durango, 81302), a number of brand-name factory outlet stores, as well as numerous well-stocked outdoor sports shops providing sales, service and, in some cases, equipment rentals. (Sports shops are listed below under *Adventures.*) Western wear, saddles and custom-made cowboy hats are also available downtown. **O'Farrell of Durango Custom Hats**, 563 Main Avenue, 81301, ☎ 970/259-5900 or 800/895-7098, uses 150-year-old hat-making equipment, which has apparently been good enough to calibrate the exact head sizes of presidents Reagan and Bush, as well as Hollywood stars.

For history buffs, the **Animas School Museum**, 31st Street and West 2nd Avenue, 81301, ☎ 970/259-2402, offers a concise selection of Anasazi artifacts, other man-made items from the early mining and ranching eras, and displays explaining the area's natural history. The building is a restored turn-of-the-century schoolhouse and one exhibit features the pioneer "Joy" cabin. For a more academic appraisal of the area's charms, the **Center of Southwest Studies**, Fort Lewis College, College Heights, 81301, ☎ 970/247-7456, is connected to the Fort Lewis College Museum and Archive. It offers one of the best collections of writings, charts, and rare documents relating to the history of the Four Corners region. In addition, the four-year college hosts special events, lectures, and concerts throughout the school year.

One of the more interesting programs at the college is a three-week summer Getaway Program for senior citizens. Participants stay in accommodations at the campus and eat meals in the cafeteria while following a schedule of two academic classes each morning, with optional arts and exercise classes in the afternoon. More than a dozen classes are offered, including Southwest archaeology, political science, basket-making and Navajo weaving. For information, ☎ 970/247-7241. **Durango Arts Center** is on the corner of 8th Street and Second Avenue, ☎ 970/259-2606. Gallery shows change every three weeks and include national traveling and juried shows, local artists, educational exhibits, and children's programs. The Arts Center also coordinates summer concerts in city parks and is a ticket outlet for cultural events. The **Municipal Pool** is at 2400 Main Avenue, ☎ 970/247-9999.

FOR MORE INFORMATION

Durango is served by the modern little **La Plata County Airport**, 16 miles east of town, with several airlines flying on a year-round basis, while other airlines serve Durango during ski season.

America West Express, ☎ 970/259-5178 or 800/247-5692, serves Durango with connections through Phoenix. United Express, ☎ 970/259-5178 or 800/241-6522, offers connections through Denver. Air 21, ☎ 800/359-2472, provides connections through Grand Junction, Colorado, Las Vegas, Nevada, and Los Angeles. American Airlines, ☎ 800/433-7300, has jet service on one flight daily to and from Dallas during the ski season only (December 15 to March 30).

Reno Air, ☎ 800/RENO-AIR, provides daily jet service through Albuquerque. Western Pacific flies through Colorado Springs.

Rental cars are available at the airport from Avis, ☎ 970/247-9761; Budget, ☎ 970/259-1841; Dollar, ☎ 970/259-3012; Hertz, ☎ 970/247-5288; National, ☎ 970/259-0068 or 800/227-7368; or Sears, ☎ 970/259-1842. Other car rental agencies are in the area: Rent-A-Wreck, 21698 US 160 West, Durango, 81301, ☎ 970/259-5858 or 800/421-7253, fax ☎ 970/247-2111; Sunshine

Motors, 20909 US 160 West, Durango, 81301, ☎ 970/259-2980; or Thrifty, 20541 US 160 West, Durango, 81301, ☎ 970/259-3504 or 800/367-2277.

Twenty-four-hour **taxi service** is provided by **Durango Transportation**, ☎ 970/259-4818 or 800/626-2066. They also have guided Mesa Verde tours, van or bus charters for five to 50 passengers, airport shuttles to Durango, Purgatory, and Telluride, and Silverton train shuttles for those who ride the train only one-way.

For information on local **Road Conditions**, ☎ 970/247-3355.

For additional information, the **Durango Area Chamber Resort Association** maintains an office at Gateway Park, 111 South Camino del Rio, Durango, CO 81302, ☎ 970/247-0312 or 800/525-8855. Their mailing address is PO Box 2587, Durango, 81302. The office maintains considerable files and brochures relating to activities and services throughout the entire region and beyond the city limits.

Discover Durango, PO Box 3337, Durango, CO 81302, ☎ 970/247-4600, provides visitor activities information and preferred reservations at no charge.

Visitor Information Network, ☎ 970/385-5544, is an automated service with details on dining, shopping, entertainment and outdoors activities in Cortez, Durango, Mesa Verde, Purgatory and Silverton.

Southeast of Durango

IGNACIO

About 10 miles south of La Plata Field on CO 172, this small town is the tribal headquarters of the Southern Ute tribe. These modern Indians have long operated a small motel, restaurant, tourist center, and a Cultural Center Museum and Gallery. They also run one of the few radio stations in the area, KSUT 89.9 FM, with something besides country music or Top 40. It's the local National Public Radio station, so scheduling includes nationally syndicated news and features, as well as creative programming.

The tribe used to run bingo tournaments on Friday nights, but that has been replaced by the newest enterprise on the reservation – a 40,000-square-foot limited-stakes casino that opened in the fall of 1993 in the remodeled Sky Ute Lodge & Casino. Now a mega-bingo purse totalling a million dollars is possible five days a week, Wednesday through Sunday. Various poker and blackjack tables, as well as more than 100 slot machines, are open daily from 8AM to 4AM.

The **Sky Ute Downs Equestrian Center**, ☎ 970/563-4502, offers riding instruction and seasonal rodeo events. The tribe hosts a four-day-long spring Bear Dance, a Sun Dance in July, and an early September Pow-Wow with members of tribes from around the country. On Wednesdays, June through August, the tribe's Southern Ute Heritage Dancers perform along with drummers and storytellers. The shows include a tour of the Cultural Center and Museum, and a barbecue dinner. The museum contains more than 500 tribal artifacts organized to trace the Ute Circle of Life. The circle is divided into four sections representing the four directions and four stages of life within the religious and cultural beliefs of the Southern Utes. The last section contains modern works, as Southern Ute history continues to unfold. For information about the various Southern Ute Enterprises, ☎ 970/563-3000 or 800/876-7017.

There's not really much happening in Ignacio, although casino gambling is changing that. One thing you can do here is order a hand-made custom pair of cowboy boots. Stop in for a fitting and select from a variety of leathers at **Custom Boots by Larry Smith**, 655 Browning Avenue, Ignacio, 81137, ☎ 970/563-9510. They're guaranteed to fit. And if you happen to be interested in Harley-Davidson motorcycles and you're in the area for Labor Day weekend in early September, you might want to check out the **Iron Horse Motorcycle Rally**. It's the brainchild of the only American Indian in the US Senate, Colorado's pony-tailed Ben Nighthorse Campbell, a Democrat turned Republican and a part-time jewelry-maker who strongly opposes mandatory helmet laws. The event has grown tremendously since the first get-together in 1993, and brings together many thousands of Harley riders and their machinery for a weekend-long party, spiced by tours and special events.

North of Ignacio and 42 miles east of Durango is the **Chimney Rock Archaeological Area**. The site is on CO 151, three miles south of US 160 East. It contains 16 excavated ruins of an Anasazi village, presumed to be related to those of Chaco Canyon. The ruins are perched atop a high mesa overlooking the Piedra River and are only accessible if you take a two-hour guided walking tour, offered four times daily, May 15 to September 15. There are two trails leading to excavated ruins and an estimated 200 undisturbed sites. One trail is a third of a mile over a smooth surface. The other trail is rougher, over loose rock, and is a half-mile. The tour includes a visit to a Forest Service lookout tower offering views of the Pueblo Ruins and the Piedra Valley. For information, ☎ 970/883-5359.

FOR MORE INFORMATION

Chamber Resort Association, 111 S. Camino del Rio, Durango, CO 81302, ☎ 800/525-8855.

Northeast of Durango

Vallecito Reservoir is 23 miles northeast of Durango at the end of Florida Road. It offers 22 miles of forested shoreline, surrounded by peaks of the San Juans, motels, a guest ranch, and campgrounds. Several operators have boat rentals. The fishing is pretty good for trout, kokanee salmon, bluegill, or crappies. The smaller **Lemon Reservoir** is just a little up the road from Vallecito and is also covered later under *Adventures On Water.*

FOR MORE INFORMATION

Vallecito Chamber of Commerce, PO Box 804, Bayfield, CO 81122, ☎ 970/884-9782.

San Juan National Forest

The San Juan National Forest extends in all directions from Durango, east to west from Pagosa Springs to Dove Creek, and from Silverton in the north to the New Mexico state line. The forest includes a federally designated scenic byway, the San Juan Skyway, which links the major towns covered in this chapter and is considered one of the top scenic drives in the nation.

The forest is laced with miles and miles of maintained hiking trails, many of which you can enjoy on mountain bikes or horseback. There are numerous lakes, rivers, and streams that offer opportunities for trout fishing, canoeing, rafting, windsurfing, and boating. Ski areas lease forest land in the vicinity of mountains ranging to more than 14,000 feet. At extreme elevations the only month of the year when it is unlikely to snow is July.

Occasional seminars are offered by the San Juan National Forest Association during the summer. These include guided hikes to view wildflowers, hiking with children, and studies of Native American cultures. For information, ☎ 970/385-1210.

FOR MORE INFORMATION

The Forest Service provides numerous recreational facilities. For information, contact **San Juan National Forest**, 701 Camino del Rio, Durango, CO 81302, ☎ 970/247-4874.

WEMINUCHE WILDERNESS

Within the San Juan National Forest, the Weminuche Wilderness encompasses one of the biggest wilderness areas in the United States, covering 459,000 acres, including 80 miles along the Continental Divide, preserved by law in a primitive state. Fixed improvements and human residency are prohibited. The mountainous Weminuche boasts elevations averaging 10,000 feet and includes more than 400 miles of trails for hikers or horseback riders. Mountain bikes, motorized vehicles, chainsaws, helicopters, and all other mechanized reminders of civilization are prohibited.

The wilderness area offers no permanent facilities, not even ready-made campsites, picnic tables or latrines, although primitive camping and licensed fishing are allowed. The Weminuche is accessible by hiking trails beginning at Vallecito Lake, 26 miles northwest of Durango, Silverton, or via a lengthy route from Purgatory-Durango Ski Area. The closest access to the wilderness area is from the Durango & Silverton Narrow Gauge Railroad, which will drop you at Needleton, south of Silverton. You can then flag the train down at the same spot for transportation back to civilization.

High country travel in the Weminuche can be demanding or even treacherous before mid-June. Unless it's been an unusually dry winter, above 10,000 feet you will usually see snow on the ground into July. Melting snow means muddy trails and fast-moving, hazardous streams you may have to ford on foot if no log bridge is available.

Once the snow is gone, colorful carpets of wildflowers begin to bloom in direct proportion to how wet the previous winter has been. Wild berries appear in mid- to late August, and last through the first tentative freezes in early September, when the leaves start to change.

FOR MORE INFORMATION

Visitor services may be found on the periphery of the Weminuche, in Silverton, Vallecito or, more commonly, in Durango.

San Juan National Forest office in Durango, ☎ 970/247-4874

Silverton

Silverton, situated at 9,032 feet and 50 miles north of Durango on US 550 North, calls itself "the mining town that never quit." This was once a prosperous boom town in the heyday of the gold and silver mines, from which millions of dollars in ore were extracted. Today, Silverton has the feel of a frontier town, if only because it's a little too down at the heels to qualify as a trendy, restored exhibit. Durango is Yuppies-ville compared to Silverton, which is more remote and occasionally inaccessible. During the hard winter of 1993 Silverton was isolated by avalanches and road closures for six days during a heavy snowstorm. Food had to be airlifted in.

Most of the time, though, you can get here from Durango or Ouray via US 550 or, during the summer on the Durango & Silverton Narrow Gauge Railroad. The town exists largely on train passengers' tourist dollars and, when the railroad stops running in October, many of the local shops and services close for the season. The town is like a step back in time. Practically every structure on Greene Street, the short main drag, has historic significance dating to the dawn of the 20th century or before, and the whole town has been certified a National Historic Landmark. Depending on how interested you are in these rather dusty and authentic-feeling structures and the plethora of gift shops and tourist-oriented businesses that now occupy them, you can spend anywhere from an hour to a day of sightseeing (you get two hours if you take the train and catch the earliest return departure for Durango).

In many of the old buildings business is still conducted on a daily basis, such as at 1129 Greene, the town's first butcher shop, built in 1893. The present occupant, the **San Juan Café & Saloon**, boasts an original hardwood floor, 13-foot pressed tin ceiling, unique antique bar and backbar, and Victorian decor. Other buildings have been preserved by the county, such as the one-time County Jail, circa 1902, now housing the **San Juan County Historical Museum**, 1567 Greene Street, Silverton, 81433, ☎ 970/387-5838. Modest displays recount pioneering life in the community, mining lore, and natural history of the San Juan Mountains.

The Silverton Standard & Miner, 1257 Greene Street, Silverton, 81433, ☎ 970/387-5477, claims to be the longest running newspaper, as well as the oldest business, on the western slope of the Colorado Rockies. The wooden structure where it resides was originally a general store in 1875 and is one of the oldest buildings in town. Today you can buy books, videos, maps, or the quirky, enduring newspaper. The building next door, now occupied by Silverton Liquors, was built in 1883 as a combined furniture store and undertaker's. And Blair Street, often referred to as Notorious Blair Street, was where the raunchiest saloons, boarding houses, and bordellos were located during the prosperous early mining years when there was "silver by the ton" being removed from the nearby mountains to be spent in town. The building at 1161 Blair was built in 1883 and was the location of Mattie's Place, also known from a sign in the window as the Welcome Saloon.

Other long-lasting structures with a more temperate historic background include the one that housed Silverton's Congregational Church, soon after its cornerstone was laid in 1880. It's now the **United Church of Silverton**, 1060 Reese Street, ☎ 970/387-5325. The **Carnegie Library**, 1111 Reese Street, ☎ 970/387-5770, was constructed in 1906 and is still the town's public library.

Much of Silverton's current appeal resides in the surrounding mountains that dwarf the town. The **Weminuche Wilderness** (see page 199) is nearby, as is the **Million Dollar Highway**, actually US 550 North, connecting to Ouray over Red Mountain Pass. Depending on what story you want to believe, the Highway got its name from a million dollars worth of gold chips mixed in with the pavement, or from the initial cost of building the road in the 1880s. Some claim the name has to do with the million-dollar views you get from a roadbed clinging to steep, hairpin switchbacks, carved out of solid rock, in the shadows cast by mountain peaks.

For a big step into the past, the **One Hundred Gold Mine Tour**, PO Box 430, Silverton, 81433, ☎ 800/872-3009, offers a one-hour underground adventure, five miles east of town, on CO 110 (Greene Street). The tour includes a ride down into the mine shaft via train. Open June through September, tours depart every half-hour in July and August, every hour during June and September. If you continue past the One Hundred Gold Mine, in another eight miles you will come to **Animas Forks**, another ex-boom town circa 1880, now a well-preserved ghost town. Numerous decrepit, photogenic buildings remain, along with an old mill, boarded-up mine shafts, and unrecognizable structures or crumbling foundations. The road is passable in a passenger car if the weather is dry, but a four-wheel-drive will provide a more secure ride, particularly if you plan to explore beyond Animas Forks. Adjacent to the ghost town is a steep and dangerous road popular for jeeping, leading to 12,800-foot **Engineer Pass** and the **Alpine Loop Backcountry Byway**. The Alpine Loop is an exceptional, challenging, 63-mile drive in the ultra-high country, beyond a doubt one of the most spectacular scenic drives in the West.

The Chamber of Commerce maintains a year-round visitor center at the Y on Highway 550, at the western edge of town. An in-town branch at 12th and Blair, near the train stop, is open during the summer.

FOR MORE INFORMATION

Silverton Chamber of Commerce, PO Box 565, Silverton, CO 81433, ☎ 970/387-5654 or 800/752-4494.

Ouray

Ouray is another one-time mining town that clings to life in the challenging mountains of southwestern Colorado, thanks largely to a vast network of underground thermal hot springs. Nestled within a deep box canyon beneath snow-topped mountains, the serene, alpine setting and therapeutic waters have brought the town a nickname – "The Switzerland of America." Regrettably, there are more than a few ersatz chalet-type homes and motels throughout the town, but for the most part you'll see more mining-era Victorian homes along unusually broad, tree-lined streets. Despite the modern structures, the entire town, which is nine blocks long and six blocks wide, has been designated a National Historic District.

Situated 25 miles north of Silverton and over the north side of Red Mountain Pass on US 550 at an elevation of 7,760 feet, the earliest permanent structure here, in 1875, was a saloon. Church services were first held in a different saloon. Worshippers sat on whiskey kegs.

Not too long ago, Ouray was only a summer destination, with much of the town shuttered during reliably harsh winters. But the ever-increasing popularity of nearby Telluride changed that. Little Telluride is located up and over on the other side of 14,150-foot Mount Sneffels, or 50 road miles from here. It attracts more skiers than it has rooms for, so a deal was worked out where skiers could stay in Ouray, or other nearby communities, and receive a half-price lift ticket. Then, some of the refugees from Telluride discovered the terrific cross-country and backcountry skiing, along with great ice climbing on frozen waterfalls nearby. A winter season was born. Now some, though not all, motels, restaurants, and other town businesses stay open year-round. It's still quiet in winter when Red Mountain Pass is closed by an avalanche and today, rather than making outdated comparisons with Switzerland, locals claim that "Ouray is like Telluride used to be."

Bigger crowds come to town in the summer, which is still the high season here, primarily for camping, hiking and jeeping, then taking a soak in the hot springs. The latter is something reportedly enjoyed by the town's namesake, Chief Ouray, a Ute Indian leader who is said to have bathed in the steaming waters. The town is very small, with only around 800 residents, far fewer than were here in 1900 when local gold mines were in full swing. The legendary, hugely profitable, Camp Bird Mine was producing three million dollars in gold yearly. Camp Bird's owner, Tom Walsh, eventually spent some of his $20 million fortune to buy the Hope Diamond.

You can easily walk the few main streets to have a look around or, if you've had it with Victoriana in Silverton, drive directly to the north end of town and jump into the largest thermal pool in town, the one-million-gallon **Hot Springs Pool**, 1000 Main Street, PO Box 468, Ouray, 81427, ☎ 970/325-4638. The facility includes two outdoor thermal pools maintained at 104° year-round, a diving and lap lane section, picnic tables, a playground, an indoor gym, and locker rooms.

Back in the center of town, the one indoor attraction that merits an hour or two of time is the **Ouray County Historical Museum**, 420 Sixth Avenue, 81427, ☎ 970/325-4576. It sits in a building that was originally a hospital built in 1887 and has an interesting collection of Victorian-era goodies, hotel logs, guns, saloon memorabilia, mining tools and equipment, as well as a recreated hospital room, general store, and law office. For a different experience of what gold mining was like, try the **Bachelor-Syracuse Mine Tour**, 1222 County Road 14, PO Box 380W, Ouray, 81427, ☎ 970/325-4500, a mile north of town, then right on County Road 14. Between May 20 and September 15 you can ride 3,350 feet horizontally on a tram car into Gold Hill. Inside, a guide describes the hard rock mining that was conducted here until the 1980s. Emerging from the shaft, you can pan for gold, dine at an outdoor café, or visit the gift shop and buy a gold nugget. The only day the mine tour is closed during its season is the 4th of July. That's because the whole town usually turns out for the biggest event of the year: water fights on Main Street. Participants wearing defensive gear, including motorcycle helmets and chest protectors, spray each other with fire hoses. Whoever hits the pavement first loses.

Speaking of water, you can walk from town to the 285-foot **Box Canyon Falls and Park**, ☎ 970/325-4464. There's a picnic area in the park, open from May to mid-October, and there are two bridges, one wooden, near the base of the falls, and one at the top made of steel. Admission is charged.

FOR MORE INFORMATION

Ouray Chamber Resort Association, Box 145, Ouray, CO 81427, ☎ 970/325-4746 or 800/228-1876.

Ridgway

Residents seem to be pretty content that there's not a whole lot going on in the town of Ridgway (6,995 feet) other than that it is fast becoming a bedroom community for Telluride (designer Ralph Lauren has an enormous ranch near here, and actor Dennis Weaver has built an ecologically sensitive home out of discarded tires and bottles which he calls an Earth Ship). There are a few shops, galleries and restaurants and the town offers the same lodging/half-price lift ticket deal with the ski area as Ouray. A quirky fact about this community, which boasts a population of 820 "in town or close by," is that streets with women's names run north-south, while streets with men's names run east-west.

The outdoor terrain is really the main attraction here, and one place to experience it is at the **Ridgway State Recreation Area**, 15 miles north of Ridgway, off US 550. Opened in 1989, the state park encompasses a large reservoir, complete with a marina, boat ramp, fish-cleaning station, beach, and several campgrounds. Winter sports available include ice-fishing, snowmobiling, and cross-country skiing. An information center is near the entrance to the park at 28555 US 550. ☎ 970/626-5822 or 800/678-2267.

FOR MORE INFORMATION

Ridgway Area Chamber of Commerce, PO Box 378, Ridgway, CO 81432, ☎ 800/633-5868.

Ridgway USA Visitor Center, 102 Village Square West, Ridgway, CO 81432, ☎ 970/626-5805.

Telluride

Trendy Telluride was not always thus. It's only in the last few years that people who pay attention to such things started calling it the next Aspen. Well, it's got all the natural attributes plus a savvy, increasingly wealthy population of 1,400 and counting to make that threat come true. Real estate prices are astronomical. Hollywood and TV stars such as Darryl Hannah and Oprah Winfrey have bought property. Tom Cruise was married here. Mr. and Mrs. Donald Trump honeymooned here. Can the *National Enquirer* be far behind? This is another wild mining town that recognized the need to encourage tourism for its survival. The community has not embraced the concept wholeheartedly. Yet, for its size, Telluride offers some of the best attractions, events, services, and activities anywhere in southwestern Colorado.

Situated at 8,745 feet on CO 145, Telluride occupies a scenic and memorable site. The town, a Registered National Historic Landmark, sits nestled in a deep and narrow canyon near the headwaters of the San Miguel River, at the base of Ingram Falls. Surrounded by the peaks of the San Juan Mountains and the Uncompaghre National Forest, Telluride was established in 1878, incorporated from humble beginnings as an incorrigible tent city and mining camp called Columbia. In 1891, the town's population topped out at 4,000. Tents and lean-tos were replaced by large, elegant Victorian homes, public buildings constructed of cut stone, fancy hotels, including the New Sheridan House, a hotel built in 1895 and still operating today, 26 saloons and a dozen brothels. Future outlaw Butch Cassidy was a mule skinner for one of the mines here. He practiced fast getaways on horseback from Main Street. Then he held up his first bank, the San Miguel Valley Bank right here in Telluride, on June 24, 1889.

In 1896, shortly after a collapse in silver prices, William Jennings Bryan, a perennial presidential candidate, stood in front of the New Sheridan House and delivered his legendary "Cross of Gold" speech, decrying the new gold standard that had decimated the silver mining operations overnight in 1893. Within 30 years the bottom had completely dropped out of the gold and silver markets. This, combined with labor union riots over plummeting wages that plagued the town and the closing of the Bank of Telluride, forced the population down to around 500 residents in 1930. The last bordello closed in 1959. The town languished through the 1960s, when you could have bought a house for $3,000. It would have been a good investment. Today there's nary a fixer-upper property in town you can touch for under $250,000.

What turned things around for Telluride was the ski area, which opened in 1972, the same year the town cancelled the annual 4th of July celebration after motorcycle gangs effectively closed down Main Street for their own private party. Firemen had to hose them down to bring things under control. Over time, as skiers discovered the exceptional terrain here, the town gradually put itself back together. Homes and buildings were restored and the **Telluride Mountain Village**, a modern upscale enclave designed to take pressure off the small downtown, was built on a glorious mountainside at 9,450 feet. It includes a hotel/spa, bed and breakfast lodge, condominiums, palatial private homes, restaurants, golf course, tennis courts, ski company offices, and a convenience store. The complex is situated seven miles south of Telluride on the other side of the ski hill, off CO 145. You can access it by skiing directly from town. Now, there is a "people-mover" gondola that directly links the town with Mountain Village. Aside from turn-of-the-century buildings and supposedly compatible modern architecture, Telluride is surrounded by ghost towns and abandoned mining camps, hiking and jeep trails, horseback and mountain bike trails, fishing holes and, of course, skiing and winter sports. These are all detailed below, under *Adventures*. As for the old buildings and houses in town, many are spruced up with multi-color paint jobs, and the compact downtown is perfect for the obligatory walk-around of an hour or two, longer if you dip into shops and galleries or the **Sheridan Bar**. It's downstairs in the hotel at 225 Colorado Avenue, ☎ 970/728-3626, a historic monument in its own right, complete with tin ceiling, tiered wooden floor, and an ornate cherrywood backbar.

Among the more interesting sites is the **San Miguel County Historical Museum**, 317 North Fir Street, 81435, ☎ 970/728-3344, occupying the old Miner's Hospital Building, circa 1895. The collection features such eclectic memorabilia as an 800-year-old Anasazi blanket, a silver nitrate film of Leo Tolstoy's life brought to town by an immigrant, a lightweight wicker casket used to transport the bodies of miners who died in high country mines, dancehall garments from the bordello district, mining artifacts, and lots of old photos. Open late May to mid-October. East of town on CO 145 is the longest waterfall in the state, 365-foot **Bridal Veil Falls**. At the top of the falls is an old hydroelectric mill that is a registered historic landmark. It is being refurbished to produce electricity again for the first time since 1954.

And if you want to get to the mountaintop without breaking a sweat, chairlift rides are offered from town to a 10,500-foot overlook via the Coonskin Chairlift. You can ride or walk down. Open Thursday to Monday, mid-June through September. Telluride's **Town Park** is where the largest outdoor summer festivals are held (see below, under

Eco-Travel & Cultural Excursions). It is also the site of a playground, children's fishing pond, baseball, soccer, basketball and volleyball facilities, two free tennis courts, and a covered picnic area with barbecue pits. In winter the town operates a skating rink and a groomed cross-country ski trail that circles the large park. Camping is available.

FOR MORE INFORMATION

Telluride Regional Airport, ☎ 970/728-3436, is the highest commercial airport in the United States, at 9,080 feet, five miles west of town. Service is provided by Mesa Airlines/America West Express, from Phoenix or Albuquerque, or Mesa Airlines/United Express from Denver. In winter only, flights are provided by Delta Connection from Salt Lake City. Contact the airport or central reservations (see below) for airline information, including options for flights connecting through Montrose, CO, 65 miles away.

Rental cars are available from Budget, 657 West Colorado, Telluride, 81435, ☎ 970/728-4642 or 800/221-2419; Hertz, Telluride Airport, Last Dollar Road, Telluride, 81435, ☎ 970/728-3163; Dollar, or Thrifty, 129 West San Juan, Telluride, CO 81435, ☎ 970/728-3266 or 800/367-2277;

Taxi service is available from **Telluride Transit, Mountain Limo**, PO Box 1662, Telluride, CO 81435, ☎ 970/728-9606, or **Skip's Taxi & Shuttle Service**, 129 West San Juan, Telluride, CO 81435, ☎ 970/728-6667, which also offers four-wheel-drive tours in a convertible, visiting ghost towns, hidden lakes, and mining ruins.

Other ways of getting around include free bicycle loaners that are kept on racks on Colorado Avenue, a free US Forest Service shuttle operating from mid-June through early September between the Visitor Center (666 West Colorado Avenue) and Bridal Veil Falls, and a new pedicab service, **Jakeshaw Pedicab**, ☎ 970/728-6149, or 970/728-7639. The pedicab service carries passengers around town, back to their campground, or on special customized tours such as the "Ten Bridges Tour," which cruises through Telluride's Historic District and explores the river trail.

For additional information contact **Telluride Visitor Services**, PO Box 653, 666 West Colorado Avenue, Telluride, CO 81435, ☎ 970/728-3041, fax 970/728-6475, or **Telluride Central Reservations**, PO Box 1009, Telluride, CO 81435, ☎ 970/728-4431 or 800/525-3455, fax 970/728-6475. Central Reservations now has the ability to book all-inclusive packages for air and ground transportation, lodging, ski lifts, festival tickets, jeeping, horseback riding and other activities.

Lizard Head Wilderness

This 42,000-acre wilderness is west of CO 145, 10 miles southwest of Telluride and 40 miles northeast of Cortez. Within the wilderness are **Mount Wilson** (one of the most challenging of Colorado's Fourteeners to climb, calling for technical expertise and equipment), **Wilson Peak**, and **El Diente Peak**, all higher than 14,000 feet, as well as other summits above 13,000 feet. Hiking, horseback riding, backpacking, and mountain climbing are popular in the area. Weather is always unpredictable here and the terrain is challenging, with many exposed ridges, loose rock, and permanent snow fields. There are practically no trail signs. Maps are necessary. The eastern portion of the wilderness area is the most accessible to hikers. The western portion is accessible only to those hikers willing to cover long cross-country routes. There are no hiking trails west of the Navajo Lake Trail and north of the Groundhog Stock Drive Trail.

FOR MORE INFORMATION

Dolores Ranger District, San Juan National Forest (see below, under *McPhee Reservoir*), or **Norwood Ranger District**, Uncompaghre National Forest, 1760 East Grand Avenue, PO Box 388, Norwood, CO 81423, ☎ 970/327-4261.

Dolores

Dolores occupies a position along CO 145, on the border of the Rockies and the Colorado Plateau. It's more of a base station for area explorations than a destination in itself – a place to buy gas, a fishing license, and maybe a meal if you not too particular. It does have a few old buildings, a fine museum, and a strange rail car known as the Galloping Goose. Part bus, car, and rail car, the Goose was at one time the vehicle of choice on the frequently snow-clogged tracks of the old Rio Grande Southern Railroad that ran through here. The main attractions are out of town. **McPhee Reservoir** (see next page) is nearby, and rafting certain stretches of the Dolores River may provide legendary adventure during the high-water season.

The **Anasazi Heritage Center**, 27501 CO 184, Dolores, 81323, ☎ 970/882-4811, was created to preserve Anasazi artifacts removed from 1,600 Anasazi sites in the Dolores River Canyon when it was flooded to create McPhee Reservoir. Operated by the BLM, it actually contains a collection of Indian tools and artifacts from the entire Four Corners region. Inside the museum are interactive exhibits employing high-tech equipment, alongside an ancient stone, called a *metate,* used for grinding corn, a loom, and a recreated pit house typical of the Anasazi era. There's a "please touch" section for children and a hologram display showing how the Anasazi looked. Up a hill from the museum, overlooking the reservoir, are the 12th-century Dominguez and Escalante Ruins.

West of the Anasazi Center on CO 184, then north on US 666 to the south edge of Dove Creek, the "Pinto Bean Capital of the World," and east on a signed dirt road for 11 miles, is the **Dolores Canyon Overlook**. From this 2,500-foot-high perch above the Dolores River, you can see the twisting, red-walled canyon, as well as the mountain ranges of southwestern Colorado and southeastern Utah.

FOR MORE INFORMATION

Dolores River Valley Chamber of Commerce, PO Box 602, Dolores, CO 81323, ☎ 970/882-4018, or stop at the **Dolores Visitor Center**, 600 Railroad Avenue, Dolores, CO 81323.

McPhee Reservoir

Situated northwest of Dolores off CO 145, this is a 4,500-acre manmade lake snuggled into a timbered shoreline. It opened in 1988 and is just starting to hit its stride with good fishing for trout, smallmouth bass, crappies, and kokanee.A range of watersports is available, including swimming, waterskiing, jet-skiing, and a no-wake canoeing area. There are hiking trails, campgrounds, and picnic areas, most in and around two full-service recreation complexes. The **McPhee Recreation Area** is on the west side of the reservoir and includes the full-service Beaver Creek Marina. **House Creek Recreation Area** is on the east side of the reservoir, 15 miles north of Dolores, off the Dolores/Norwood Road (Forest Road 506). There are also five other fishing access points spaced at intervals around the lake.

FOR MORE INFORMATION

Dolores Ranger District, San Juan National Forest, 521 Central Avenue, PO Box 210, Dolores, CO 81323, ☎ 970/882-7296.

Cortez

Eight miles south of Dolores on CO 145 at US 160, where the mountains meet the desert, Cortez calls itself "The Gateway To Indian Country." The promotional language is actually true in this case, mainly because of the number of ancient and modern Indian sites that are within day-trip distance of this small agricultural town. It is estimated that 40,000 Anasazi lived in the Montezuma Valley, in and around the site of modern day Cortez, from 900 to 1300 AD. Today, 7,000 residents call Cortez home.

To the east of town is the La Plata Range of the San Juans, reaching over 13,000 feet. To the west, the vast high Sonoran Desert of the Colorado Plateau stretches to an unimaginably distant horizon.

One of the most useful places to go in town is the **Colorado Welcome Center**, 928 East Main, Cortez, 81321, ☎ 970/565-4048 or 800/346-6528. The center is operated by the Cortez Chamber of Commerce. It offers free maps, brochures, coffee, and information about the Four Corners region. There are Indian dances or theatrical gunfights at 7PM every night in the summer at the city park next to the center. There is also a municipal pool with a highly regarded waterslide.

A little-known but fascinating in-town site is just a block off Main, at the **Cortez Center-University of Colorado Museum**, 25 North Market Street, 81321, ☎ 970/565-1151. The small, informative museum offers interpretive exhibits on the progression of Anasazi history, from the earliest Basketmakers through the classic Pueblo period. The museum also has videos describing Anasazi sites in the area. Indian storytellers and artists give presentations during the summer at 8:15PM.

The small downtown area can be covered easily on foot in an hour or two. There are several interesting antique shops here, and on the east side of town, on US 160, several trading posts sport huge, garish signs.

FOR MORE INFORMATION
Colorado Welcome Center, 928 East Main, Cortez, CO 81321, ☎ 970/565-4048 or 800/346-6528.

Hovenweep National Monument

The rugged red-walled canyons, scrubby desert lands, and mesas north of the San Juan River were occupied by numerous bands of pre-Columbian Pueblo Indians until their disappearance in the 1300s. The entire region, including private property holdings, is dotted with Indian ruins, including many, many more than are open to the public. One public site that is worth the lengthy trip on bad roads is **Hovenweep National Monument**.

The park is situated among slickrock and desert, 50 miles west of Cortez via McElmo Canyon Road (County Road G), which starts three miles south of Cortez off US 160. Alternatively, use the Pleasant View Road (County Road CC), 20 miles north of Cortez off US 666, to County Road 10, which leads to the site. Some of these roads are poorly marked or unmarked, so take a map with you.

Hovenweep was created in 1923 and straddles the Colorado-Utah border. It includes 784 acres and six major groups of unusual ruins indicating the prior residence of a large community, possibly Anasazi, who stopped here after leaving the cliff dwellings at Mesa Verde. The ruins here are further distinguished by their unusual designs of square, oval, circular, and D-shaped towers, showing refined masonry techniques. Today, there are walls standing 20 feet high, although any mortar that had been used to hold the rocks together 700 years ago has long since deteriorated.

Hovenweep is just one of the fantastic Anasazi sites in the Southwest. It's easy to imagine Indians living here in these haunting towers, surveying the expansive high desert, perhaps watching out for the approach of enemies.

Square Tower Ruin is the most famous and frequently photographed ruin here. It is the best preserved and the only site accessible by car. Relatively easy hikes along well-marked, rocky trails lined with cacti and low-slung trees lead to all the other ruins. The two crumbling pueblos of the **Cajon Ruins**, across the state line in Utah, are the least well preserved, having been heavily vandalized before the monument was established. On the Colorado side are the **Holly**, **Hackberry Canyon**, **Cutthroat Castle**, and **Goodman Point Ruins**.

There is a ranger station where you can pick up trail maps, and inside is a small display explaining the terrain and ruins here. There is a campground but no visitor services – save for a soda machine. There are trading posts at Hatch, 16 miles west, or Ismay, 14 miles southeast, but they keep irregular hours. Bring provisions from Cortez and start out with a full tank of gas. Hiking is allowed, but only on maintained trails. This is also a good place for bike riding, which is restricted to maintained roads. Make sure you have plenty of water, especially during summer months, when it gets extremely hot out here.

Write c/o **Mesa Verde National Park**, CO 81330, ☎ 970/529-4461.

Lowry Ruins

Sixteen miles north of Hovenweep on County Road 10, then one mile west on County Road CC (or nine miles west of US 666 at Pleasant View) lies a tiny National Historic Landmark – Lowry Pueblo Ruins. The roads leading to Lowry are unmarked. The site is somewhat austere – no campground, no visitor center, and no park ranger. The gravel road from Pleasant View is a good one, but it is not maintained in winter. The site does have a picnic table.

Lowry is thought to have been occupied by only 100 or so farmers, who grew the standard array of corn, beans, and squash for only 50 years until 1140 AD. Today, Lowry is visited by very few, and therein lies its special charm.

The Lowry site has one of the largest circular *kivas*, which were communal gathering spots, yet discovered in the Southwest. The ruins also contain 40 rooms, some of which had three stories, and eight smaller *kivas*. There is also a rare painted *kiva,* which is protected by a modern roof to help preserve five layers of old, faint plaster paintings inside.

FOR MORE INFORMATION

Bureau of Land Management, 701 Camino del Rio, Durango, CO 81302, ☎ 970/247-4082.

Ute Mountain Tribal Park

Twelve miles south of Cortez on US 160 is the entrance to an extraordinary ancient Indian site that dwarfs nearby Mesa Verde National Park and surrounds it on three sides. It is regarded as sacred ground by the Ute Mountain Utes, whose arid reservation lands spread across the extreme southwestern corner of Colorado. It has been virtually untouched for hundreds of years.

The park extends along the now-dry Mancos River Valley and contains only a few excavated surface ruins and cliff dwellings decorated with petroglyphs and paintings. Hundreds of additional sites remain unexcavated. Long protected and now carefully operated by Indians, the area has maintained a completely different sensibility than other Anasazi sites administered by the federal government. If you are intrigued by the Anasazi and their ruins, this is the one site that should not be missed. Its evocative simplicity reverberates with an unequalled authenticity and the Indian guides add a resonance that is not generally provided by uniformed federal park rangers.

Visitors are not allowed into the tribal park on their own. You must reserve space for guided half- or full-day tours. Your guide meets you outside the park and drives through the 125,000-acre site in his own vehicle. A small group of participants, limited to 20 per tour, follow in their own vehicles. A full-day tour takes six hours and crosses nearly 100 miles of sage-scented, rugged high desert. There are frequent stops as you wander over an ancient Anasazi domain, blanketed with thousands of distinctive pottery shards, tool fragments, corn cobs, and other shattered remnants of a vanished race. The guide points out buried pit houses and burial mounds, leads short hikes to hidden petroglyph panels from 1200 AD, rock paintings, and strategically placed guard towers. Toward the end of the tour, you visit the only excavated ruins in the park, walking single file along a narrow trail in a shady canyon. There are several short ladders you must climb to reach the trail leading to a handful of ruins. Those who wish to may climb a 30-foot ladder leading to an incredible, unrestored Anasazi ruin that has been left intact, exactly as it was when people lived here 800 years ago.

Carry water, food, and start with a full tank of gas. A day here may be physically demanding, especially in the summer when temperatures commonly top 100°. The only water in the park is in a tank near the start of the road.

Aside from group tours, you may reserve an Indian guide for day-long or overnight backpacking, biking, or horseback trips through prehistory.

The newest addition to the Ute Mountain Ute Reservation is a limited stakes casino. The small, active casino is almost directly opposite the entrance for the Ute Mountain Park, 11 miles south of Cortez on US 160/666. It's open 8AM to 4AM daily and offers slots, video poker, blackjack, poker, and bingo. Phone **Ute Mountain Casino**, ☎ 970/565-7000 or 800/258-8007 for information.

Due west of the Ute Mountain Tribal Park, directly behind the new casino, is a curious landmark visible for 50 miles from the east or west. **Sleeping Ute Mountain** rises almost 10,000 feet from the horizontal desert floor. Some people don't see the resemblance, but for others it really does look like a sleeping Ute on his back, his head to the north, his feet to the south, with strong arms folded across his proud chest. It can be seen clearly from Hovenweep, Ute Mountain Tribal Park, and Mesa Verde, but the best view is probably from the parking lot of the casino!

FOR MORE INFORMATION

Ute Mountain Tribal Park, Towaoc, CO 81334, ☎ 970/565-3751, extension 282, or 800/847-5485.

Mesa Verde National Park

Situated seven miles west of Cortez, off US 160, this is by far the most visited tourist attraction in the region. Mesa Verde National Park draws nearly one million visitors yearly to its prominent, broad-topped mesa, haunting side canyons, expansive scenic vistas, and ancient Indian ruins. Situated in the high canyon country between Cortez and Mancos, the park offers scenic paved roads and short trails leading to a large concentration of Indian ruins.

This site contains the most mysterious of all Anasazi structures – the puzzling and inaccessible cliff dwellings. These are literally holes cut into the vertical canyon walls and no one really knows how the Anasazi got to these sites – it is presumed they used very long ladders – or why they bothered. Were they seeking protection, or simply privacy? Only the strange, remote architecture remains, raising questions, but providing no clear-cut answers.

Utes and Navajos have known about these ruins for much longer than archaeologists, who have been studying them for only 100 years. But Indians don't like to hang around places where other Indians have died, so they left the site alone. Local cowboys tracking stray cattle discovered this place only in the late 1880s. It was declared the nation's first national park reserved to protect man-made artifacts in 1906.

Many of the cliff dwellings, and other canyon rim ruins of a more conventional nature, may be viewed from paved overlooks you can drive to on well-maintained roadways. Numerous other architectural remains are harder to see, requiring arduous hikes ranging in altitude from 6,000 feet to 8,600 feet. Trails to certain ruins involve clambering up and down narrow steps cut out of the rugged terrain. Still other sites are reached only by sturdy but insecure-looking ladders.

The park represents generations of Anasazi who progressed over centuries from living in elemental caverns or hand-dug pit houses. The earliest residents wove baskets of wildly prolific yucca or hemp that thrived here; archaeologists named them Basketmakers.

No evidence of a written language has ever been found, but some of their stories are told in cave paintings that have survived. Other artifacts – coiled clay pots and pottery shards, yucca fiber sandals, stone tools, skeletons, shriveled corn cobs, and irrigation courses on the mesa tops that have remained intact in the ultra-dry high desert – have been dated to 550 AD. Along with the impressive structural ruins, these things provide clues to explain the lifestyles and behavior of these primitive residents.

The good stuff – the five major cliff dwellings and numerous mesa top villages – is 20 miles up the entrance road from US 160. It's at least a 45-minute ride to reach the major ruins, assuming there is no traffic, which means any time except the summer. At the peak time, the crowds can be daunting as the bulk of visitors make the switchback pilgrimage. Summer can be brutally hot; fall is ideal. Winter is the most deserted, some believe the most mysterious; it definitely affords a more personalized experience than August, though some ruins are closed and park services are reduced in winter.

It's four miles from the Highway to **Morefield Village**, where a huge, full-service campground for tents, cars, and RVs is located. It's the only campground in the park and has all amenities, including a gas station. Several hiking trails start around here. Nearby, at the peak of the winding entrance road, is **Point Lookout**. It's a one-mile round-trip hike to look out over the lip of the mesa at four states, ranging from the desert flats and slot canyons of Arizona, through New Mexico, Utah and the 13,000-foot La Plata Mountains in Colorado. Today the area is known as the Four Corners. To the Utes who adopted this land many years after the Anasazi had declined, the view from this spot revealed "the rim of the little world."

It's another nine miles to the **Far View Visitor Center**. Most of the numerous services available in this area are open only from April to October. These include a motel, restaurant, gas station, store, and informative displays.

Open in summer only, there's a turn-off for **Wetherill Mesa** at Far View. From the turn, it's a serpentine 20 miles or so to the Long House Ruins, Step House, and Badger House sites spanning almost the entire range of Anasazi occupation. Visits to Long House are restricted to ranger-guided tours only.

A mini-tram takes visitors on a four-mile loop of the area, with numerous stops where you can get out and walk a half-mile to the various ruins. These include mesa-top pit houses, estimated to be nearly 1,400 years old, and structures from the Classic Pueblo period, circa 1200 AD.

If you keep going straight for seven miles on the main park road from Far View, you will reach **Chapin Mesa** – the site of an **Archaeology Museum** and the Park Headquarters. Both of these are open year-round. The museum has a variety of displays representing just about everything that has ever been recovered from the park. Artifacts, old photos, documents, and maps enumerate the known and presumed chronology of the Anasazi, along with the history of the park.

A short trail from the museum leads to **Spruce Tree House**, a big ruin nestled under the rim of a canyon. You can climb around it, peek in the tiny windows and low doorways, go down into a *kiva*, or simply look at the site from an overlook. Spruce Tree House is open year-round.

It's a half-mile from the museum to the turn-offs for two separate six-mile loops of **Ruins Road**. The easterly loop leads to the largest cliff dwelling in the world, **Cliff Palace**. It's a half-mile round-trip hike, climbing four 10-foot ladders and stone steps to reach the site. **Balcony House Ruins**, on the same loop, is situated high in a cliff. You have to climb ladders and crawl through a little tunnel to get to it; the only way to do this is on a guided tour. The westerly loop leads to **Square Tower House, Sun Point**, and **Sun Temple Ruins**.

Hour-long, ranger-guided tours start every 30 minutes to Long House and Balcony House. A ranger is on duty at Spruce Tree House and Cliff Palace during summer. In winter, guided tours are offered to Spruce Tree House only, weather permitting.

The park is open year-round, but campsites, motel accommodations, and gas are only available inside the park from May through October.

FOR MORE INFORMATION

For information on tour schedules, other ranger-led programs, special activities, and weather conditions, contact **Mesa Verde National Park**, CO 81330, ☎ 970/529-4461, 970/529-4475 or 970/529-4465. For additional information on the area of Dolores, Cortez, Mesa Verde, and Mancos, contact **Mesa Verde County Visitor Information Bureau**, PO Box HH, Cortez, CO 81321-0990, ☎ 800/253-1616.

Mancos

Mancos, seven miles east of Mesa Verde on US 160, doesn't look like much more than a couple of neon motels and gas stations. But there are some unusual things going on here, including one of the best restaurants in the entire Southwest, **Millwood Junction**, and several idiosyncratic shops. South of town, the **Mancos Valley Stage Line** offers horse-drawn stagecoach rides. At **The Bounty Hunter**, 115 West Grand Avenue, 81328, ☎ 970/533-7215, or 800/BEST-HAT, you can order a high-quality, customized cowboy hat or other cowboy duds. A few doors away, at **Buck's Saddlery** (120 West Grand Avenue, 81328, ☎ 970/533-7958), you can order a custom-fitted saddle.

The commercial heart of Mancos, Grand Avenue, is where these and several other Western shops are found. It is all of two short blocks long and is two blocks south of US 160, off Railroad Avenue (CO 184).

FOR MORE INFORMATION

Mancos Merchants Association, PO Box 196, Mancos, CO 81328, ☎ 970/533-7434, or stop at **Mancos Visitor Center,** 200 Main Avenue.

Hesperus

Fifteen miles east of Mancos on US 160 is the small town of Hesperus, consisting of a gas station with a convenience store and restaurant, post office, a low-slung cinder block motel, and a café. Little **Hesperus Ski Area** is here along with a peaceful, little-known place to stay, **Blue Lake Ranch**. The modest little café, **Chip's Place**, attracts an eclectic clientele of locals and savvy travelers engaged in the quest for the ultimate burger. Chip's is attached to the Canyon Motel, a small property with small rooms at small rates.

It's 11 miles east from Hesperus on US 160 to Durango, the last link on the San Juan Skyway loop.

Adventures

On Foot

Some of the most beautiful and least used trails for alpine hiking are found in southwestern Colorado, including challenging ascents of 14,000-foot peaks. Easier routes offer their own rewards in beauty, seclusion, or historical appeal.

HIKING TIPS

▫ Most hikes range from 5,000 feet to more than 12,000 feet in elevation. Some people may show symptoms of altitude sickness, progressing from a headache to nausea, vomiting, disorientation and loss of consciousness, or death. The quickest remedy is to get to a lower altitude. The best preventative is to acclimate to the elevation by allowing two to three days of relative inactivity before you start hiking.
▫ Be prepared for extreme changes in weather.
▫ Don't drink untreated water.
▫ Keep your distance from wildlife. If you scare or surprise a wild animal the response may be unpredictable or dangerous. Keep campsites clean and put all food away to prevent unwanted nocturnal visits from bears, skunks or other critters.

Colorado's Fourteeners, by Gerry Roach, Fulcrum Publishing, is an excellent book for serious alpine backcountry hikes.

The following trail listings are by no means complete – you could easily spend many summers exploring and never follow the same track twice.

DURANGO-SILVERTON

The **San Juan National Forest** and **Weminuche Wilderness Area** offer some of the most rugged and rewarding hiking in the area, ranging from verdant riverside trails to barren alpine tundra. Hiking or backpacking excursions of one hour to several weeks duration are feasible.

For information, contact the **Animas Ranger District, ☎** 303/970-4874.

The 469-mile **Colorado Trail** connects Durango with Denver. The southwest portion of it begins west of Durango, off Junction Creek (25th Street), west of Main Avenue. The terrain is tough, but you can hike portions of the trail, which traverses alpine wilderness between 7,000 and 11,000 feet.

Perins Peak Trail is a five-mile loop starting at the end of 22nd Street in Durango. The short but arduously steep trail passes through evergreen glades and entails clambering up a 10-foot cliff for a picturesque panorama of Durango and the La Plata Mountains.

Red Creek Trail runs around six miles one-way to the top of Missionary Ridge, for spectacular views of the entire Animas Valley. Access is from Florida Road (East Third Avenue), 10 miles north of town, to the sign for Colvig Silver Camps, then turn left and continue two more miles to the trailhead.

Needleton Trail, elevation 8,200 feet, is 13 miles south of Silverton. The easiest way to reach the trailhead is by the Durango & Silverton Narrow Gauge Railroad to Silverton. An alternative is a subsidiary line, the Animas River Railway, which travels from the small town of Rockwood, 16 miles north of the train station in Durango, to Elk Park, north of Needleton, at half the cost. **Elk Creek Trail** may be accessed from the train at Elk Park. It covers eight miles to the Continental Divide above Elk Creek Valley.

The **Needle Creek Trail** from Needleton is one of the more popular ones in the Weminuche Wilderness. The 14-mile trail leads to Chicago Basin. From there it is between two and five miles to Mount Eolus, 14,084 feet, Sunlight Peak, 14,059 feet, or Windom Peak, 14,087 feet. Hikers can flag the train down at Needleton for the return trip to Durango or Silverton. Topographic maps are required for most routes and are available from the Forest Service or sport shops in either town.

Two other trailheads also offer somewhat lengthier access to Eolus, Sunlight, and Windom, but bypass the train.

Purgatory Trail (elevation 8,000 feet) starts at Purgatory Campground across from Purgatory-Durango Ski Area, on the east side of US 550 and 26 miles north of Durango. The **Cascade Creek Trail** is four miles one-way, mostly down, to the Animas River, then up seven miles farther on the Animas River Trail to Needleton, the Weminuche, and the Fourteeners.

Vallecito Trail is at 7,900 feet, at Vallecito Campground. To get here you drive 20 miles east of Durango on Florida Road (East Third Avenue) to Vallecito Reservoir. Drive five miles farther to the junction on the west side of the reservoir, bear left for three miles to the campground. The trails in this area are the longest and least used leading to the Weminuche. It's a 35-mile trek to reach the base of a 14,000-foot peak from here, making this a viable option only for those seeking an extended backpacking trip.

Little Molas Lake, off US 550 between Purgatory and Silverton, provides a passage to the Colorado Trail via the **Clear Creek Trail**. The trailhead is at South Mineral Creek Campground.

Many day-hikes start around Silverton, switch back through forests and meadows, then climb into high country or to alpine lakes. The **Ice Lake Trail** from South Mineral Campground is a good day-hike. Another possible day-trip is the hike to Highland Mary Lakes, starting at the end of Cunningham Gulch.

Access to the Weminuche from Silverton is possible on trails from Cunningham Gulch Road, the Stony Pass jeep road, and the Kendall Mountain jeep road.

FOR MORE INFORMATION

Backcountry Experience, 1205 Camino del Rio, Durango, CO 81302, ☎ 970/247-5830, features top-quality backpacking, climbing and mountaineering equipment and clothing. The store is a great source for outdoor information, with a staff who know the local outdoors. Good selection of maps and books. Rental camping equipment is available.

Pine Needle Mountaineering, 835 Main Avenue, Durango, CO 81302, ☎ 970/247-8728 (in the Main Mall), features high quality outdoor gear for backpacking, climbing, and ski touring, along with sportswear, maps, and books. Some rental equipment is available.

Gardenswartz Sports, 863 Main Avenue, Durango, CO 81302, ☎ 970/247-2660, is another good place to check for outdoor gear, backpacking and camping equipment, fishing rods, reels and tackle, topographical maps, licenses, outdoor clothing, including boots, and backcountry snow gear. The staff can provide you with area-wide outdoor information, including details on guided fishing trips.

Outdoor World, 1234 Greene Street, Silverton, CO 81433, ☎ 970/387-5628, has gear and specializes in outdoor recreation in the Silverton area.

The San Juan National Forest also offers numerous opportunities for rock climbers. Guided climbs, group and private rock and ice climbing classes for all levels of climbers are offered by **SouthWest Adventures** (see below, under *Adventures: On Wheels*). Rock classes are designed for a four-day progression beginning with Level I, an introduction to basic climbing techniques, then on to refined techniques and skills in Level II, followed by an advanced rock program, and finally an ascent of the 800-foot face of Snowdon Peak. This includes an introduction to multi-pitch climbing in an alpine setting. Other scheduled climbing trips include a three-day seminar in the West Needles Mountains, focusing on basic rock climbing and rappelling techniques, and modern snow climbing techniques; a five-day seminar on alpine rock and snow climbing in Ice Lake Basin north of Durango; three-day Vestal Basin ascents for those with a minimum of Level II rock climbing abilities; a five-day Chicago Basin ascent that includes transportation on the Durango-Silverton train; summit climbs of Mount Eolus (14,083 feet), North Eolus (14,039 feet), Windom Peak (14,082 feet), and Sunlight Peak (14,059 feet); customized climbing and hiking trips in the Needles mountains.

OURAY, RIDGWAY, TELLURIDE, DOLORES

Although these towns are far apart, if you travel by road, they share the same mountains. There are many, many hiking trails to choose from.

One of the most accessible is **Lower Cascade Falls Trail**, only a half-mile each way, beginning in the town of Ouray at the top of Eighth Avenue. You hike down over big rocks, to the bottom of the falls.

The **Portland Trail** is probably easier than Lower Cascade, though longer at five miles. It starts on the east side of Ouray, at Amphitheater Campground, gaining around 700 feet in elevation.

Also beginning at Ouray's Amphitheater Campground is the 2½-mile **Upper Cascade Trail**. The 1,500-foot elevation gain makes for a rather steep, short hike, but affords fine views of the valley and the falls. Don't try this hike on your first day at this elevation.

Mount Sneffels (14,150 feet) is seven miles west of Ouray, or five miles north of Telluride. Two area trailheads offer the best access.

The south side of Sneffels is accessed through **Yankee Boy Basin Trail**. It's situated at 10,700 feet and is not so easy to find. Turn south on CO 361, off US 550, half a mile south of Ouray. From there it's 17 tricky miles to the trailhead. Inquire locally for specific directions and road conditions.

East Dallas Creek Trail (9,340 feet) provides access to the north side of Sneffels. To get here you go nearly five miles west on CO 62 from the intersection with US 550 in Ridgway, then south on CO 7 (East Dallas Creek Road) for another nine miles. Again, inquire locally for explicit directions and road conditions.

Telluride has 250 miles of trails originating in town, ranging from easy walks to strenuous backcountry excursions. The most popular route is probably the short trek to **Bridal Veil Falls**. The round trip from **Pandora Mill** at the east end of Telluride covers two miles, up a steep dirt road, gaining 1,000 feet in elevation. It should only take around two hours. At the top is an old hydroelectric power plant. The scenic falls are the largest in the state, tumbling 500 feet out of the hills.

If you want to keep going after you reach the power plant, **Blue Lake Trail** starts a quarter-mile beyond it. It's the trail that forks to the left. Stay to the left at the next fork in the trail and it's a 90-minute hike to Blue Lake.

Another short trek to scenic views is the **Jud Weibe Trail**, a loop which covers 2½ miles, starting at the north end of Telluride's Aspen Street, at Cornet Creek.

Bear Creek Trail is at the south end of Pine Street, where the road turns from pavement to dirt. The trail, at its worst near the bottom, leads to a waterfall. It's a 4½-mile round-trip.

Liberty Bell Mine Ruins Trail begins off Tomboy Road at the north end of Oak Street. Go up Tomboy Road and turn left at the first dirt road. Allow at least five hours for the round trip.

Thirteen miles southwest of Telluride, in the Lizard Head Wilderness Area (see above), lie three Fourteeners: Wilson Peak, (14,017 feet), Mount Wilson (14,246 feet), and El Diente Peak (14,159 feet). Climbing these mountains is serious business, with some routes requiring technical equipment and maneuvering.

The best access to these mountain trails is through **Silver Pick Trail** (10,650 feet), approximately eight miles south of CO 145, midway between Telluride and Placerville, on Forest Road 622 along Big Bear Creek. Another option is **Kilpacker Basin Trail** (10,080 feet), 5½ miles west of CO 145, nine miles north of Rico. The trailhead is 2½ miles north of Burro Bridge Campground and 3½ miles north of Dunton on Forest Road 535. Rico is a tiny mountain town with some modest services, listed under *Where to Stay & Eat*. Dunton is a ghost town that was recently purchased by European real estate developers. They plan to turn it into an upscale planned community.

Navajo Lake Trail (9,340 feet), a mile north of Burro Bridge Camp-ground on Forest Road 535, also leads to the peaks of El Diente or the Wilsons. An easier alternative is climbing only to Navajo Lake, at 11,154 feet. The trailhead is 7½ miles west on Dunton Road (Forest Road 535) from CO 145, north of Rico. Alternatively, it's 12½ miles east of Dolores on West Fork Road, and then 24 miles north on Forest Road 535 to the campground and trailhead. It's a 10-mile round-trip hike to the lake, sitting in the shadow of 14,159-foot El Diente.

An interesting yearly event that participants attempt on foot is the Imogene Pass Run, held in the second week of September. It is not meant to be a hike, but rather an 18-mile mountain foot race. It starts in Ouray and ascends a four-wheel-drive road to the top of Imogene Pass (elevation 13,100 feet).

FOR MORE INFORMATION

Telluride Mountaineer, 219 East Colorado Avenue, Telluride, CO 81435, ☎ 970/728-6736, offers sales, rentals and service across the street from Town Park.

Skip's Taxi & Shuttle Service (129 West San Juan, Telluride, CO 81435, ☎ 970/728-6667) can provide trailhead drop-offs and pick-ups for hikers.

☞ Scheduled and customized hiking trips for women only are offered by **Women in the Wilderness**, a Telluride-based outfitter. Taught by women for women, the trips are designed so that even the most cosmopolitan camper will feel at home in the wild with experienced and enthusiastic leadership, gourmet campfire cooking and lightweight backpacking. The program is structured so that women can build confidence in their own abilities in a non-competitive environment. Evenings are devoted to campfire songs with flute accompaniment. For information, contact Ulli Sir Jesse, ☎ 970/728-4538. In describing her trips, she says, "It's not army boot camp. It's a very human experience."

CORTEZ

The best hiking around here is outside of town. Good hikes lead to Anasazi Indian ruins; others offer an introduction to sloping slickrock and the canyon country, found in greater concentrations west of here in southern Utah. One of the nice things about this part of southwestern Colorado is that it borders mountains and desert. Hiking atop plateaus and mesas provides expansive, unobstructed views of up to 200 miles.

Hovenweep Trails are a network of well marked trails within the National Monument and offer hikes of varying lengths through rugged, but comparatively level terrain. It is very hot during summer; the best times for hiking are spring and fall. Winter – if there's not too much snow on the ground – can also be rewarding. Trail maps are available from the ranger station at Square Tower Ruins. Hiking trails lead to the Cajon Ruins in Utah, or the Holly Ruins, Hackberry Canyon Ruins, Cutthroat Castle Ruins and Goodman Point Ruins of Colorado.

Ute Mountain Tribal Park also has a trail network with interesting backpacking possibilities. Access is restricted to those who hire a Ute guide to accompany them. Trails lead to the few excavated ruins in the park, as well as to numerous unexcavated sites buried along 25 miles of the Mancos River Valley. One of the most popular trails starts at the park entrance and traverses 13 miles along the river. Aside from archaeological sites along the way, including modern Ute rock carvings, the little-used park is a haven for wildlife, including deer and antelope.

Hiking in **Mesa Verde National Park** is carefully restricted to maintained trails and, despite the size of the park, no backcountry hiking is allowed. Hikers must stay on five trails and register at the park ranger's office. Nevertheless, the park trails can offer the peaceful ambiance of pinyon and juniper groves, striated canyons, towering mesas, and the largest concentration of excavated Indian ruins in the Southwest. It gets brutally hot in summer – don't think that because there are restaurants and services within the park you can get away without carrying water and a supply of high energy food.

Several short trails are detailed above under *Mesa Verde National Park*. Among others, which tend to see slightly less usage because of their length, are the following:

A 2½-mile loop, **Petroglyph Point Trail** continues beyond the heavily traveled path to Spruce Tree House near the park headquarters. It crosses along the rim of Spruce Tree Canyon, hugging the top of the mesa. You will see Anasazi rock carvings at Petroglyph Point, the midway point of the loop.

The two-mile **Spruce Canyon Trail** veers off in the opposite direction from Spruce Tree House. It covers some steep terrain as it takes you down below the mesa top into the heavily foliated Spruce Tree Canyon, then back up again to the park headquarters.

An excellent free brochure, titled "Guide to Scenic Hiking Trails in Mesa Verde Country," is available locally.

LLAMA TREKS

Durango, Silverton & Telluride

Let a llama lug your load. They're cuter than they are friendly, but they never complain that you brought too much stuff.

One-day hikes, customized backpacking trips, or llama leasing are offered by **Turnbull Llama Company**, 455 High Llama Lane, Durango, 81302, ☎ 970/259-3773.

Buckhorn Llama Company, 1834 County Road 207, Durango, 81301, ☎ 970/259-5965, offers a variety of guided, fully outfitted llama treks, including excursions of four to eight days in the Chicago Basin area of the Weminuche Wilderness and trips of four days or longer into Anasazi and canyon country.

Telluride-based **Women in the Wilderness** (see above, under *On Foot*) offers one scheduled llama trek in July, in the San Juan Mountains, for women only.

On Horseback

Travel on the back of a well-trained horse for an hour or days on end. For some, this is the ultimate way to experience the backcountry. Several ranches specialize in horseback riding for guests who generally book all-inclusive week-long stays. These are included below, under *Accommodations*.

Among the best local outfitters are the following:

DURANGO

Weminuche Wilderness Adventures, 17754 County Road 501, Bayfield, 81122, ☎ 970/884-2555 (May to November), or PO Box 1899 Wickenburg, AZ 85358, ☎ 602/684-7259 (December to April). Starting above Vallecito Reservoir, guided and fully outfitted trips of 5-10 days pass through alpine meadows into ponderosa pine, blue spruce, and Douglas fir forests. These give way to alpine tundra above the timberline. Deer, elk, coyotes, and bighorn sheep frequent these trails. Custom trips can be arranged.

Hermosa Creek Outfitters, PO Box 2295, Durango, 81302, ☎ 970/259-5393. Specializing in big-game hunting, this outfitter also offers family horseback trips of one to five days in the San Juans, photo adventure tours focusing on wildlife, and high alpine scenery, including workshop sessions with a top local photographer, or fly-fishing trips to remote streams.

Over the Hill Outfitters, 3624 County Road 203, Durango, 81301, ☎ 970/247-9289, offers a variety of horseback trips, from 1½-hour breakfast or supper rides to customized family pack trips along the Continental Divide in the San Juans. Summer fishing trips are also available. Located at the Ponderosa KOA Campground.

Rapp Guide Service, 47 Electra Lake, Durango, 81301, ☎ 970/247-8454 or 970/247-8923, fax 303/259-2953. Customized trips of a half-day or longer, or scheduled pack trips of three to six days, are offered in the Upper Animas River Canyon, Silver Mesa, the Needles Mountains along the Continental Divide to Starvation Gulch, or the Ute Mountain Tribal Park.

Engine Creek Outfitters, PO Box 3803, Durango, 81302, ☎ 970/259-2556 or 303/259-3500, offers hourly breakfast, lunch, and dinner rides, or summer pack trips two to five days in the area of 12,000-foot peaks around Cascade Creek and Engineer Mountain. It is based in Cascade Village (see below, under Durango Accommodations).

San Juan Outfitting, 186 County Road 228, Durango, 81301, ☎ 970/259-6259, runs big game hunting trips, high-country pack trips in the Weminuche Wilderness, an eight-day Continental Divide ride covering 100 miles from Wolf Creek Pass to Silverton, or a variety of customized trips for fishing and photography.

Mayday Livery (4432 County Road 124, Hesperus, 81326, ☎ 970/385-6772) has horseback rides by the hour, half-day rides, and customized guided pack trips.

Buck's Livery, US 550 at Purgatory, Durango, 81301, ☎ 970/385-2110, fax 970/259-5675, offers one-hour, two-hour, half-day, or day-long trail rides, sunset steak or trout dinner rides, high-country fishing trips, or three- to five-day pack and prospecting trips.

Outlaw West Livery, 180 Forest Lakes Drive, Bayfield, 81122, ☎ 970/884-9631 (summer), or 970/884-2074 (winter), specializes in shorter trips of one hour, two hours, half-day or a full day from Vallecito Reservoir. They also offer three-hour breakfast rides, guided fishing trips, or full-service pack trips of three, five or seven days duration.

Southfork Stables, 28481 Highway 160 East, Durango, 81302, ☎ 970/259-4871, offers hour-long rides scheduled five times daily in summer, as well as breakfast rides, half-day rides, full-day rides, including lunch, an evening chuckwagon supper ride, or a moonlight champagne ride. Customized, guided, fully outfitted pack trips and horse leasing are available.

Clinics focusing on horseriding skills are offered by Edna Van Noort, who operates the **Quarter Moon Equestrian Center**, 3320 County Road 203, Durango, 81301, ☎ 970/382-0949 (barn), or 970/247-7942 (home).

SILVERTON

LK Outfitters, 1646 Cement Street, Silverton, 81433, ☎ 970/387-5861.

San Juan Outdoor Recreation Center, PO Box 45, Silverton, 81433, ☎ 970/387-5866 or 800/697-5672.

Silverado Outfitters, 1116 Mineral, Silverton, 81433, ☎ 970/387-5747 or 970/247-1869, offers hourly and half-day horseback rides at Molas Lake, 10 miles south of Silverton on US 550. Also available are dinner or breakfast rides, and overnight trips, including a pack trip from Durango to Silverton, with the return on the narrow-gauge train.

Silver Trails, 600 Cement Street, Silverton, 81433, ☎ 970/387-5869.

Sultan Mountain Livery, 4th Street, PO Box 33, Silverton, 81433, ☎ 970/387-5480, offers customized horseback trips.

George Pastor Mountain Guide, 830 Empire Street, Silverton, 81433, ☎ 970/387-5556, provides outfitting and guide services.

OURAY

Ouray Livery Barn, 834 Main, Ouray, 81427, ☎ 970/325-4606 or 970/626-5695, offers horse rides of one hour, two hours, half-day, full day, and pack trips. Also offered are dinner rides on Deep Creek Mesa. The livery barn was built in 1883, and is still operated in much the same manner of those days. Some of the trails in this area follow the top of the Continental Divide.

RIDGWAY

San Juan Mountain Outfitters, 2882 CO 23, Ridgway, 81432, ☎ 970/626-5360, offers half-day, full-day, and overnight pack trips. You get a free Ouray Hot Springs swim pass with each ride, a nice, soothing touch, especially if you are unaccustomed to riding and experience predictable muscle aches or soreness.

TELLURIDE

D&E Outfitters, 805 West Pacific Avenue, Telluride, 81435, ☎ 970/728-3200. One-hour, full-day, and overnight pack trips. Also dinner rides and horse-drawn wagon trips.

Telluride Outside (666 West Colorado, Telluride, 81435, ☎ 970/728-3895) operates trail rides and pack trips.

Telluride Horseback Adventures, ☎ 970/728-9611, offers customized trips beginning on CO 145, about five miles south of Telluride. The guy who runs this operation is named Roudy, and he is the same gentleman who has been known to ride his horse into Telluride's Sheridan Bar (see below, under Eco-Travel & Cultural Excursions).

DOLORES, CORTEZ & MANCOS

The Outfitter, 410 Railroad Avenue, Dolores, 81323, ☎ 970/882-7740, offers guided horseback rides and overnight pack trips into 18 miles of the Lower Dolores Canyon. The 2,000-foot-deep canyon is accessible only by horseback or on foot, with colorful rock walls and Anasazi caves. The canyon bottom overflows with ponderosa pine, sage, and wildflowers. It provides habitat for eagles, hawks, black bear, and mountain lions. The Dolores River flows through and the trout fishing is excellent. Tours include camping accommodations and meals.

Gene Story, Box 300, Dolores, 81323, ☎ 970/882-4990, is a guide and outfitter.

Triple Heart Ranch, Box 117, Dolores, 81323, ☎ 970/882-4155, offers guide and outfitting services.

The Trappers Den, 37101 US 160, Mancos, 81328, ☎ 970/533-7147, offers horseback riding in the Mancos Valley, a mile east of Mesa Verde.

Echo Basin Stable and Roping Arena (see below, under *Mancos Accommodations*), 2½ miles east of Mancos on US 160 and three miles north on Echo Basin Road, leads one- , two- or three-hour trail rides along the west fork of the Mancos River, four-hour lunch rides to higher elevations, all-day rides in high country, breakfast or dinner rides, and overnight extended pack trips in the La Plata and San Juan Mountains. They also offer riding lessons, team roping, barrel racing, team penning, and horse shows.

CATTLE DRIVES

Parts of the movie *City Slickers* were filmed in and around Durango, and some of the stars were local residents, namely the cattle. If you really want to experience the life of a cowboy, there's no better way than to hitch onto a real Western cattle drive.

Southfork Riding Stables & Outfitters (see above, under *On Horseback: Durango*), runs a spring cattle drive in conjunction with Decker Ranch. Guests participate in gathering, herding, and driving 400 head of cattle across 50 miles of open territory. Framed by the San Juan and La Plata Mountains, the terrain is hilly. After gathering the herd, you then drive it to a corral where you can help with the branding. A horse-drawn chuckwagon follows along the trail, packing your personal belongings, camping gear, and food.

On Wheels

RAIL TRIPS

Railroads used to be a lifeline for remote mountain communities. Most of them are long gone, but one remains – the **Durango & Silverton Narrow Gauge Railroad**, 479 Main Avenue, Durango, 81301, ☎ 970/247-2733. The carefully restored steam engines and train cars are a Registered National Historic Landmark, as well as a National Civil Engineering Landmark.

Nearly a quarter of a million travelers ride these rails through the San Juan National Forest yearly, covering 45 miles of track in a style very little changed from its inception in 1882. It first chugged into existence to transport an estimated $300 million in gold and silver during the mining era.

The trip is among the longest narrow-gauge routes in the world, as well as one of the most picturesque rail trips anywhere. Passengers can travel in colorful, perfectly restored orange and black Victorian-style coaches, some dating to the 1880s or in open gondola cars. These are drawn by an immense coal-fired, steam-powered locomotive – an Iron Horse – built for the Denver & Rio Grande Railroad.

The restored engines that are used date from 1923 to 1925. You can't call a repair shop for parts so the rolling stock is maintained in tip-top running order at a 15-stall roundhouse in Durango. Parts are fabricated there and you can observe the various maintenance and restoration procedures on a yard tour. The 45-minute tour is available daily, May through October, behind the train station, at 479 Main Avenue in Durango. It includes the locomotive service and storage areas, turntable, machine shop, and car shop, replete with unusual tools and equipment for working on the uncommon coaches and locomotives.

The train route parallels the Animas River for most of the way, hugging the three-foot-wide rails through slim canyons and clean-scented evergreen forests, powering slowly through isolated stretches of the national forest that are inaccessible by road. Other than the train, the only ways into this land are by foot or on horseback. The sound of the train's forlorn whistle, its clanking steel, flying cinders, and swelling gray fog of coal smoke recall uncomplicated days when legendary wealth rode these rails.

The slow-moving rail tour is 3½ hours one way, climbing around 3,000 feet from Durango to Silverton. After a two-hour layover in Silverton, the train returns to Durango.

There are as many as five Silverton departures daily from May 1 to October 31. An abbreviated trip is offered between Thanksgiving and early April, from Durango to Cascade Canyon, a 52-mile round trip. Fall, when the colors of foliage are spectacular, and winter, when the route is blanketed in snow, are particularly pretty times to travel.

The Cinco, Animas, and Nomad are private cars available for charter. The Alamosa Parlor Car, circa 1880, is a deluxe, refurbished bar car that is available daily, offering first-class service and alcoholic beverages.

You may purchase a round-trip ticket and layover in Silverton for as many nights as you want. For those who find the one-way trip sufficient exposure to old-time railroads, a bus from Silverton to Durango is available June 7 through September 25. This and other options for delivery of your car to Silverton or Durango, or one-way train trips combined with a jeep tour, are available through **Discover Durango, ☎** 970/247-4600.

During the summer, one departure daily is offered on the **Animas River Railway**, from Rockwood to Elk Park, in the Weminuche Wilderness. This trip is not heavily publicized, but it does eliminate the slow crawl through Durango and immediately plunges into the prettiest part of the Durango-to-Silverton route. It is favored by backpackers who hop off at Needleton or Elk Park for access to the Weminuche, and it is considerably less expensive than the full Durango-Silverton fare.

JEEPING/FOUR-WHEEL-DRIVE TRIPS

The Iron Horse, of course, takes you only where its tracks are laid. If you really want to cover some ground in a short time in the backcountry, travel by jeep or four-wheel-drive. Always check with local authorities about road conditions before you set out. Some high passes may not open at all, while others could remain snow-clogged well into August after a severe winter. Normally, though, even the highest routes will be open by July.

Durango

Rocky Mountain High Tours, PO Box 3337, Durango, 81302, ☎ 970/247-0807 or 800/530-2022, fax 970/247-5082, offers jeep tours or jeep rentals. Half-day guided tours go into the San Juans near Silverton, past pioneer cabins and abandoned mines, up to the ghost town at Animas Forks (elevation 11,300 feet). Another option is to participate in a jeep safari. You rent a jeep and follow behind a guide in his jeep. You can go off on your own or follow the leader, sort of like a modern-day wagon train. The safari is a day-long excursion that includes background information on history, wildlife, vegetation, and folklore of the area. Make your choice for lunch at an old, historic mountain inn, or a catered picnic lunch beside an alpine lake or in an old miner's cabin.

New West Adventures, PO Box 2744, Durango, 81302, ☎ 970/385-4940 or 800/748-1188, suggests reservations a day in advance for its guided tours. These include a four-hour wildlife safari at dawn or dusk (seeking out deer, elk, eagles, hawks, coyotes, foxes, bobcats, and bears) with breakfast or dinner included, or a day-long Silverton/Ghost Town Tour, covering the Alpine Loop (see below, under Silverton). Also available are special three- to four-hour photographic tours and seasonal photo seminars with professional instructors teaching field techniques for shooting summer wildflowers or fall colors. They will provide a guide and jeep to drive you to a remote trailhead, then lead you on a hike or backpacking trip, with or without llamas.

Rocky Mountain High Tours, PO Box 3337, Durango, 81302, ☎ 970/247-0807, offers jeep tours and rentals based out of Tamarron Resort, Purgatory-Durango Ski Resort, Needles store and Silverton. Fall foliage packages include jeep rental, accommodations at the Alma House or Wyman Hotel in Silverton, and meals at Silverton's Handlebars or Zhivago restaurants.

ATV Adventures, PO Box 2756, Durango, 81302, ☎ 970/247-9000, extension 141, operates guided tours on all-terrain vehicles from Purgatory-Durango Ski Resort in the summer, from mid-June through mid-September. Also known as ATVs, these small four-wheel vehicles carry one person, minimum age 18, with a valid driver's license, on two- or four-hour-long excursions into the high San Juan Mountains around the ski area. The trips typically visit abandoned mines, an old stagecoach stop, and other historic and scenic sites. The ATVs come equipped with an automatic transmission, and participants are provided with a helmet, goggles and a rain slicker. It's a wise idea to wear sturdy shoes, long pants and a long sleeved shirt. Reservations are recommended.

Silverton

Jeeping is popular around here, with more than 700 miles of accessible jeep roads in the area and several firms offering rentals.

The **Alpine Loop Backcountry Byway** is a 65-mile trip over gravel and dirt roads, some of which may be rocky, rutted or washed-out, necessitating a four-wheel-drive. The route, open July through October, connects the towns of Silverton, Ouray, and Lake City. It crosses Engineer Pass, at 12,800 feet, and Cinnamon Pass, at 12,620 feet. Highlights include many miles of road above the tree line, amid alpine tundra, as well as numerous abandoned mining sites, including the ghost town at Animas Forks, and old mining camps, cabins, mines and tramlines.

Stony Pass is another jeep route from Silverton, which crosses the Continental Divide at 12,000 feet, then follows the headwaters of the Rio Grande River to the mountain town of Creede. It's east of town, on County Road 110 to Howardsville, then turn right on Cunningham Gulch Road. After two miles you will come across Stony Pass Road on the left.

Black Bear Pass, connecting the top of Red Mountain Pass with Telluride, one-way only, is extremely challenging, beautiful, and dangerous in a jeep. The road is narrow, with long, steep drops. Some switchbacks require three-point turns. Some people do it on a bicycle. If your vehicle doesn't make it you may find yourself doing the trip on foot. Approach with respect and caution.

Ophir Pass, 11,740 feet, connects Silverton and Ophir, nine miles south of Telluride. It starts approximately five miles north of Silverton, off US 550, on an unmarked turn-off across from a sign that says "Red Mountain Summit Five Miles." It's 45 miles to Ophir, but the road's not too bad as far as jeep roads go. This is one of the more popular backcountry jeep roads.

FOR MORE INFORMATION

Triangle Jeep Rentals, 864 Greene Street, Silverton, CO 81433, ☎ 970/887-9990 or 970/387-5498.

Silverton Lakes Jeep Rentals, PO Box 126, Silverton, CO 81433, ☎ 970/387-5721, open May 1 to October 15.

San Juan Tours & Trading Company, 1333 Greene Street, Silverton, CO 81433, ☎ 970/387-5565 or 800/4X4-TOUR.

Rocky Mountain High Tours, 1215 Blair Street, Silverton, CO 81433, ☎ 970/387-5562.

Ouray

This area considers itself the jeeping capital of the world and the number and variety of routes in the area prove the claim. You can take trips to old gold mines and ghost towns, hugging narrow ledges over sheer drop-offs on harrowing roads that seem more appropriate for mountain goats than motor vehicles. In short, just the sort of terrain that four-wheel enthusiasts dream about. One of the easiest routes is through **Yankee Boy Basin**, beginning at Camp Bird Road, south of town, off US 550. It takes you along Canyon Creek to the legendary Camp Bird Mine, then through a series of meadows along the base of looming mountains. **Imogene Pass** offers a more challenging tour over a 13,509-foot pass to Telluride. It starts at the Camp Bird Mine and is not for the inexperienced.

FOR MORE INFORMATION

San Juan Scenic Jeep Tours, PO Box 143, Ouray, CO 81427, ☎ 970/325-4444 or 970/325-4154, is a possibility for those who prefer an experienced driver behind the wheel. They offer half-day and full-day tours on pre-set or customized itineraries. They also offer jeep rentals.

Switzerland of America Jeep Rentals & Tours, 226 7th Avenue, PO Box 780, Ouray, CO 81427, ☎ 970/325-4484 or 800/432-5337, is a major operator, offering a wide variety of guided tours, as well as a large selection of rentals by the half-day, daily, or weekly. Also, historic "Tin Lizzie" tours in a 1916 Model T Ford, guided fly-fishing tours, and hiker drop-off and pick-up.

Colorado West, PO Box 1850, 322 Fifth Avenue, Ouray, CO 81427, ☎ 970/325-4014 or 800/648-JEEP, offers off-road tours or jeep rentals, including mapping services. On these tours passengers ride in an open-top vehicle in which one may sit or stand.

Polly's Jeep Rentals, 1805 Main Street, Ouray, CO 81427, ☎ 970/325-4061, rents out jeeps.

Budget Rent-A-Car, PO Box 290, Ouray, CO 81427. ☎ 970/325-4154 or 800/221-2419, rents four-wheel-drive vehicles.

Timber Ridge Jeep Rentals, PO Box 606, Ouray, CO 81427, ☎ 970/325-4523, rents jeeps.

Red Hot Ryder Jeep & Snowmobile Rentals, 5th & Main Street, Ouray, CO 81427, ☎ 970/325-0350 or 800/325-4385.

Along with all the jeeping around here, one operator is offering guided backroad trips to ghost towns and isolated mountain backcountry in little four-wheel ATVs with automatic transmissions. These all-terrain vehicles resemble nothing so much as a motorcycle with four wheels, or perhaps a snowmobile for bare ground and, as ecologically unsound as these noisy, nubby-wheeled vehicles probably are, they are also a lot of fun. Two people can ride on one machine, and helmets, gloves, raincoats, and coolers are provided. You bring your own snacks. For information contact **Fantastic Four Wheelin'**, 722 Main Street, Ouray, 81427, ☎ 970/325-4284.

Telluride

There are hundreds of jeep roads in the Telluride vicinity. Some connect with the Silverton or Ouray routes listed above. The Chamber

Resort Association (see above, under *Touring: Telluride*) or jeep tour operators can provide complete information.

A challenging and popular jeep route is **Imogene Pass** (13,059 feet) from Telluride to Ouray. It is accessed on the Telluride side by going north on Oak Street to the Imogene Pass Road. The road passes the Tomboy Mine ruins and then gets serious. This is a difficult and dangerous road. Although the scenery is rewarding, do not take this drive lightly.

FOR MORE INFORMATION

Budget Rent-A-Car, 657 West Colorado, Telluride, CO 81435, ☎ 970/728-4642 or 800/221-2419, rents four-wheel-drives for jeeping.

Telluride Outside, 666 West Colorado, Telluride, CO 81435, ☎ 970/728-3895, rents four-wheel-drives and operates half-day, full-day, customized and private guided tours. Also offers backpacker drop-offs and four-wheel-drive, sit-down dinner tours to the Alta Lakes Observatory, or sunset, cowboy, and barbecue dinner tours to Deep Creek Mesa.

Thrifty Car Rental, 129 West San Juan, Telluride, CO 81435, ☎ 970/728-3266 or 800/367-2277, rents jeeps, all-wheel-drive minivans, four-wheel-drive Cherokees, and runs guided four-wheel-drive tours.

Skip's Taxi & Shuttle Service, 129 West San Juan, Telluride, CO 81435, ☎ 970/728-6667, runs four-wheel-drive tours in a convertible, visiting ghost towns, hidden lakes, and mining ruins.

Mountain Limo, PO Box 1662, Telluride, CO 81435, ☎ 970/728-9606, offers four-wheel-drive tour services for the Telluride region.

STAGECOACH RIDES

Mancos Valley Stage Line, 4550 County Road 41, Mancos, 81328, ☎ 970/533-9857 or 800/365-3530, has tours in an old-fashioned horse-drawn stagecoach, circa 1860. They leave from just south of Mancos into Weber Canyon, below Mesa Verde, and run from May through September. Among the options are overnight trips, including meals and accommodations in a four-bedroom log cabin; three-hour lunch trips; three-hour dinner trips; or a brief ride, without meals. Advance reservations are required for meal trips.

WAGON RIDES

Mayday Livery, 4317 County Road 124, Hesperus, 81326, ☎ 970/385-6772. Spend a few days on the seat of a real chuckwagon, rolling through the San Juans, Canyon de Chelly, or Monument Valley. The Taylor family, who operates these tours, are long-time local residents whose rolling and livestock have been used in numerous TV commercials and movies. Each trip is custom-designed for your group.

Deep Creek Sleigh & Wagon Rides of Telluride, 130 West Colorado, Telluride, 81435, ☎ 970/728-3565, operates horse-drawn wagon rides into the San Juans at sunset, where a bonfire is built and a Western dinner is served.

MOUNTAIN BIKING & BICYCLING

Durango

Durango likes to call itself the mountain biking capital of America. Because of the abundance of steep forest roads and backcountry trails, a number of professional bike riders live and train in the area. The town has hosted the **Iron Horse Bicycle Classic** every Memorial Day weekend for more than 20 years. It started with about a dozen riders racing the narrow-gauge train to Silverton, and has now grown into an internationally recognized event that attracts several thousand professional and amateur bike riders. They still race the train and still climb tenaciously over two 10,000-foot passes. Many other participants compete only with themselves and are happy enough just to finish the race – even if they arrive in Silverton hours after the train. In addition, Durango hosted the first unified World Mountain Biking Championship in 1990. The championship track at Purgatory Ski Area is open to bike riders in the summer.

The **Animas Valley Loop** is rated as easy, but that doesn't mean you should attempt it on your first day at 6,500 feet coming from sea level. People who live here and ride at this elevation all the time consider it easy. You stay on county roads all the way, over essentially level terrain with rolling hills. Total elevation gain is 280 feet on the full 30-mile loop. There is an alternative 15-mile loop.

The 30-mile route goes north on County Road 250 from Durango on the east side of the Animas Valley. You cross US 550 at Baker's Bridge (where parts of the movie *Butch Cassidy and the Sundance Kid* were filmed). On the west side of US 550, you take County Road 203 south to Durango, down the west side of the scenic, red-rock valley.

Also starting right in town, the **Animas City Mountain Loop** is a short but steep trail for advanced riders. Follow the signs off East 4th Avenue, north of 32nd Street. The 5½-mile trail gains 1,250 feet in elevation, but your sweat is rewarded with a bird's-eye panorama encompassing Falls Creek, the Animas Valley, and the West Needle Mountains.

Old Lime Creek Road is considered intermediate terrain. This is an old stagecoach road parallel to US 550 at Coal Bank Pass (10,630 feet) north of Purgatory and south of Silverton. It's 11 miles one-way, with the Silverton side 2,000 feet higher than the Purgatory side. Most riders start 11 miles south of Silverton at the turn-off from US 550 on the east side of the road. The shady route drops from over 10,000 feet to just under 9,000 feet (with some uphill stretches along the way), past forested hillsides, streams, and the brick remains of the low Chinese Wall. The wall was once all that prevented horse-drawn wagons and carriages from tumbling hundreds of feet down the sheer hillside.

Purgatory-Durango Ski Area (26 miles north of Durango on US 550, ☎ 970/247-9000 or 800/525-0892) offers an entire network of well-marked mountain bike trails during the summer. You can tackle the world championship course or ride a chairlift up with your bike and ride down. Purgatory supplies maps of such routes as the Championship Trail (an advanced eight-mile loop), Hermosa Cliff Overlook (a nine-mile intermediate trail that takes you to a stunning viewpoint atop the Hermosa Cliffs), Harris Park Loop (a four-mile intermediate trail down the north face of the ski mountain and into the Hermosa Valley), Hermosa Creek Trail (covering 20 miles of expert single-track trail named by *Snow Country* magazine as one of the five best mountain bike rides in the United States), and several beginner trails. They also offer guided tours.

Bike rentals are available at Purgatory from **Purgatory Sports**, ☎ 970/247-9000 or 970/385-2183. Although these rentals do include mountain bike uplifts on Purgatory's chairlift, these are more expensive than similar rentals available in Durango.

Mountain Bike Specialists, 949 Main Avenue, Durango, 81301, ☎ 970/247-4066, operates a full-service bike shop year-round in Durango, with rentals and guided tours, which include bikes, helmets, lunch, trail-side snacks, rain gear, and sag wagon. In addition to half-day and full-day tours, they offer the following itineraries (these include accommodations and most meals):

Ute Mountain Tribal Park Tour is a fully outfitted day-long trip from Durango to the park. You drive to the park, then ride 26 miles round trip up and down the river valley, stopping to view Anasazi archaeology and wildlife. The trip comes complete with an Indian guide.

The *Iron Horse Tour* is a three-day trip, including accommodations in Silverton and Purgatory. The first day you ride the narrow-gauge train to Silverton with your bike. You can ride to a ghost town, a mountaintop, or just around town that afternoon. The second day you ride the Old Lime Creek Road to Purgatory. You can bike around the area, fish, or ride a horse that afternoon. The third morning you ride the chairlift with your bike to the top of the ski mountain and then bike your way south toward Durango, ending five miles north of town at Trimble Hot Springs, for a well-earned soak in a natural hot springs pool.

A five-day bike tour encompasses the entire 232-mile *San Juan Skyway Loop*. You ride the train to Silverton, then bike to Ouray. Day two ends in Telluride. Day three ends in Mancos. On day four you visit Mesa Verde National Park, then return to Mancos. On the last day you return to Durango. Some diehard bikers attempt to cover this five-day route in one day, in which case it is affectionately called the death ride.

Custom tours are also available to such sites as wildflower meadows in July and August, mining camps, or special photo tours.

A six-day bike tour encompassing the San Juan Skyway, beginning and ending in Durango, is offered by **Backroads Bicycle Touring** (1516 5th Street, Berkeley, CA 94710-1713, ☎ 415/527-1555 or 800/245-3874, fax 415/527-1444). It includes a ride on the narrow-gauge train, accommodations at local inns, and two nights at Mesa Verde National Park.

FOR MORE INFORMATION

Hassle Free Sports, 2615 Main Avenue, Durango, CO 81301, ☎ 970/259-3874 or 800/835-3800.

Durango Cyclery, 143 East 13th Street, Durango, CO 81301, ☎ 970/247-0747.

SouthWest Adventures (780 Main Avenue, Durango, CO 81302, ☎ 970/ 259-0370 or 800/642-5389) rents mountain bikes for an hour, a half-day or full day. Also available are guided tours of a half-day or full day.

Pedal the Peaks, 6th & Main Avenue, Durango, CO 81301, ☎ 970/259-6880, offers sales, service and rentals of mountain bikes.

Second Gear, 600 East 2nd Avenue, Durango, CO 81301, ☎ 970/247-4511, rents used mountain bikes and also sells second-hand recreation equipment, bikes, skis, camping and river gear.

Durango Mountain Bike Camp, 621 Columbine Road, Durango, CO 81301, ☎ 970/259-0238, runs instructional bike riding programs for children and adults. This might be a good idea for beginners or riders who want to sharpen their skills before tackling the local cycling challenges.

Silverton

There are many, many miles of trails and jeep roads for bike riding around Silverton, but the most diverse is probably the **Alpine Loop Scenic Byway**. You can ride over two 12,000-foot passes, visit ghost towns, wildflower meadows, and alpine lakes. See above, under *Jeeping* for details on the Alpine Loop and other Silverton area jeep routes good for mountain biking.

In Silverton, contact **San Juan Outdoor Recreation Center** (PO Box 45, Silverton, 81433, ☎ 970/387-5866 or 800/697-5672) for mountain bike tours and rentals.

Ouray

All the jeep roads around Ouray are also good for bike riding. You can veer off the Alpine Loop near Engineer Pass and ride down around 5,000 feet in 10 miles to Ouray.

Downhill Biking, 722 Main Street, Ouray, 81427, ☎ 970/3254284, rents mountain bikes for a half-day, full day or weekly. Also available are tours in which riders are driven up a mountain for a downhill-only ride back to town.

Biking Ouray, by Marcus Wilson, Wayfinder Press, is a guide to mountain biking in Ouray and Ridgway. It contains detailed descriptions of 20 trails for novices to experts.

Telluride

Telluride is loaded with incredible bike routes, many of which are strenuous.

One of the easier ones is to **Bear Creek Falls**. It's two miles up a road to the falls from the south end of Pine Street.

The steep dirt road that leads to **Alta Lakes** passes through a ghost town. The road is five miles south of Telluride, off CO 145 at the Alta sign.

Black Bear Pass is a longer, more difficult ride. You follow the jeep road leading to Bridal Veil Falls. It's at the end of Colorado Avenue, past the Idarado Mine. You can stop at the top of the falls and at the power plant, then, on your way back down, follow the switchback to the right at the one-way sign just below the power plant. The road gets very steep going over Ingram Falls, then passes through an immense alpine basin before reaching US 550, at the top of Red Mountain Pass, midway between Silverton and Ouray.

Ophir Pass is less difficult than Black Bear Pass, but still challenging. Follow CO 145 south. Turn left at Ophir and keep going until you reach US 550 in Silverton.

Tomboy Road and Imogene Pass starts at the north end of Oak Street, continues past ghost town ruins at Tomboy, and then up Imogene Pass. From the top you rapidly descend into Ouray.

BIKE OUTFITTERS

Free Wheelin' Bike & Board Shop, 101 East Colorado, Telluride, CO 81435, ☎ 970/728-4734, specializes in mountain bike sales, service, rentals, and tours.

Olympic Sports (150 West Colorado, Telluride, CO 81435, ☎ 970/728-4477 or 800/828-7547) rents mountain bikes and makes repairs.

Telluride Outside (666 West Colorado, Telluride, CO 81435, ☎ 970/728-3895) rents mountain bikes and runs tours, including a 17-mile downhill mountain bike tour from the top of Lizard Head Pass, featuring a 2,000-foot descent along an old railroad line.

Paragon Ski & Sport, 213 West Colorado, Telluride, CO 81435, ☎ 970/728-4525, sells, services, and rents mountain bikes.

A unique, eight-night, seven-day mountain bike tour is offered by **San Juan Hut Systems**, Box 1663, 117 North Willow Street, Telluride, 81435, ☎ 970/728-6935. It's a 205-mile trip from Telluride to Moab, Utah, with nightly accommodations in a series of five wooden huts and one 20-foot, fabric-frame octagon shelter on a platform. The tour stays mainly on Forest Service or BLM dirt roads. The modest huts are 35 miles apart along a route designed for intermediate riders in good shape.

Advanced technical single track is found in the vicinity of each hut for highly skilled cyclists. There is no vehicle support, so riders should be knowledgeable in maintenance and repair. Participants are required to carry their own pump, patch, and repair kit, as well as warm clothes, rain gear, and three quarts of water.

You can bring your own food; or the complete package tour includes three meals a day, hut facilities, sleeping bag, trail map and descriptions. It does not include a guide, although one is available for an additional fee.

There are a lot of climbs while getting out of Telluride, then the route levels somewhat into slickrock canyon country, high red-rock deserts of sage, juniper, and pinyon. It's a memorable and challenging ride. You can also rent a bike and all the necessary equipment for the whole hut tour, or rent bikes by the hour, half-day or day.

Dolores, Cortez & Mancos

Cortez-Mancos-Dolores Half-Century, is a 43-mile intermediate road ride, for road or mountain bikers. You start in Cortez on US 160, travel east past the entrance to Mesa Verde, and continue on through rolling meadows and ranch land into Mancos. In Mancos, head north on CO 184 to Dolores. The return to Cortez is south, and mostly downhill for around 10 miles into Cortez on CO 145.

The 17-mile **Cutthroat Castle Ruins & Negro Canyon Loop** starts 17½ miles south of US 666 at Pleasant View off County Road BB, on the way to Hovenweep National Monument. The route is marked with bicycle emblem signs. You pass Cutthroat Castle Ruins on the way into Hovenweep Canyon, cross rolling hills, and the same stream several times. Then you climb out of the canyon and back down into the cottonwood groves and stream beds of Negro Canyon, before climbing several hills and returning to County Road BB.

Ute Mountain Tribal Park has rides that are similar to those offered by Mountain Bike Specialists (see above, under *Durango*), minus the outfitting services. These are run by the Ute Tribe, ☎ 970/565-3751.

Dolores River Canyon has an easy 22-mile ride along the river, with opportunities to play in the water or picnic. The route is well-marked with bicycle emblem signs. Park your car at the Dolores Canyon river access. It's 34 miles north of Cortez on US 666, then east at the sign that reads "Public Lands Access, Dolores River Canyon, and Overlook."

There are several bike trails at **McPhee Reservoir** and **House Creek Recreation Area**, but they're not well marked. It's a good idea to have topographic maps. Contact the San Juan National Forest office in Dolores, ☎ 970/533-7716, for details.

Two six-mile loops on **Ruins Road** offer easy biking to various Indian ruins at the top of Mesa Verde. It is, however, 21 miles of steep, advanced terrain from the turn-off on US 160 to the area around Chapin Mesa, where the loop roads are located. It's really crowded in the summer and not much fun sharing the narrow roads with cars, trucks, and motor homes. Try spring or fall – the weather's more comfortable, and there's much less traffic. No bicycles are allowed on the Wetherill Mesa Road, and no off-road bike travel is permitted within the national park.

For information, bike rentals, service, or sales try **Southwest Bicycle**, 450 East Main, Cortez, 81321, ☎ 970/565-3717; the **Bike Hiker**, 402 South Park, Cortez, 81321, ☎ 970/565-9342; **Kokopelli Bike & Board**, 30 West Main Street, Cortez, 81321, ☎ 970/565-4408.

On Water

Floating slowly through ancient gorges decorated with Anasazi art or racing along a whitewater river pouring out of the high country have become justifiably popular. Tours are available for an hour, two hours, a half-day, full day, or overnight for up to a week.

Durango & Silverton

The **Upper Animas**, from Silverton to Rockwood, is considered by experts to be the most exciting and advanced whitewater run available commercially in the Rockies. The stretch offers two days of expert kayaking over numerous Class V rapids, covering 28 miles of isolated, difficult, and hazardous terrain through exquisite wilderness. The next three miles after Rockwood are not navigable.

The Animas River is also called the "River of Lost Souls." About six miles north of Durango, from Trimble Lane south for 10 miles, the much slower Animas can be canoed.

The **Lower Animas**, passing through Durango, is milder still, suitable for rafts, kayaks, or canoes, although a small section south of the US 160 Bridge is not to be taken lightly. It drops through several rapids and is used for professional kayak races each spring, usually in the first week of June. Even smooth spans of river can be stimulating and risky during spring run-off (mid-May to mid-June).

The following Durango area tour companies offer river trips:

SouthWest Adventures, 780 Main Avenue, Durango, 81302, ☎ 970/259-0370 or 800/642-5389, runs two-hour or half-day river trips on the Lower Animas, rated Class III, in oar or paddle rafts. Also available is a one-day guided voyage in self-bailing rafts on the Upper Animas, rated Class IV and V, covering 12 miles of extreme, continuous whitewater. The trip includes shuttle via the narrow-gauge railroad. They also conduct one- , two- , or three-day kayak schools for beginners or experienced kayakers seeking technical proficiency.

Durango Rivertrippers, 720 Main Avenue, Durango, 81302, ☎ 970/259-0289, offers two-hour or half-day trips on the Lower Animas in oar or paddle rafts.

Mountain Waters Rafting, 108 West 6th Street, Durango, 81302, ☎ 970/259-4191 or 800/748-2507, offers two-hour, half-day, full-day, and dinner trips on the Lower Animas. A two-day Class V whitewater trip on the Upper Animas, for which a pre-trip swim and physical are required, is also available. Depending on water levels, the trip is run from late June to mid-July. They also have inflatable kayaks for the lower Animas. In Silverton, contact Mountain Waters Rafting, 1314 Greene Street.

Flexible Flyers, 2344 County Road 255, Durango, 81302, ☎ 970/247-4628, offers one- or two-hour trips on the Lower Animas.

American Adventure Expeditions, 701 Main Avenue, Durango, 81302, ☎ 970/247-4789 or 800/288-0675, runs two-hour or half-day raft trips, or two-hour trips in inflatable kayaks on the Lower Animas. Also available are one-or two-day trips on the Upper Animas. Customized multi-day trips can be arranged.

RiversWest, 520 Main Avenue, Durango, 81302, ☎ 970/259-5077, offers one-hour, two-hour, or half-day raft trips on the Lower Animas. Some of the trips include brunch.

Peregrine River Outfitters, 64 Ptarmigan Lane, Durango, 81321-6928, ☎ 970/385-7600 or 800/598-7600, fax 970/259-7600, operates one- to 11-day river trips on the Upper Animas and Dolores rivers, as well as two-hour and half-day trips on the Animas River through Durango. Trips are in oar boats or paddle boats. Also available at a small extra charge on the lower Animas trips are inflatable kayaks. Multi-day trips include meals, waterproof storage for cameras, and all river-related gear.

Watermelon Adventures, ☎ 970/946-RAFT, operates two-hour Animas River raft trips that leave from the parking lot of the Albertson's supermarket in Durango.

Among out-of-town tour operators, **Wilderness Aware Rafting**, PO Box 1550A, Buena Vista, 81211, ☎ 719/395-2112 or 800/462-7238, runs

Upper Animas and Dolores River (see below) trips for four to 18 participants.

For those determined to go it alone, **Four Corners River Sports**, 360 South Camino del Rio, Durango, 81301, ☎ 970/259-3893 or 800/426-7637, conducts novice, intermediate, and advanced whitewater kayak and canoe classes.

Telluride & Dolores

The **San Miguel River** starts near Telluride and flows 70 miles to Naturita, with some whitewater and waves in May and June. Most trips are an hour or two.

The **Dolores River** flows through steep sandstone canyons, past Anasazi ruins and petroglyphs. It is reminiscent of the desert Southwest, as opposed to the alpine flavor of other rivers in southwest Colorado. The Dolores loses its punch quickly, though; its well-known and dramatic whitewater rapids that are treacherous in May and June can be mild in July.

The **Upper Dolores** flows 37 miles from Rico to Dolores, through some of the region's prettiest mountains, into desert canyons. It's usually a two- to three-day trip. There are, however, an additional 171 miles of the river that can be floated through incredible canyon country, and containing some of the biggest rapids, such as the infamous Snaggletooth. The entire stretch can be done in around a week.

FOR MORE INFORMATION

Olympic Sports, 150 West Colorado, Telluride, CO 81435, ☎ 970/728-4477 or 800/828-7547, offers whitewater rafting trips.

Telluride Outside, 666 West Colorado, Telluride, CO 81435, ☎ 970/728-3895, operates whitewater rafting trips.

Telluride Whitewater, 224 East Colorado Avenue, Box 685, Telluride, CO 81435, ☎ 970/728-3985, runs guided one- to six-night river trips on the San Miguel, Dolores or Upper Animas rivers.

Humpback Chub River Tours, 202 South 4th Street, Dolores, CO 81323, ☎ 800/882-7940, offers river trips on the Dolores.

Four Corners Rafting, ☎ 800/332-RAFT, operates a 19-mile day-trip between Bradfield and Dove Creek on the Dolores River.

Dvorak's Kayak and Rafting Expeditions, 17921 Highway 285, Nathrop, CO 81236, ☎ 719/539-6851 or 800/824-3795, fax 719/5393378, has a number of river trips in the Four Corners.

Dolores River trips are offered for five, eight, 10, or 12 days, from mid-April to mid-June. A special eight-day "Classical Music Journey" is offered in early June, featuring daily concerts.

Echo Canyon River Expeditions, 45000 US Highway 50 West, Canon City, CO 81212, ☎ 719/275-3154 or 800/748,2953, runs early season (spring) two-day river trips on the San Miguel River, out of Telluride.

BOATING, FISHING & FLY-FISHING

Everyone over 14 years old needs a Colorado fishing license. These are available from most sporting goods stores and many convenience stores. There are several varieties of resident and non-resident licenses, including one-day or five-day licenses. For additional information contact **Colorado Division of Wildlife**, Southwest Region, 2300 South Townsend Avenue, Montrose, 81401, ☎ 970/249-3431.

Always consult local fishermen on where the fish are biting. There's generally some good fishing in the following waters:

Animas River Drainage

The Animas River offers the best fishing for rainbow and brook trout right in Durango or south of town. Fishing in the Animas River Canyon (north of Durango), accessed by Forest Service trails or the narrow-gauge railroad, is not as good, due to heavy mineralization in the water.

Cascade Creek, 26 miles north of Durango off US 550, is stocked with rainbow, brook, and cutthroat trout. Access is by Forest Service trails near Purgatory.

Florida River, northeast of Durango, above Lemon Reservoir, has good fishing for rainbow, brook, and cutthroat trout adjacent to the national forest campground.

Hermosa Creek Drainage, west of Purgatory Ski Area, has many small trout streams off various Forest Service roads and trails.

Lime Creek, accessed north of Purgatory or south of Silverton from Old Lime Creek Road, is usually worthwhile for trout fishing.

Mineral Creek, five miles west of Silverton on US 550 and County Road 585 to South Mineral Creek Campground, has good trout fishing, with lots of fisher-folk angling for rainbows and brookies.

Molas Creek, accessed via Forest Service trails from US 550 at Molas Pass, is good for brook trout fishing.

Durango & Silverton Lakes & Reservoirs

Andrews Lake (at 10,774 feet), seven miles south of Silverton on US 550, then south on a gravel access road, is a 14-acre lake stocked with rainbow and brook trout.

Clear Lake (at 12,000 feet) west of Silverton on US 550, and west on Forest Service Road 585, is a 42-acre lake stocked with rainbow and brook trout. You need a four-wheel-drive to get to the lake.

Electra Lake is a private 816-acre lake at an elevation of 8,320 feet. A fee is charged to fish for rainbow, brook, and cutthroat trout. It's 20 miles north of Durango on US 550.

Haviland Lake (at 8,100 feet) has 65 acres stocked with rainbow and brook trout. Head 19 miles north of Durango on US 550, then east on a gravel access road.

Ice Lake (at 12,260 feet) is a 15-acre lake stocked with brook trout. It's west of Silverton on US 550, then west on Forest Service Road 585 and up a steep Forest Service trail.

Lemon Reservoir is a 662-acre lake at an elevation of 8,145 feet. It's popular for rainbow and brown trout, or kokanee salmon. It is 17 miles northeast of Durango on County Road 240 to County Road 243.

Big & Little Molas Lakes are 10 miles south of Silverton on US 550. Big Molas (at 10,905 feet) is a 20-acre lake. Little Molas covers 10 acres at an elevation of 10,500 feet. Catch-and-release trout fishing is encouraged.

Vallecito Reservoir, covering 2,723 acres at 7,662 feet, is home to rainbow and brown trout, kokanee salmon, and northern pike. It's 22 miles northeast of Durango on County Road 501. There are boat ramps around the lake, as well as several commercial marinas, including the following:

❑ **Angler's Wharf**, 17250, County Road 501, Bayfield, 81122, ☎ 970/884-9477. Located at the north end of Vallecito Reservoir; services include boat rentals for fishing or pleasure, pontoon boats, canoes, and paddle boats, information on daily fishing conditions, free fishing instructions, guide services, as well as equipment sales and rentals, licenses and bait.

❑ **Shorty's Vallecito Marina**, 14518 County Road 501, Bayfield, 81122, ☎ 970/884-2768 or 303/884-4161. Services offered include fishing licenses, public boat ramp, docking facilities and mooring, free fishing lessons, equipment rental, tackle and bait sales, and fishing or pontoon boat rentals.

❑ **Mountain Marina,** 14810 County Road 501, Bayfield, 81122, ☎ 970/884-9450 or 970/884-9389. They rent fishing boats, pontoon boats, pleasure boats, canoes, fishing gear, guides, and sell tackle, bait and licenses.

Pine River Drainage

The **Pine River,** south of Vallecito Reservoir, is accessed via paved and gravel roads. North of the reservoir, access is via Forest Service trails. Catch-and-release trout fishing is encouraged.

East Creek, east of Vallecito Reservoir, contains brook trout. It is accessed via Forest Service trails.

Vallecito Creek is accessed via Forest Service trails north of the reservoir. Catch-and-release trout fishing is encouraged.

Ouray & Ridgway

A number of stocked lakes include the following:

Ptarmigan Lake, below Imogene Pass.

East Dallas Lake, at the Willow Swamps Campground, is four miles west of Ridgway, then seven miles south on East Dallas Divide Road.

Silver Jack Reservoir is 12 miles north of Ouray on US 550, then east on Forest Service Road 858.

Ridgway Reservoir, 15 miles north of Ridgway on US 550, has a full-service marina and boat ramp.

Telluride

The **San Miguel River,** west of Telluride to Placerville, is stocked in July. Fly-fishing for rainbow, brown, cutthroat, and brook trout is good between Telluride and Norwood.

Other potentially trout-filled waters include:

Leopard Creek, west of Dallas Divide, toward Placerville, to the San Miguel River.

Alta Lakes, southwest of Telluride off CO 145.

Trout Lake, set at 10,000 feet, south of Telluride, allows boats.

Dolores & Rico

Bear Creek, northeast of Dolores and Mancos, is accessed via Forest Service trails. Catch-and-release trout fishing is encouraged.

Coal Creek, between Rico and Lizard Head Pass, contains rainbow trout and is accessed through Dunton.

Roaring Forks, northeast of Priest Gulch on CO 145, contains cutthroat trout and is accessed via Forest Service Road 435.

The **Dolores River**, which starts high in the mountains, near Lizard Head Pass, travels through Rico, along CO 145 to Dolores and McPhee Reservoir. It is considered one of the best 100 trout streams in America for rainbows, snakeriver cutthroats, and German browns, many in the three- to four-pound range. It offers Gold Medal trophy fly-fishing for trout on the 12-mile stretch of river from McPhee Dam to the bridge on County Road 505, known as Bradfield Bridge.

Fishermen may use flies and artificial lures only, and everything you catch here must be thrown back. Westward from Bradfield Bridge you may keep your limit of browns or rainbows, without limitation on the type of tackle used.

Dolores River & Tributaries

West Fork of the Dolores, between Dolores and Dunton along Forest Service Road 536, is stocked with rainbow, brown, and cutthroat trout. Camping is available.

Barlow Creek, northeast of Rico off CO 145, contains native trout.

Stoner Creek, north of Dolores on CO 145, contains rainbow and brook trout and is accessed by Forest Service trails.

Taylor Creek, also north of Dolores on CO 145 and also containing rainbow and brook trout, is accessed by a gravel road, Forest Service Road 545.

Lake & Reservoir Fishing

Ground Hog Reservoir, 32 miles north of Dolores on paved Forest Service Road 526 to gravel Forest Service Road 533, contains rainbow and cutthroat trout in 668 acres and is set at 8,718 feet. There is a boat ramp, marina (motors are permitted), and there are campsites as well as modest cabin rentals available. The area may be closed in early spring or late fall if there has been heavy snow.

Jackson Gulch Reservoir, a 216-acre lake set at 7,822 feet, is six miles northeast of **Mancos** on County Road 42, at Mancos State Recreation

Area. There is a boat ramp for access to rainbow trout and small yellow perch. Camping is available.

Joe Moore Reservoir, five miles north of Mancos on CO 184 and County Road 40, is 45 acres, set at 7,688 feet. Best fishing is in early summer for rainbow trout, largemouth bass, perch, crappie, bluegill, and green sunfish.

McPhee Reservoir is northwest of Dolores on CO 184. It features cold- and warm-water fishing and it's stocked with trout, kokanee salmon, largemouth and smallmouth bass, perch, bluegill and catfish. Boat and equipment rentals and guide services are available from Beaver Creek Marina, ☎ 970/882-2258, and there is a no-wake zone exclusively for canoeists. Bass 15 inches and under must be released.

Puett Reservoir is 14 miles northwest of Mancos on CO 184. It's a 145-acre lake at 7,260 feet elevation. A rough road keeps many away from fishing for walleye, yellow perch and northern pike. There is a boat ramp and camping is available.

Summit Reservoir is 11 miles northwest of Mancos on CO 184. It's 350 acres and is at 7,386 feet elevation. Restrictions apply to fishing for rainbow trout, smallmouth bass, channel catfish, and crappie. There is a boat ramp and camping is available.

Toten Reservoir is two miles east of Cortez on US 160, then north on County Road 29. It's a 220-acre lake at 6,156 feet elevation, with warmer water than high mountain lakes, so it can be stocked with walleye, bluegill, yellow perch, crappie, and largemouth bass. There is a boat ramp.

OUTFITTERS

Duranglers, 801B Main Avenue, Durango, CO 81301, ☎ 970/385-4081. This is a full-service fly-fishing store, offering equipment sales and rentals, custom fly-tying, up-to-the-minute stream reports, and guided trips.

Rocky Mountain High Tours, ☎ 970/247-0807, with bases in Durango, Purgatory and Silverton, offers single-day or multi-day wilderness fly-fishing tours. Equipment rentals are available, along with fly-fishing instruction.

Don Oliver Fishing Guide, PO Box 3448, Durango, CO 81302, ☎ 970/382-0364, offers customized half-day or full-day fly-fishing trips which include flies and lunch. Equipment rentals and fly-fishing instructions are available.

Anasazi Angler, 607 Sunnyside Drive, Durango, CO 81302, ☎ 970/385-4665, offers professionally guided wade and float trips.

Animas Anglers, 720 East 7th Avenue, Durango, CO 81031, ☎ 970/247-2250 or 970/259-0999, specializes in wade and float trips.

Fly-fishing Durango, Inc., 255 Valle Avenue, Durango, CO 81302, ☎ 970/382-0478, offers guided fishing trips on the San Juan River and overnight fishing trips in the San Juan Mountains.

Olympic Sports, 150 West Colorado, Telluride, CO 81435, ☎ 970/728-4477 or 800/828-7547, offers guide services and fly-fishing schools, rental equipment, licenses, and expert advice on local fishing.

Telluride Outside, 666 West Colorado, Telluride, CO 81435, ☎ 970/728-3895, offers guided trophy fly-fishing trips on the San Miguel, Dolores and San Juan rivers, or on mountain lakes. Also offered are one- , two- , or three-day fly-fishing schools, featuring instruction in casting, entomology, reading the water, fly-tying, vernacular of fly-fishing, presenting the fly, equipment, and knot tying. After your lessons you practice techniques on the San Miguel River and mountain lakes. Also: Licenses, supplies, flies and gear rentals, as well as winter fly-fishing trips on the San Juan River below Navajo Lake.

Sawpit Fly & Rod Co., PO Box 344, Placerville, CO 81430, ☎ 970/728-6011, is one mile west of Telluride on CO 145, offering flies, supplies, guides, rentals, as well as custom rods, remote belly boating, and horseback trips.

Tellair Inc., PO Box 2130, Telluride, CO 81435, ☎ 970/728-5358, offers customized, guided fly-in fishing trips on the San Juan River in New Mexico, the Green River in Utah, and other sites.

The Outfitter, 410 Railroad Avenue, Dolores, CO 81323, ☎ 970/882-7740, offers guided fly-fishing trips on the Quality Waters of the Dolores River.

The Tackle Shack, 11290 CO 145, Cortez, CO 81321, ☎ 970/565-6090, offers fishing and marine supplies, live bait, camping gear, and water sports items.

HOT SPRINGS

Mineral-laden hot water flowing from underground springs soothes the body and the mind – especially after a tiring day in the mountains.

Trimble Hot Springs, 6475 County Road 203, Durango, 81301, ☎ 970/247-0111, fax 970/247-4493, offers modern services at a historic mineral hot springs. It is a National Historic Site and was reputedly frequented by Ute Chief Ouray in the 19th century, as well as by a 20th-century celebrity clientele, including Marilyn Monroe. An old hotel on the site burned down long ago. The facilities, which are open year-round, include an Olympic-size natural hot springs pool, a therapy pool, private hot tubs, massage therapy, body and skin treatments, physical therapy, and a fitness program including yoga instruction. Each summer, in July, Trimble hosts a weekend-long jazz festival. You can stay cool swimming, or soak and perspire while listening to hot jazz, some provided by nationally known artists.

Wiesbaden Lodge, PO Box 349 (6th Avenue and 5th Street), Ouray, 81427, ☎ 970/325-4347, is a motel situated directly over a geothermal spring. The facility includes a steamy, shallow, underground vapor cave and an outdoor swimming pool heated by the hot springs. The pool's warm enough for swimming outdoors throughout the year, even in mid-winter with snow piled high all around.

On Snow

There's usually more than enough snow for several months of winter sports in southwestern Colorado, with many areas averaging more than 300 inches yearly. Of course, it doesn't fall at one time, but it does tend to accumulate until spring. Planning a winter trip between January and March would give you excellent odds of encountering prodigious white stuff for all your snow-time pursuits.

Downhill ski areas are well-maintained and carefully patrolled. Cross-country skiing is becoming increasingly popular, but be warned that backcountry routes can be both spectacular and dangerous. Careful preparation and extra caution are highly recommended. A variety of other snow sports are also available through outfitters or on your own. Equipment rentals are available at the ski areas or from numerous shops in Durango, Ouray, Telluride, or other communities.

DOWNHILL SKIING

Some people consider the powder terrain in these parts to be the best you can find anywhere.

Purgatory-Durango Ski Resort, PO Box 166, Durango, 81302, ☎ 970/247-9000 or 800/525-0892. Located 26 miles north of Durango on US 550, Purgatory seems to have been in the throes of management problems for most of the last decade – that is until the newest regime at the ski area. These guys have virtually transformed Purgatory into a world-class ski destination. Among other things, Purgatory was instrumental in guaranteeing American Airlines enough money to offer daily jet service between Durango and Dallas in the winter. These convenient flights, providing more direct access to Durango from virtually everywhere, are now available from December 15 to March 30. Another package is offered in conjunction with Southwest Airlines, consisting of inexpensive flights to and from Albuquerque, a rental car to drive to and from Purgatory (around 200 miles each way), lift tickets and accommodations.

With new lift construction completed in 1995, Purgatory offers better access to all parts of the mountain for skiers, including experts. And the resort continues to increase its snow-making capability.

Purgatory's bread and butter is and always will be its gorgeous alpine terrain, fantastic weather (it's generally 10-15° warmer this far south, as compared with more northerly Rockies ski areas) and reliable intermediate powder skiing provided by an average of around 300 inches of snow each winter. A new quad speed-lift, four triple chairlifts and five double chairlifts provide access to 75 trails spread over 745 acres of ski terrain. Vertical drop is 2,029 feet, and the terrain is 20% beginner, 50% intermediate, 30% advanced. Facilities include a ski school, equipment rentals, nursery, slope-side condominiums, snowmobiling, sleigh rides, and groomed cross-country ski trails.

☞ A big thing for families is that children under 12 can ski for free. Other package deals are equally attractive, a rarity in an industry where raising the price of lift tickets yearly is more predictable than snow. One of Purgatory's packages is called a Total Ticket and is included with any purchase of a four-day or longer lift ticket. With this deal guests can exchange one day of skiing for any of seven activities. These include a ticket on the Durango & Silverton Narrow Gauge Train, a tour to Mesa Verde National Park, a day at Trimble Hot Springs, a dinner sleigh ride, a snowmobile tour, cross-country skiing, or gambling at the Sky Ute Casino.

Hesperus Ski Area, 9848 US 160, Hesperus, 81326, ☎ 970/259-3711. This little ski hill, 12 miles west of Durango on US 160, has a vertical drop of only 900 feet, but it's steep. Lift tickets are about half the cost of those at Purgatory or Telluride, and there are lights for night skiing until 9:30PM. The area is mostly used by local kids and you feel as if this is your private mountain. Cross-country trails are nearby.

Telluride Ski Resort, PO Box 307, Telluride, 81435, ☎ 970/728-3856 (for snow reports ☎ 970/728-3614). Telluride offers one high-speed quad-lift, two triple chairs, six double chairs, and one poma lift to 62 trails spread over 1,050 acres. A gondola connects the town of Telluride with the Mountain Village. Close access to the mountain is available from the center of town or from the Telluride Mountain Village.

The area contains 21% beginner, 47% intermediate, and 32% advanced terrain, including some of the steepest slopes in the Colorado Rockies. The vertical drop is 3,522 feet and the longest run is nearly three miles. Facilities include a ski school, equipment rentals, and a nursery. The area sponsors weekly NASTAR races, maintains groomed cross-country trails, and offers helicopter skiing, snowmobiling, hockey, ice skating, and sleigh rides.

Telluride has skiing on three mountain faces for different levels of ability. This includes 400 acres on Gold Hill for expert skiers, providing a real backcountry ski experience, complete with glades and chutes. The ski area is well-run and the scenery here is incomparable.

Accommodations can sometimes be scarce in little Telluride, so the ski area has teamed up with local communities to offer packages, including out-of-town lodging with half-price lift tickets. See below, under *Accommodations*, for participating properties in Ridgway, Ouray, Rico, Dolores and Cortez.

If you need rental equipment for downhill skiing, numerous shops in Durango or Telluride, or at the ski areas, provide rental equipment. As for cross-country ski gear, telemark equipment, snowshoes, and snowboard, all this and more is readily available from shops throughout southwest Colorado. Copious listings are available from tourist offices or the ski areas.

CROSS-COUNTRY SKIING

The following listings include some of the most scenic and safest cross-country ski routes in southwestern Colorado. Groomed trails are generally perfectly safe, but remember that backcountry conditions are unpredictable and can change rapidly; on the spot research is essential before any backcountry ski trip.

Foremost, consider the weather. It can turn from clear to stormy before you know it, obliterating a trail and an unprepared skier's sense of direction in minutes. Sunny, warm days may provide glorious ski conditions but can also increase avalanche dangers after heavy snowfall.

The current snowpack needs to be considered, particularly in relation to wind conditions, which may have a profound effect on your pleasure and safety.

On any cross-country ski trip, dress warmly with layered clothing. Carry high energy foods, and be prepared for the worst, so you can have the best time.

Durango & Silverton

Hillcrest Golf Course, 2300 Rim Drive, Durango, 81301, ☎ 970/247-1499, is at the top of College Drive (6th Street) in Durango. The undulating hills and flats are great for cross-country skiing and overlook the fairy tale, snow-covered town.

Bear Ranch, 42570 US 550, Durango, 81301, ☎ 970/247-0111, is practically across the street from Purgatory Resort. Groomed cross-country trails are available, along with sleigh rides.

The **San Juan National Forest** contains numerous backcountry ski trails, but knowledge of snow and avalanche conditions is essential. The trails around Haviland Lake, 17 miles north of Durango on US 550, are good for beginners who can ski near the campground area. Check out some of the hiking and jeep trails listed above for other ideas, or consult with Forest Service personnel. ☎ 970/247-4874 for rates and ski conditions. **Tamarron Resort**, 40252 US 550, Durango, 81301, ☎ 970/259-2000 or 800/678-1000, has a hilly, championship golf course used for cross-country skiing in winter.

Purgatory Nordic Center, at Purgatory-Durango Ski Area (see above), features 16 kilometers of machine-groomed tracks.

The Silverton area offers many more miles of diverse and challenging cross-country ski terrain. Avalanche dangers are usually high, but there are certain safer areas. There are numerous trails fanning out from Molas Pass, six miles south of Silverton on US 550. One fairly easy trail leads to Little Molas Lake, on the west side of the Highway and a half-mile up a snow-covered road.

South Mineral Creek Road (near Silverton), from US 550 to the Forest Service campground, offers five miles of easy terrain.

Ouray

Red Mountain Pass is a serious cross-country skiers' haven. You can usually see ski tracks all over the place, but these are left by knowledgeable backcountry skiers. St. Paul Lodge (see below under *Accom-*

modations) offers rustic backcountry accommodations and challenging cross-country ski terrain, but not for rank beginners.

There are hundreds more miles of cross-country ski trails around Ouray and Ridgway. Ouray has formed the Ouray County Nordic Council to coordinate a system of trails in the Ironton/Red Mountain Pass area south of town, which has easy-to-challenging terrain. Get information and equipment rentals from local sport shops or the **Ouray Visitor Center**, Box 145, Ouray, 81427, ☎ 970/325-4746 or 800/228-1876.

Ridgway, Telluride, Rico & Dolores

East Dallas Creek Trail is five miles west of Ridgway off CO 62, to County Road 7. You can drive up the road for a few miles, then ski five miles farther. It is fairly steep, but lacking in the extreme avalanche danger found on other routes. It's a lot easier coming down than going up.

San Juan Hut Systems, Box 1663, 117 North Willow Street, Telluride, 81435, ☎ 970/728-6935, maintains an extensive, demanding cross-country, telemark and nordic trail system between Telluride and Ouray. They operate five rustic ski huts placed strategically between the towns, approximately a one-day ski apart, or huts may be accessed individually via Forest Service roads or hiking trails. Huts have padded bunks, propane cook stove, propane lamp, wood stove, firewood, and all necessary kitchen implements. You melt snow for water. Latrines are little more than stumps you hold onto while balancing over a hole in the snow. Sleeping bags can be rented and food can be provided, along with guide services.

The hut system is designed to accommodate skiers of all abilities, but we recommend intermediate skiing skills at the least. Above each hut is terrain for advanced, intermediate, expert, and extreme powder skiing, or telemark skiing.

All skiers must be aware of changing weather conditions, as well as snow and avalanche conditions. This is not light touring terrain; it requires nordic skis with metal edges. You need to pack extra clothing, sufficient food, and any gear you might need for unexpected weather conditions or an emergency bivouac. A full line of rental equipment is available, including avalanche transceivers and shovels.

There are 15 kilometers of groomed cross-country trails at the top of the **Telluride Ski Area's Sunshine Express Lift**, as well as another 15 kilometers of groomed trails at the **Telluride Mountain Village Golf Course**.

Cross-country skiing around **Lizard Head Pass** can also be splendid but hazardous along backcountry trails. Avalanche danger is low if you stick to the huge open meadows on either side of CO 145. **Cross Mountain Trail** starts on the west side of the Highway, two miles south of Lizard Head Pass, and is a mostly uphill trail for 1,200 feet. It is four miles to the recommended turn-around point at a level clearing. Avalanche danger increases beyond this point, but the eight-mile round trip is a good intermediate to advanced route.

There's good intermediate terrain around **Dunton**. A four-wheel-drive is required to reach areas north of Dunton on West Fork Road, 33 miles north of Dolores, or via CO 145 to Dunton Road (Forest Service Road 535), and 20 miles west to Dunton. Park at the end of the plowed road. You can ski on Forest Service Road 535, past the intersection with Forest Service Road 611, bearing right after two miles to head toward Burro Bridge Campground. An alternative route for novice skiers starts the same way but bears left on Forest Service Road 611. The first mile of skiing is through aspen glades and into open meadows; beyond is hilly telemark skiing terrain in sight of Dolores Peak.

Scotch Creek, 2½ miles south of Rico off CO 145 on the east side of the Highway, is a historic toll road once used to carry supplies to the Rico mining district. The novice/beginner trail follows the left side of the creek for three miles, passing between high canyon walls. Turn around where the trail crosses the creek.

Taylor Mesa is 15 miles south of Scotch Creek, north of CO 145. A seven-mile beginner/intermediate trail climbs gradually through evergreens, aspen, and cottonwoods for 3½ miles to Little Taylor Trail on the right. It gets steeper beyond this point, so beginners may want to turn back. Stronger skiers can continue up Taylor Creek.

Boggy Draw Norwood Road, north of Dolores, offers up to 20 miles of gently rolling terrain along unplowed roads and open fields suitable for family outings. Follow Forest Service Road 526 north from Dolores to the intersection with Forest Service Road 527. Ski north on the Norwood Road or east on 527.

Mesa Verde National Park & Mancos

The entrance road to Mesa Verde National Park is plowed in winter, but other park roads are not. You can drive up to the empty **Morefield Campground** and ski around there on a mile or so of easy terrain. Alternatively, continue up the main road for 20 miles to **Chapin Mesa**. Atop the mesa, you can ski around the park's Ruins Road on the six-mile **Balcony House Loop**. Snowfall is generally not too heavy here and may not remain on the ground terribly long. Call the park, ☎ 970/529-4461, 970/529-4475 or 970/529-4465, for snow conditions and required permission to ski.

Chicken Creek Canyon, 1½ miles north of Mancos on CO 184, then three miles farther on Chicken Creek Road, offers 20 miles of maintained trails for all levels of skiers. These include six miles of double-track and skate lanes, as well as five miles of single-track in various loops and spurs. These are the only groomed trails in the area. Detailed maps are available from stores in the town of Mancos.

Railroad Trail is 5½ miles east of Mancos on US 160, at the summit of Mancos Hill. Drive north a quarter-mile to the end of the plowed road and park there. You can ski on Forest Service Road 316 for a mile, then turn east (right) onto Forest Service Road 568, which is eight miles one-way. The trail follows an old railroad grade through an oak brush plateau and aspen groves, dropping 480 feet in the last mile to the Cherry Creek Picnic Area. An alternative is to ski uphill for six to eight miles on Forest Service Road 316, but this route is only recommended for advanced or strong skiers.

SNOWMOBILING, DOGSLEDDING, ICE CLIMBING & SLEIGH RIDES

There are hundreds of miles of snowmobile trails in southwestern Colorado. Snowmobile tours are available from Purgatory-Durango Ski Resort and Telluride Ski Resort.

Durango Snowmobile Adventures, 2206 County Road 207, Durango, 81302, ☎ 970/247-0271, offers guided snowmobile tours in the San Juan Mountains.

Ice Pirates, 47 Electra Lake Road, Durango, 81302, ☎ 970/247-8923, runs "unique and unusual snowmobile adventures."

Telluride Outside, 666 West Colorado, Telluride, 81435, ☎ 970/728-3895, also has snowmobile tours, including one- or three-hour dinner tours to Skyline Ranch and full evening dinner tours to the Alta Lakes Observatory. They will customize tours to suit your needs.

Red Hot Ryders Jeep & Snowmobile Rentals, 5th & Main Street, PO Box 732, Ouray, 81427, ☎ 970/325-0350 or 800/325-4385, features snowmobiling at elevations ranging from 7,000-12,000 feet on a parcel of private property covering 17,000 acres. They also have winter wildlife jeep tours.

Customized trips are offered by **Sunset Kennels Dog Sled Rides**, 25 Sunset Acres, Hesperus, 81326, ☎ 970/588-3641. Also available are one-hour, half-day, or overnight trips.

Winter Moon Sled Dog Adventures, c/o Telluride Outside, runs one-hour, half-day, and full-day dogsled tours. It also offers private dogsledding lessons.

SouthWest Adventures, 780 Main Avenue, Durango, 81302, ☎ 970/259-0370 or 800/642-5389, teaches scheduled two- to five-day classes in alpine ice climbing and waterfall ice climbing. Other ice courses and private guiding are available.

Ouray is known around the world for its ice climbing on Box Canyon Falls and more than a dozen other accessible areas for ice climbing. This is quite serious stuff, requiring ropes and harnesses. Contact the **Visitor Center**, Box 145, Ouray, 81427, ☎ 970/325-4746, for information.

One- to five-day courses in technical ice climbing, winter peak ascents, and guided alpine tour services are offered by **Fantasy Ridge Mountain Guides**, PO Box 1679, Telluride, 81435, ☎ 970/728-3546. Also available: technical summer rock climbing instruction and non-technical ascents to 14,000-foot peaks.

Horse-drawn sleigh rides are offered by **Mayday Livery**, 4317 County Road 124, Hesperus, 81326, ☎ 970/385-6772, and **Buck's Livery**, US 550 at Purgatory, Durango, 81301, ☎ 970/385-2110.

Deep Creek Sleigh Rides of Telluride, 130 West Colorado, Telluride, 81435, ☎ 970/728-3565, offers sleigh rides twice each evening. A steak dinner served in a heated tent is included.

In the Air

Durango Soaring Club, Inc., 27290 Highway 550, Durango, 81301, ☎ 970/247-9037, offers glider rides over the Animas Valley from an airfield three miles north of Durango. Thirty- or 60-minute flights are available seven days a week, May 15 to October 15.

Gregg Flying Service, Animas Air Park, Durango, 81302, ☎ 970/247-4632, has scenic flights or airplane charters to locations throughout the Four Corners and as far as the Grand Canyon from a small airfield a few miles south of town. Also: flight instruction and aircraft maintenance services.

Durango Air Service, La Plata Field, Durango, 81301, ☎ 970/247-5535, offers scenic flights for a minimum of two people from an airport

15 miles southeast of town. Charters and airplane rentals, flight instruction, and aircraft maintenance services are also available.

New Air Helicopters, PO Box 3268, Flight Line Road, Animas Air Park, Durango, 81302, ☎ 970/259-6247, has helicopters for charter and offers scenic tours of 15 or 30 minutes in speedy jet helicopters that cover a lot of ground in a short time. A novel idea is to ride the narrow-gauge train to Silverton and arrange for a helicopter flight back to Durango – the best of both worlds. Other services include photo tours and remote site transportation.

Air Durango, PO Box 2138, Durango, 81302, ☎ 970/385-1749, offers year-round hot-air balloon flights every day (weather permitting). To take advantage of the calmest weather of the day, launches take place at 6:30AM from the Durango High School parking lot on Main Avenue. Typical one- to 1½-hour flights float over Durango and the train station, revealing the mountainous terrain that surrounds the city and the Animas Valley, landing south of town. A traditional champagne toast is included.

New West Adventures, PO Box 2744, Durango, 81302, ☎ 970/385-4940 or 800/748-1188, and **Rocky Mountain High Tours**, ☎ 970/247-0807, can book balloon flights.

San Juan Balloon Adventures, PO Box 66, Ridgway, 81432, ☎ 970/626-5495, or 970/728-3895 (in Telluride), or 800/831-6230, offers hot-air balloon flights of a half-hour, one hour, or a deluxe Balloon 'n Brunch flight over the Ridgway Valley.

Telluride Soaring, Telluride Regional Airport, ☎ 970/728-5424, 970/728-3895 or 800/831-6230, offers glider rides over what they claim to be "the most spectacular scenery in the country." They may be right.

Mesa Verde Soaring, ☎ 970/565-6164, at Cortez Airport, three miles south of Cortez on US 160, offers sailplane rides over the world of the Anasazi Indians.

Cortez Flying Service, PO Box 997, Cortez, 81321, ☎ 970/565-3721, offers scenic flights and charter services in fixed-wing aircraft.

Eco-Travel & Cultural Excursions

DURANGO

American Southwest Adventures, PO Box 3471, Durango, 81302, ☎ 970/247-5274 (or contact Durango Travel, 563 Main Avenue, 81301, ☎ 970/259-0090 or 800/748-2021), offers customized educational and photographic tours of one day or longer throughout the Four Corners region. Itineraries include sites such as Mesa Verde, Ute Mountain Tribal Park, Chaco Canyon, Monument Valley, Canyon de Chelly, canyons of southeastern Utah and numerous ghost towns. Their focus is on photography, ecology, wildlife, and Native American cultural history. The trips, which include transportation in an air-conditioned four-wheel-drive, lunch, entrance fees, and photographic assistance, are led by an environmental education specialist who is also a professional photographer. Reservations are required.

Durango Pro Rodeo, PO Box 299, Durango, 81302, ☎ 970/247-1666. A pro rodeo takes place Tuesday and Wednesday nights, from early June to late September, at the La Plata County Fairgrounds, 25th Street and Main Avenue, Durango. The competition features all seven rodeo events: calf roping, saddle bronc riding, bareback riding, bull riding, bull dogging, team roping, and barrel racing.

Hiss the villain at the **Diamond Circle Theatre**, 699 Main Avenue, PO Box 3041, Durango, 81302, ☎ 970/247-3400, which features live turn-of-the-century melodramas from early June to late September.

Bar D Chuckwagon, 8080 County Road 250, Durango, 81301, ☎ 970/247-5753, offers a popular chuckwagon supper of barbecue beef, beans, and biscuits, and a Western show that's been running every summer for more than 25 years. The show includes original songs, Western classics, yodeling, and comedy skits. There's also a miniature train ride, art gallery, leather shop, t-shirt store, blacksmith shop, and a record shop selling Bar D Wrangler records.

There is not a great deal of nightlife in the Durango area, but one of the most popular spots on summer evenings is a throwback to simpler times, the **Rocket Drive-In Theatre**, 26126 US Highway 160, Durango, ☎ 970/247-0833. The sound from small clip-on speakers is tinny, but where else can you see a double feature these days? Basically, the whole town comes out for these shows, so the audience is a show in itself. Children under 12 usually get in for free, and the intermission snackbar trailers, exhorting viewers to extricate themselves from their cars for hot dogs, popcorn and soft drinks, appear to be authentic 1950s vintage.

There are quite a number of Western bars in Durango, making bar-hopping a cultural experience of its own. The classic **Diamond Belle Saloon**, 699 Main Avenue, Durango, 81301, ☎ 970/247-4431, makes you feel as if you are entering Dodge City when you pass through its swinging doors. Inside, a honky-tonk pianist is pounding the ivories. Bar girls are dressed in scanty 1880s costumes. Even the male bartenders wear garters on their sleeves.

Sundance Saloon, 601 East 2nd Avenue, ☎ 970/247-8821, features live country Western dance music, or country rock, Monday through Saturday nights.

Some of the clubs where you are likely to find bands playing are:

Farquahrts, 725 Main Avenue, Durango, ☎ 970/247-5440, features nightly live entertainment, usually rock 'n roll or reggae bands.

The Silver Saddle, 3416 Main Avenue, Durango, ☎ 970/382-2702.

Horny's Dancehall & Saloon, 800 South Camino del Rio, Durango, ☎ 970-382-8217, actually keeps a longhorn cow penned outside while nationally known country bands perform inside.

Billygoat Saloon, 38948 US 160, Bayfield, ☎ 970/994-9155, is 15 miles east of Durango in the small town of Gem Village. It looks a lot like a 1960s-style biker bar/roadhouse and frequently offers live music.

SILVERTON

A Theatre Group, 1069 Greene Street (upstairs in the American Legion Building), Silverton, 81433, ☎ 970/387-5337 or 800/752-4494, is one of Colorado's few year-round mountain-town theatre companies, comprised of local, university, and professional talent.

OURAY & RIDGWAY

San Juan Odyssey, Main Street at 5th Avenue (the Old Opera House), Ouray, 81427, ☎ 970/325-4607, uses five screens, 15 projectors, and surround-sound stereo to bring the San Juans to you.

Chipeta Opry Show, 630 Main Street, Ouray, 81427, ☎ 970/325-7354 or 800/356-8729, is a two-hour live variety show offered nightly from Memorial Day (late May) to mid-October. The performance's Western theme manages to include an Elvis impersonator and a patriotic gospel finale.

The Big Barn Entertainment Emporium, CO 52 at US 550 in Trail Town, PO Box 257, Ridgway, 81432-0257, ☎ 970/626-3600, is a family-style, Western dancehall.

TELLURIDE

Skiing is the winter activity that revived the prosperity of Telluride, but in summer, a weekly roster of festivals lures thousands of people to town. During the biggest events, such as the Bluegrass, Jazz or Film Festivals, every room in town is booked months in advance, so plan early if you want to participate, or be prepared to camp out or stay somewhere out of town. Contact the **Telluride Chamber Resort Association** (PO Box 653, 666 West Colorado Avenue, Telluride, 81435, ☎ 970/728-3041, fax 970/728-6475) for updated information.

TELLURIDE FESTIVALS

Festivals vary from the wildly popular to the obscure, and schedules change each summer, but here is a sampling of what you might expect in a typical year.

Native American Writer's Forum features workshops, discussions, and readings.

Steps to Awareness includes 30 workshops related to self-generated healing, including topics such as native herbal remedies, shamanism and birthing.

Mountainfilm offers movies and discussions devoted to mountain adventure and the environment.

A *Balloon Festival* features hot-air balloons over the valley.

Talking Gourds is a cross-cultural gathering of poets, storytellers, and performance artists, offering three days of discussions, workshops, and presentations.

The *Telluride Theatre Festival* includes theatrical seminars and presentations in acting, playwriting, direction, and design.

The *Telluride Bicycle Classic* features pro-am races.

The *Telluride Bluegrass Festival* is one of the biggest local events of the year; attendance is limited to 10,000 and it's always a sell-out. Outdoor performances in Town Park are by well-known and aspiring banjo pickers, mandolin manipulators, and other sympathetic performers. There are also workshops for adults and children.

Deep West Arts Circuit offers modern dance performances.

A **Telluride Mountain Bike Festival** features organized group bike rides, bike polo, bike rodeo, and pro races.

Telluride Wine Festival includes tastings, matching wines with foods, and a champagne brunch.

KOTO Community Concert Series features outdoor concerts sponsored by a local radio station.

Fireman's Fourth of July is just an excuse for a traditional small town celebration, including a parade, children's games, rides on an antique fire truck, a barbecue, and after-dark fireworks.

Lunar Cup Ski Race features pros and amateurs competing at 12,500 feet in dual slalom, telemark, and snowboard events – in July!

Shakespeare on the Shellman Stage is performed by the Telluride Repertory Theatre in Town Park.

The **Superwinch/Rotary Club 4x4 Tour** includes guided off-road driving.

A **Telluride Ideas Festival** has featured workshops on creating a sustainable rural community.

The **Telluride Jazz Celebration** is a weekend of music, with some big names, performed outdoors in an incomparable setting.

A **Chamber Music Festival** features intimate concerts.

Jimmy Huega's Mountain Bike Express has three-person teams competing in a four-hour relay marathon.

The **Telluride Mushroom Festival** is actually one of the longer running festivals, now featuring a parade, a cook-and-taste feast, mushroom-hunting expeditions, and workshops on edible, poisonous, and psychoactive mushrooms.

Magic Arts Festival closes the streets downtown for Western arts displays, street performers, and magicians.

The **Telluride Film Festival** is internationally renowned. Screenings include national and international premieres, world archive treasures, experimental films, retrospectives, and three yearly tributes. Screenings and accommodations are booked solid far in advance by a mix of Hollywood and international film celebrities, critics, and hard-core film-goers.

The **Imogene Pass Run** covers 18 miles over the 13,000-foot pass.

A yearly **Living in Harmony Concert** is organized by Peter, of Peter, Paul & Mary, and features the folk singer performing along with children and local musicians.

A **Hang Gliding Festival** draws the world's top pilots. They come year after year for this week of high flying, which includes the World Aerobatic Hang Gliding Championships.

A **Behind Closed Doors Home Tour** visits historic and contemporary houses, which are opened to the public for a weekend during the prime foliage season.

A **Telluride One-World Festival** has international music by top stars from all over the world in Town Park and local clubs.

A **Wild West Weekend** celebrates the days of the Old West, with cowboys, Indians and a smattering of Hollywood celebrities on hand to raise money for the Telluride Arts Foundation. Scheduled events include a rodeo, chuckwagon barbecue, dances, and live music.

The **Telluride Brewer's Festival** features numerous micro-brewery beers and live music.

As much fun as all this is, at the insistence of vociferous local residents, one weekend each summer is set aside for a **Nothing Festival**. Nothing special is planned.

Tours, Classes & Programs

Telluride Outside, 666 West Colorado, Telluride, 81435, ☎ 970/728-3895, runs two-hour geologist-guided expeditions for stream-side gold panning and special geology tours to explain the processes that formed the region.

Telluride Institute, PO Box 1770, 283 South Fir Street, Telluride, 81435, ☎ 970/728-4402, fax 970/728-4919, is a non-profit think tank that sponsors the Deep West Arts Circuit, with performing, composing and other creative arts programs. Regional studies and education programs are also offered.

The **Ah Haa School For the Arts**, PO Box 1590, 135 South Spruce, Telluride, 81435, ☎ 970/728-3886, offers classes for adults and children in painting, ceramics, photography, bookmaking, drawing, print making, silver casting, basket making, creative writing, and other subjects.

Herb Walker Tours, PO Box 399, Telluride, 81435, ☎ 970/728-4538 or 970/728-4559, runs educational herb/nature hikes. Participants learn to identify and use wild plants and mushrooms while exploring the many trails in the Telluride area. These hikes range from leisurely walks in town to climbing in the high country. Topics include how to differentiate between poisonous and beneficial plants, medicinal/culinary uses, folklore, and preparation.

Nightlife

Nightlife is pretty lively in Telluride. Among the options available within three or four blocks of Colorado Avenue are the following:

Fly Me To The Moon Saloon, 132 East Colorado Avenue, Telluride, ☎ 970/728-6666, is considered by some to be Colorado's best nightclub. It features a springboard dance floor and live music.

One World Café has live music from around the world.

Club B.I.O.T.A. (Blame It On The Altitude), revels in live bluegrass music and country dancing lessons.

Café Kokopelli, features good coffee and live jazz.

San Juan Brewing Company, and **Baked & Brewed in Telluride** serve locally brewed beers. See below, under *Restaurants*.

The Sheridan Bar, 231 West Colorado Avenue, Telluride, ☎ 970/728-3911, is part of an old historic hotel, and it feels a lot like the old west, particularly when one of the local cowboys decides to ride his horse into the place. **The Sheridan Opera House**, at the same location, features occasional live theatrical or musical performances, and shows movies at other times.

CORTEZ & MESA VERDE

The Crow Canyon Archaeological Center, 23390 County Road K, Cortez, 81321, ☎ 970/565-8975 or 800/422-8975 (Durango office: Main Mall, Suite 221, 835 Main Avenue, Durango, 81301, ☎ 970/259-2449), is an innovative archaeological research and education center focusing on the prehistoric Anasazi Indians. One-day programs include examining 700-year-old artifacts and archaeological site visits. These are offered Tuesday, Wednesday, and Thursday, from the first week in June to the last week of October. Week-long programs include hands-on work at an actual excavation site, one of which is Sand Canyon Pueblo, the largest ruin ever found in the Southwest. They conduct workshops on Native American crafts, including pottery, weaving, basketry, and jewelry. Cultural explorations led by archaeologists and Native Americans are also offered. Reservations are required at least a day in advance for day programs.

For information about Indian dances and cultural, historical and archaeological programs on summer evenings at the CU Cortez Center and the Colorado Visitor Center, in Cortez, see above under *Touring*.

Mesa Verde National Park offers several guided tours and multi-media shows from mid-April to mid-October. Information is available at Far View Lodge (see below, under *Accommodations*).

Where to Stay & Eat

Southwest Colorado counts on tourism to pay the bills, and therefore provides all levels of accommodations, from free and primitive wilderness campgrounds to luxury resorts charging hundreds of dollars a day. Most places fall somewhere between these limits. There are many independent or chain motels, most quite ordinary, as well as historic hotels, bed & breakfasts, condominiums, cabin rentals, and dude ranches. Many of the ranches offer a Western variant of the all-inclusive vacation, with meals, horseback riding, backcountry excursions, and other activities for a flat price.

Summer is considered high season throughout southwestern Colorado except for accommodations close to Purgatory and Telluride, where rates increase when the snow flies.

Some bargains can be found in winter when accommodations are considerably less expensive in Durango than slope-side at Purgatory. Inexpensive round-trip bus service from town to the ski area is available or you can drive the 26 miles; US 550 is kept well-plowed. As for Telluride accommodations in winter or on busy summer festival weekends, look outside of town to save money and have an easier time securing a reservation.

A disturbing trend in the accommodations industry is that, as the region's popularity increases, rates are rising astronomically. Modest Durango properties are charging $90-$100 for a bare bones motel room during busy summer weekends – the same room that might be available for only $35-$40 in winter.

Depending on what you want to do in southwestern Colorado, you could probably stay in one or two places and drive from these bases to anywhere suggested in this chapter. There are many, many individualistic places to stay, and these are the ones included here. The widest range of accommodations is in Durango, which boasts around 6,000 beds. In Silverton, prices are deservedly inexpensive and dining can be a challenge. Ouray is growing and has several interesting places to stay, while Telluride offers numerous well-equipped condos, bed & breakfasts, and some ultra-deluxe accommodations.

Cortez is closest to Indian Country. Accommodations tend to be moderately priced standard motels, but there is one unique bed & breakfast (Kelly Place) outside of town. Mesa Verde National Park has a motel that fills up far in advance during the summer; in April-May or September-October, you're more likely to get a room on the spur of the moment.

Restaurants appear to be on the upswing in these parts, too. Although southwest Colorado still contains a share of restaurants that are no better than adequate or worse, there are some good ones to be found. Prices tend to be within reason, although some of the better restaurants are jacking-up prices.

There are many more accommodations and restaurants in this area than what follows. At some of these hotels you can stay for as little as $35 nightly in low-season (though double or triple that in high-season) or receive change from a $10 bill for dinner. Contact local Visitor Centers or Chambers of Commerce for complete listings.

Accommodations

DURANGO

In-Town

The classiest historic hotel in southwestern Colorado is the **Strater Hotel**, 699 Main Avenue, PO Drawer E, Durango, 81302, ☎ 970/247-4431, 800/247-4431 (in Colorado) or 800/227-4431. It's been a Durango landmark since 1881 and is actually classified as a museum; Marketing Director Rod Barker is the curator. Each of the 93 rooms is different and all are furnished with antiques, comprising one of the largest collections of Victorian walnut furnishings in the world. Rooms have modern bathrooms and cable TV. No pool, but there is a spa room with Jacuzzi. There is a constantly improving hotel-quality restaurant here. The food is as good as anywhere in Durango, and the setting can't be beat. **Henry's** serves three meals a day and even if you do not stay here, you should certainly come in for a meal and a look around. At the very least try to stop in for a drink at the **Diamond Belle Saloon** and perhaps an old fashioned Western melodrama at the **Diamond Circle Theatre**. Both are on the premises. Reserve early during summer.

The General Palmer Hotel, 567 Main Avenue, Durango, 81302, ☎ 970/247-4747 or 800/523-3358, is also a Victorian-style hotel a block south of the Strater. It has a cozy, antique-filled lobby right on Main Avenue, a block from the Silverton train, but its 39 rooms contain reproductions, not antiques. Certain "inside rooms" lack windows. It's still a very nice place, and it has an interesting, tiny, claustrophobic old elevator. Expensive.

Jarvis Suite Hotel, 125 West 10th Street, Durango, 81301, ☎ 970/259-6190 or 800/824-1024, has studios, one-and two-bedroom suites with small rooms, homey living rooms, and full kitchens. Situated downtown just five blocks from the train station. Expensive.

The Durango Hostel, 543 East 2nd Avenue, Durango, 81301, ☎ 970/247-9905, is cheaper than many campgrounds, though not much more deluxe. Dorms or private rooms, with a shared kitchen, are available. Inexpensive.

Leland House, 721 East Second Avenue, Durango, 81301, ☎ 970/385-1920 or 800/664-1920, fax 970/385-1967, is a friendly 10-room B&B in a remodeled 1927 building. It has antique-furnished rooms with kitchenettes, or three-room suites with full kitchens. Situated a block off of Main Avenue, a five-minute walk to the train station. Good breakfasts served across the street at the Rochester Hotel. Expensive.

Rochester Hotel, 726 East Second Avenue, Durango, 81301, ☎ 970/385-1920 or 800/664-1920, fax 970/385-1967, is a beautifully renovated 15-room Western-style hotel in an old, historic building that was most recently a flop house. Located just across the street from the Leland House, this hotel is operated by the same people, and guests here get the same tasty breakfast, only they don't have to walk across the street for it. The large rooms have high ceilings and each one is decorated to represent a different Western movie filmed around Durango, such as *Butch Cassidy and the Sundance Kid*. Expensive.

In addition, there is a strip with one after another modest motel on North Main Avenue, some with pools. Contact the Chamber of Commerce for complete listings.

The best of the more predictable accommodations in Durango is the **Red Lion Inn**, 501 Camino del Rio, ☎ 970/259-6580. The property overlooks the Animas River in Durango, with an indoor pool, exercise room and sauna, a decent restaurant, a good happy hour with free hors d'oeuvres in the bar, the best Sunday brunch in town (see below, under *Restaurants*), and an outdoor café, open during the summer only, where you can hear the river running by a few feet away. It's a half-block from the train station. Expensive.

Out-of-Town

Tamarron Hilton Resort, 40252 US 550, Durango, 81301, ☎ 970/259-2000 or 800/678-1000, is a large, luxurious, contemporary Western golf resort hotel, with 350 large rooms and multi-bedroom condo units. All have kitchens or kitchenettes. Scenically situated 16 miles north of Durango, facilities include an indoor/outdoor pool, saunas, whirlpool, children's program, golf, tennis, cross-country ski trails, horseback riding, ski shuttle to nearby Purgatory, airport transportation, and two dining rooms. Rates tend to be well above moderate. If it's out of your range, this is a nice place to stop for a drink. There are free hors d'oeuvres in the **Yellow Belly Saloon** from 5-7PM. Expensive.

Tall Timber, SSR Box 90A, Durango, 81302, ☎ 970/259-4813, is completely secluded on the banks of the Animas River, north of Durango. Most people ride the narrow-gauge railroad or a helicopter to get here. The alternatives are to hike or ride a horse; the closest road is five miles away.

When you finally get here, you discover a top-rated, luxurious hideaway for a maximum of 30 guests. With only 10 modern multi-bedroom units, each with fireplace and deck, five-star dining, indoor/outdoor pool, sauna, whirlpool, putting green, executive nine-hole golf course, tennis court, exercise room, skiing and hiking trails, horseback riding, fishing, heli-picnics, and heli-hiking, it certainly offers plenty to keep you busy. Premium rates include meals and transportation to the resort. There is a four-day minimum stay. Very expensive.

Lightner Creek Inn, 999 County Road 207, Durango, 81301, ☎ 970/259-1226, fax 970/259-0732, features eight luxurious guest rooms in an elegantly remodeled 1903 farmhouse. Set on 20 acres of wooded property, the inn is a five-minute ride from Durango, and is consistently rated among the top bed & breakfasts in the state. Expensive.

Steward Ranch Cabins, 4385 County Road 207, Durango, 81301, ☎ 970/247-8396 or 970/247-8962, offers 40 acres of privacy, a one- or two-bedroom log cabin with fireplace, kitchen, barbecue, and picnic table. Parts of the movie *City Slickers* were filmed here, just west of Durango, off US 160. Inexpensive.

Diamond Lodge Guest Ranch, 2038 Sierra Verde Drive, Durango, 81301, ☎ 970/259-9393 or 800/426-9765, is 17 miles northwest of Durango at 9,200 feet elevation. This modern guest ranch contains 24 bedrooms with private baths. The ranch has Sunday-to-Sunday lodging from late May to mid-September, including horseback riding, cookouts, trout fishing, and hiking. Moderate.

Colorado Trails, 1261 County Road 240, Durango, 81301, ☎ 970/247-5055 or 800/323-3833, fax 970/385-7372, is 12 miles northeast of Durango, and has operated as a well-regarded family guest ranch since 1960. Facilities accommodate 75 guests per one-week minimum stay and include cabins with single rooms or two-room suites, all meals, a horseback riding program, waterskiing and tubing, heated pool and spa, archery, riflery, trapshooting, fishing, tennis, square dancing, hayrides, camp-outs for kids, music shows, dancing, chuckwagon dinners, children's and teens' programs. Moderate.

Wit's End Guest Ranch, 254 County Road 500, Bayfield, 81122, ☎ 970/884-4113. Located at Vallecito Reservoir, this year-round resort features luxuriously furnished log cabins with stone fireplaces, decks, brass beds, and kitchens. There's a good dining room, a hot tub/Jacuzzi, fishing, evening entertainment, horseback riding, pool, tennis, and waterskiing. Cross-country skiing and snowmobiling are available in winter. Expensive.

Wilderness Trails Ranch, 776 County Road 300, Durango, 81301, ☎ 970/247-0722, has been a guest ranch since 1950. Located on the edge of the Weminuche Wilderness, the ranch accommodates 50 guests per minimum week-long stay in two-, three-, or five-bedroom log cabins, or duplexes. Activities include special children's and teens' programs, horseback riding, square dancing, staff shows, campfire sing-alongs, an overnight camp-out, volleyball, fishing, waterskiing, and four-wheel-drive trips. There is a heated pool and all meals are included. Guests may participate in a cattle round-up the last week in September. Moderate.

D'Mara Resort, 1213 County Road 500, Bayfield, 81122, ☎ 970/884-9806, offers several modern cabins with kitchens. These accommodate two to eight people and are set on the edge of Vallecito Reservoir. There is a two-night minimum stay in summer. Inexpensive.

Purgatory Village Hotel, PO Box 2082, Durango, 81302, ☎ 970/247-9000 or 800/879-7874, at the ski area, offers luxurious one-, two-, or three-bedroom suites with balconies, wood-burning fireplaces, kitchens, in-room saunas, and whirlpool baths. Moderate-expensive.

Cascade Village, 50827 US 550, Durango, 81301, ☎ 970/259-3500 or 800/525-0896, has a variety of accommo dations from large studios to three-bedroom luxury condos with a full kitchen, cable TV, stereo, fireplace, balcony, and private Jacuzzi tubs. There is a heated pool, a steam room, and an exercise room. Guests have easy access to Café

Cascade (see below, under *Durango Restaurants*), a strong contender for the best restaurant in these parts. Expensive.

MESA VERDE, MANCOS & HESPERUS

Far View Lodge, PO Box 277, Mancos, 81328, ☎ 970/529-4421, is the only motel inside Mesa Verde National Park, open May to October. Ordinarily it wouldn't rate a second glance, but the spectacular mesa-top location does recommend it. There are 150 rooms and a restaurant. Moderate.

Lake Mancos Ranch, 42688 County Road N, Mancos, 81328, ☎ 970/533-7900 or 800/325-WHOA, accommodates 55 guests in private cabins, and offers fishing, jeeping, hiking, and cookouts. Meals are included in weekly rates, but horseback riding is extra. Most guests, however, do come here to ride horses, and the riding program is top notch. Pool, volleyball, horseshoes, and a children's program, including camp-outs, are also available. The main summer family season runs from early June through August. The last month of the season, September, the ranch stays open, but for adults only. This is when most serious riding is done, and the guests tend to be regulars who return each year at this time to ride and see the fall colors, which are usually spectacular in the vicinity of the ranch. The Sehnert family has been running the ranch since the 1950s, and a black and white photograph on the wall in the main lodge shows a youthful Johnny Carson with two of his sons. They vacationed here in the early 1960s. The ranch is still a friendly, unpretentious 1950s-style place. Moderate.

Echo Basin Dude Ranch, 43747 County Road M, Mancos, 81328, ☎ 970/533-7800 or 800/426-1870, has lodge rooms, bunkhouse or cabin accommodations, and tent or RV sites on 600 acres north of Mancos. Activities include fishing in a stocked lake, horseback riding, boating, hayrides, cookouts, snowmobiling, hiking and backpacking, and there is a swimming pool. Inexpensive.

Jersey Jim Fire Lookout Tower, c/o US Forest Service, Mancos Ranger District, PO Box 320, Mancos, 81328, ☎ 970/533-7716, is not very fancy, but it certainly offers a spectacular view. Located 20 miles north of Mancos in an old, obsolete, 55-foot-tall fire lookout, it's just a small room, with a stove, refrigerator, lanterns, and bird's-eye views of four states. There is no running water, but you can hoist the water and supplies you bring along from the ground with the original pulley system. You bring your own sleeping bag and everything else you want. Make reservations far in advance for this ultimate retreat, which is generally booked solid a year in advance, although there are occasional cancellations. Inexpensive.

The Gingerbread Inn Bed & Breakfast, 41478 CO 184, Mancos, 81328, ☎ 970/533-7892 or 800/644-2065, is a mile north of Mancos on the way to Dolores. Inexpensive.

The Bauer House, 100 Bauer Avenue, PO Box 1049, Mancos, 81328, ☎ 970/533-9707 or 800/733-9707, is a B&B in a restored 1890s Victorian mansion. It contains three rooms, as well as a penthouse with a kitchen and bar, all with private baths. Moderate.

Blue Lake Ranch, 16919 CO 140, Hesperus, 81326, ☎ 970/385-4537, fax 970/385-4088, is a well-hidden B&B 20 miles west of Durango. Call for exact directions. To protect guests' privacy, there's no sign on this luxurious 100-acre hide-away. It consists of a main house with four suites, a separate log cabin overlooking a small lake, and several other cottages scattered around exquisite flower and herb gardens. Breakfast usually includes eggs from ranch chickens, homemade jams, and jellies.

La Plata Vista Ranch, 13400 County Road 120, Hesperus, 81326, ☎ 970/247-9062, is a "hand-crafted solar hacienda," in a quiet, undeveloped area. Breakfast is included and dinner is available with advance reservations.

OURAY & RIDGWAY

Ouray is becoming saturated with moderately priced lodging options, lots of newly restored B&Bs, condos, long-neglected hotels being brought back to life, and semi-rustic cabins nestled in secluded forest settings close to town. Check with the Visitor Center for complete listings. You can ski for half-price at Telluride if you stay in Ouray or Ridgway.

St. Elmo Hotel, 426 Main Street, Ouray, 81427, ☎ 970/325-4951, is a beautifully restored, well-run, nine-bedroom, 1898 Victorian bed & breakfast that's open year-round. The building is listed in the National Historic Register, and contains lots of stained and etched glass. Moderate.

Wiesbaden Lodge and Spa, Box 349, Ouray, 81427, ☎ 970/325-4347, has a wonderful underground vapor cave fed by the hot springs that run below this hillside property. There's also a large outdoor mineral hot pool. The motel rooms are standard, but several lodge rooms are interesting, including one with a rock wall hewn out of the mountainside that has rivulets of steaming mineral water running down it. Moderate.

Alpenglow Condominiums, 215 5th Avenue, Ouray, 81427, ☎ 970/325-4664 or 303/325-4972. Open year-round, it offers modern one- , two- , or three-bedroom condos with kitchens, private decks, fireplaces, and cable TV. Moderate.

Box Canyon Lodge & Hot Springs, 45 Third Avenue, Ouray, 81427, ☎ 970/325-4981 or 800/327-5080, is most notable for its four outdoor mineral hot springs tubs. Some of the rooms or suites have a fireplace and some have kitchenettes. It's open year-round. Moderate.

Damn Yankee Bed & Breakfast, PO Box 709, 100 6th Avenue, Ouray, 81427, ☎ 970/325-4219 or 800/845-7512, offers eight deluxe rooms in a modern chalet with queen beds, down comforters, and private baths. Most rooms have a fireplace. There's a piano in the parlor, a third-floor observatory lounge, hot tub and sauna. No pets or children are allowed. Expensive.

Hill House, PO Box 373, Ouray, 81427, ☎ 970/325-4350 or 970/325-4584, is a four-bedroom, 2½-bathroom house, situated two miles north of Ouray, that is available for rent. Inexpensive.

Historic Western Hotel Bed & Breakfast, 210 Seventh Avenue, Ouray, 81427, ☎ 970/325-4645, contains 14 rooms in the oldest wooden structure in a town with lots of old wooden buildings. It was once one of the better hotels in the area, but fell into disrepair over the years. Now it's a B&B complete with fancy wood detailing, a wide balcony, and an old tin ceiling. Moderate.

Ouray Hotel, 303 Sixth Avenue, PO Box 1862, Ouray, 81427, ☎ 970/325-0500 or 800/216-8729, is now restored to its original 1893 splendor. Moderate.

The Manor Bed & Breakfast, 317 Second Street, PO Box 745, Ouray, 81427, ☎ 970/325-4574, is situated in a renovated Victorian home. Breakfast, tea and cookies, down comforters on the beds, Jacuzzi. Moderate.

Ouray Realty Rentals, 634 Main Street, PO Box 77, Ouray, 81427-0077, ☎ 970/325 -4141, offers luxury two- or three-bedroom condos near the hot springs pool, as well as one- to five-bedroom houses and cabins, all fully furnished, with kitchens. Inexpensive-expensive.

The Brown Cabin, 16298 US 550, Ouray (mail and inquiries c/o Property Manager, PO Box 1614, Telluride, 81435-1614, ☎ 970/626-5437), is a rustic log cabin situated high above the river, three miles north of Ouray. The place is equipped for four guests. It comes with linens, a wood stove and a deck overlooking the Uncompaghre Valley. Inexpensive.

Chipeta Sun Lodge, 304 South Lena, PO Box 2013, Ridgway, 81432, ☎ 970/626-3737 or 800/633-5868, calls itself a "classy Southwestern solar adobe lodge." The place was built as a showplace for a solar home development across the street. The walls are two feet thick, the rooms are sunny, with private baths, and all reveal substantial unobstructed views of the San Juan Mountains. There's a hot tub in an adobe tower, and breakfast is served in a bright solarium. In summer, guests can use the lodge's mountain bikes for free, and a number of other excursions can be arranged at no charge. These are called "Epic Adventures" and they represent one of the best deals around. For the price of a room, free outings are guided by the lodge hosts, Lyle and Shari Braud. These include summer excursions such as easy biking in Ridgway State Park, a technical single-track descent covering 2,500 feet on Dallas Trail, biking on jeep roads to nearby towns, or wildflower hikes. In winter, trips might include day-long cross-country ski treks to the San Juan Mountain Huts, skiing on Red Mountain Pass to ghost towns or on a set track in Telluride, followed by a dunk in some hot springs. Detailed maps are available for self-guided adventures. Moderate.

San Juan Guest Ranch, 2282 CO 23, Ridgway, 81432, ☎ 970/626-5360, is a classic, small guest ranch. It's not fancy, but it is modernized and comfortable. Activities include a comprehensive horseback riding program in the remote San Juans, weekly overnight cook-outs, private trout fishing, ballooning, jeep tours, and swimming in Ouray's Hot Springs Pool. Three meals a day are included in summer. In winter, the ranch operates as the San Juan Ranch Bed & Breakfast, featuring cross-country skiing, ice skating, ice climbing, sleigh rides and sledding. Breakfast is included, along with half-price Telluride lift tickets. Moderate.

Orvis Hot Springs, 1585 County Road 3, Ridgway, 81432, ☎ 970/626-5324, has a few rooms for guests. Inexpensive.

For a clean, modern, standard motel room, the **Ridgway-Telluride Super 8 Lodge**, PO Box 608, 373 Palomino Trail, Ridgway, 81432, ☎ 970/626-5444 or 800/368-5444, is well-situated on US 550 in Ridgway, just south of the turn to Telluride on CO 62. Facilities include an indoor pool, Jacuzzi and sauna, and a free continental breakfast is included with a room. Moderate.

RICO, DOLORES & CORTEZ

Rico is a tiny old mining town 25 miles south of Telluride on CO 145. There's fine alpine scenery and adventurous territory nearby, but not much of a town. In winter, when half-price Telluride lift tickets are offered, it might not be such a bargain if Lizard Head Pass – the only way to reach Telluride – is closed by avalanches. You can also lock onto the half-price tickets if you stay in Dolores or Cortez, but it's an even longer ride to the slopes. Although there are a fair share of unimaginative motels in Cortez, there are now numerous personalized accommodations in this area, too. Again, most are moderately to inexpensively priced.

Rico Motel & Cabins, Silver Street, PO Box 303, Rico, 81332, ☎ 970/967-2444, has motel rooms with refrigerators, microwave ovens and coffee pots, or small self-contained cabins. The property is open year-round. Inexpensive.

Rico Hotel and Restaurant, 124 Glasgow Avenue, Rico, 81332, ☎ 970/967-3000, is a funky B&B in an old miner's boarding house. The restaurant serves lunch and dinner. Inexpensive-moderate.

Rhode Inn Bed & Breakfast, 20 South Glasgow, Rico, 81332, ☎ 970/967-2352, was built by a silver baron in 1884, when Rico was a boom town. Today it's a restored Victorian house, complete with antiques, and five guest rooms (three with private baths). Moderate.

Green Snow Oasis & Cabins, 27602 CO 145, Rico, 81332, ☎ 970/562-3829, offers four cabins with kitchenettes and baths on the Dolores River, about six miles south of Rico. The cabins have wood stoves and can sleep up to six people. Good trout fishing right outside the door. Inexpensive.

Laughing Coyote Lodge, PO Box 21, Dolores, 81323, ☎ 970/882-7321 or 800/373-7321, is actually 35 miles northwest of Dolores, making it possibly the most remote lodge in all of Colorado, accessible by road in summer only. Winter guests need to ski or snowmobile to reach the seven-room property set on 40 acres. The lodge can accommodate as many as 26 guests at a time and offers two kitchens where you can prepare your own meals if you like, or meals will be prepared for you. The lodge is available to groups only from November 15 to May 15, and offers fine backcountry skiing, snowmobiling, snowshoeing or ice fishing on Groundhog Lake, which is about a mile from the lodge. The rest of the year, the lodge is a base for hiking, mountain biking, jeeping, fishing, or horseback riding trips, which can be arranged by proprietors Paulette and Kevin Barlow. The lodge is rustic but comfortable (some rooms have shared baths), and it is one of the most unusual properties in all the Southwest, the perfect spot for those who want millions of acres to themselves. Inexpensive-moderate.

Rio Grande Southern, 101 Fifth Street, Dolores, 81323, ☎ 970/882-7527, is an old railroad hotel and the oldest building in town. The six little guest rooms come with full breakfast in the hotel's restaurant. Inexpensive.

Lebanon Schoolhouse Bed & Breakfast, Roads 25 & T, Dolores, 81323, ☎ 970/882-4461 or 800/349-9829, is a European-style country inn. The restored 1907 building has historic significance. Inexpensive.

Lost Canyon Lake Lodge, PO Box 1289, Dolores, 81323, ☎ 970/882-4913, is a contemporary two-story log lodge with four guest rooms, all with private baths. It overlooks Lost Canyon Lake Reservoir at 7,300 feet elevation. Rates include breakfast and snacks. Moderate.

Rag 'O Muffin Ranch, 26030 CO 145, Dolores, 81323, ☎ 970/562-3803, offers two housekeeping units, with kitchens, in a log cabin on 12 acres, bordering the Dolores River. Moderate.

Mountain View Bed & Breakfast, 28050 Road P, Dolores, 81323, ☎ 970/882-7861 or 800/228-4592, is set on 22 acres, with hiking trails, an outdoor sun deck and hot tub, and a front porch swing. Moderate.

Kelly Place, 14663 County Road G, Cortez, 81321, ☎ 970/565-3125 or 800/745-4885, is a most unusual, eight-room bed & breakfast. It is set on 100 acres, west of Cortez, in red rock and slickrock country. You can help excavate Indian ruins on the remote property, study weaving, pottery-making, canning, quilting, tanning, farming with draft horses, or blacksmithing. Reservations are required. Moderate.

SILVERTON

Alma House, 220 East 10th Street, Silverton, 81433, ☎ 970/387-5336, is a cozy, restored Victorian hotel in a 1908 building. Largely done in antiques, the Alma upholds the old custom that it's okay for some rooms to share a bathroom. Open mid-May to late September. Room service is available and pets are welcome. Inexpensive.

The Grand Imperial Hotel, 1219 Greene Street, Silverton, 81433, ☎ 970/387-5527, is a more ornate Victorian restoration than the Alma House. It has 40 rooms with private baths, some with oak pull-chain toilets. There is a restaurant and a saloon with a bullet hole in the bar. Open year-round. Inexpensive-moderate.

Wingate House Bed & Breakfast, 1045 Snowdon Street, Silverton, 81433, ☎ 970/387-5713, is an antique-filled B&B in a century-old home, with breakfast included at the French Bakery (see below, under *Silverton Restaurants*), or you can use the kitchen to prepare your own meals. Moderate.

The Wyman Hotel, 1371 Greene Street, Silverton, 81433, ☎ 970/387-5372, off-season 970/249-5423, is Silverton's only AAA-rated lodging. Rooms in the 1902 building have private baths, something of a novelty around here, and VCRs with free tapes. Open mid-May to mid-October. Moderate.

Teller House Hotel, 1250 Greene Street, Silverton, 81433, ☎ 970/387-5423 or 800/342-4338, is above the French Bakery, where breakfast is included with a room. Bathrooms are down the hall and dorm rooms are available. The 800# also represents **Wingate House** and **Smedley's**, 1314 Greene Street, Silverton, 81433, ☎ 970/387-5423, another antique building offering suites with private baths and kitchens. Moderate.

St. Paul Ski Lodge, PO Box 463, Silverton, 81433, ☎ 970/387-5367, offers rustic backcountry lodging set at 11,440 feet, above Red Mountain Pass and accessible only by hiking or cross-country skiing. This is an historic mining structure, cunningly remodeled with second-hand materials to accommodate 22 guests in dorm rooms, with an indoor outhouse, sauna, hot showers, and kerosene lamps. The lodge provides excellent access to challenging cross-country skiing in the heart of the San Juans and hosts periodic avalanche and medical seminars. Inexpensive-moderate.

TELLURIDE

Telluride, as the class act of southwestern Colorado, offers a number of higher priced accommodations. Keep in mind there are few typical hotel/motel rooms. The closest you can find to the ordinary is perhaps at The Peaks (see below), which is a modern hotel, but also happens to be one of the top resort spas in the country. There are a number of mostly upscale B&Bs and also many well-equipped condos and private homes.

Skyline Guest Ranch, Box 67, Telluride, 81435, ☎ 970/728-3757 or 970/728-6728, is the prettiest and classiest guest ranch in southwestern Colorado. The beauty comes from its serene location. Set at 9,600 feet, it is surrounded by broad meadows and lofty peaks eight miles south of Telluride, off CO 145. The ranch provides a rarefied western experience. The hosts, the Farney family, are extremely knowledgeable about all manner of outdoor activities in the area, and they are particularly skilled at making guests feel comfortable. The food is great, too, not just gray cowboy food.

It offers small but cozy lodge rooms or private cabins, with down comforters on the beds. There is a stocked trout-fishing lake on the property, and horseback riding, pack trips, hiking, mountaineering, jeep trips, a sauna and hot tub. Make reservations as early as possible here. This is a popular place, with many repeat guests. The dining room is open to non-guests by reservation. Expensive-moderate.

San Sophia, 330 West Pacific Avenue, Telluride, 81435, ☎ 970/728-301 or 800/537-4781, is a distinctive, elegant, modern B&B with 16 luxurious rooms. All rooms have private baths, brass beds, and a cable TV. There is a rooftop observatory, library, lounge, and a garden with a Jacuzzi. A complimentary afternoon happy hour is offered. Expensive.

New Sheridan House, 231 West Colorado Avenue, Telluride, 81435,- ☎ 970/728-4351, is an old, historic hotel built in 1895. It's terrifically atmospheric, including some rooms with shared baths. Expensive.

Telluride Lodge, 747 West Pacific Avenue, Telluride, 81435, ☎ 970/728-4446, 970/728-4400, or 800/662-8747, offers rooms with full kitchens and cable TV; some have fireplaces. Hot tubs and a steam room are available. Moderate-expensive.

The Peaks at Telluride, PO Box 2702, Telluride, 81435, ☎ 970/728-6800 or 800/789-2220, fax 970/728-6175, was formerly the Telluride Doral Resort & Spa. It remains an ultra-modern 177-room luxury hotel at the Mountain Village with a 42,000-square-foot spa, indoor/outdoor pool, Jacuzzis, saunas, steam rooms (including a eucalyptus steam room that is simply out of this world), massage therapy, beauty treatments, racquetball, an indoor climbing wall, two restaurants, ski-in/out access, and all situated on the 18-hole Mountain Village golf course. The spa has been rated among the top 10 in the United States by the picky readers of *Condé Nast Traveler*, and it really is a wonderful facility in a stunning mountain location, making this easily one of the top resorts in the area. Much of the time, pampered guests can be seen padding around the lavish property in slippers and thick terrycloth bathrobes. Rates are high, but a surprising number of discounts are available year-round. Some special "ski free" packages may be available, as well as other holiday, ski and vacation packages. The hotel operates a free shuttle service to the town of Telluride. Expensive-very expensive.

If you're really enamored of Telluride and have the money to back your tastes, the **Franz Klammer Lodge**, ☎ 970/728-9508 or 800/405-4199, bills itself as Telluride's first private residence club. It commands a prime ski-in/ski-out location in the Mountain Village, and offers two- and three-bedroom private residences with stone fireplaces, fully equipped kitchens and 10-foot-high wood ceilings. Club amenities include a health club and heated outdoor pool, ski valet, 24-hour concierge, and pre-arrival grocery service. Very expensive.

Telluride Mountain Village Resort Management Company, 550 Mountain Village Road, Telluride, 81435, ☎ 970/728-6727 or 800/544-0507, represents luxury properties in the Mountain Village. Offerings include studios, one- to four-bedroom condos, and private homes. Expensive.

Resort Rentals, 673 West Pacific Avenue, Telluride, 81435, ☎ 970/728-4405, manages rentals of luxury properties, from studio condos to four-bedroom homes. Expensive.

Pennington's Mountain Village Inn, PO Box 2428, Telluride, 81435, ☎ 970/728-5357 or 800/545-1437, offers 12 large suites with private decks, stocked refrigerators, and a full breakfast every day. There is an indoor spa at this luxury property on the Mountain Village golf course. Expensive.

Telluride Central Reservations, PO Box 1009, Telluride, 81435, ☎ 970/728-4431 or 800/525-3455, fax 970/728-6475, can reserve all-inclusive packages providing for lodging, air and ground transportation, tickets to events, activities, and travel insurance.

Restaurants

DURANGO

There are probably at least 50 restaurants in Durango, with new ones setting up shop regularly. It's a competitive market, so prices are frequently low to moderate, rarely expensive. Several national franchises are represented throughout town. I'm not including the more touristy restaurants, where you pay more for the show than the good food.

In-Town

A lot of the dining in Durango still seems to focus on meat and pota toes; for vegetarians or other cholesterol-conscious travelers, the best option is to cook for yourself. **Durango Natural Foods**, 575 East 8th

Avenue, Durango, ☎ 970/247-8129, offers the largest selection of goodies for you. Also in town is **Nature's Oasis**, 1123 Camino del Rio, Durango, ☎ 970/247-1988, a natural foods store with a deli and a juice bar.

Season's Rotisserie & Grill, 746 Main Avenue, ☎ 970/382-9790, is a sleek and cleanly operated winner in a restored Durango storefront. Not particularly elaborate, the dining room's oak floors and library chairs give it a no-nonsense feel, enhanced by the location of the grill, where all the food is prepared, in a corner of the room. Serves wood-grilled chicken, duck, pork chops, pasta dishes, and vegetarian entrées. The garlic mashed potatoes are a must. Good wine list, full bar, attentive service. Moderate.

Cyprus Cafe, 726 East 2nd Avenue, ☎ 970/385-1920, serves some of the healthiest food in town, good salads with lots of unusual green things in them, pastas and, in summer, fresh herbs and vegetables grown in their own garden. The food is briskly seasoned and tasty. Dining on the small outdoor patio is sometimes accompanied by live jazz. Moderate.

The Red Snapper, 144 East 9th Street, ☎ 970/259-3417, specializes in several varieties of seafood, along with Durango's best salad bar and epic desserts (save room for "Death by Chocolate"). Ask what's really fresh before you order. Wine list and full bar. Moderate-expensive.

Griego's North, 2603 North Main, ☎ 970/259-3558, is an evocative converted drive-in serving tasty, but not ungreasy tacos, burritos, and burgers. Not only does this place look like something out of *Happy Days*, the prices are as close as you'll find in this town to 1959. Inexpensive.

Durango Diner, 957 Main Avenue, ☎ 970/247-9889, serves classic diner fare, a whole potato's worth of hash browns with your breakfast eggs, lunch specials, burgers, sandwiches, and homemade pies. Try the green chili. I think it's made out of mashed peppers and chicken soup. Bart and Gary, who preside over the grill, are now bottling the stuff. It's available in supermarkets – Durango's answer to *Ben & Jerry*. Sit at the counter if you want to find out what's really going on around town. Inexpensive.

Carver's Bakery and Brew Pub, 1022 Main Avenue, ☎ 970/259-2545, serves good coffee, baked goods, big salads in a bread bowl, sandwiches, and several varieties of beer brewed slowly in a back room. Service is, shall we say, casual, but then none of the guests ever appear to be in much of a hurry, either. An outdoor patio in back is nice for sipping a brew while you're waiting, and waiting, for breakfast, lunch or dinner. Inexpensive.

The Old Tymer's Café, 1000 Main Avenue, ☎ 970/259-2990, serves good nachos, burgers, and booze in an old historic building. This is not exactly a spectacular restaurant, but it is always crowded with locals. The food is basic, but Old Tymer's does serve the best French fries in town. Outdoor patio dining in warm weather. Inexpensive.

There was an active Chinatown in Durango in the late 19th century, when the railroads were being built. The best of today's several Chinese restaurants in town is the **May Palace**, 909 Main Avenue, ☎ 970/259-4836. Inexpensive-moderate.

Mai Thai, 1050 Main Avenue, Durango, ☎ 970/247-8272, is a tiny hole-in-the-wall joint that has been winning rave reviews from locals for its curries, vegetarian selections and spicy noodles. Inexpensive.

Durango Coffee Company, 730 Main Avenue, ☎ 970/259-2059, used to serve the best cup of coffee in town. Nowadays it's impossible to tell who has the best coffee. The proliferation of coffee shops in such a small town is astonishing. This upscale kitchenware shop and coffee emporium supplies a lot of local restaurants. A few small tables squeezed by retail displays of pots and pans, and a bench out front, are the only seats. They still serve an excellent cup of coffee. Inexpensive.

Steaming Bean, 915 Main Avenue, ☎ 970/385-7901, is a casual, take-off-your-shoes coffee house with classic garage-sale decor in a sort of Western-punk motif. Inexpensive.

Durango Bagel, 106 East 5th Street, ☎ 970/247-9889, is just a few doors east of the train station at the south end of Main Avenue, and serves the best fresh bagels in the Four Corners – real bagels. Also excellent cream cheese, sandwiches, including lox, muffins, pastries, cookies, ice cream in summer, and the coffee is some of the best around (they probably get it from the Coffee Company, too). Inexpensive.

Red Lion Inn, 501 Camino del Rio, ☎ 970/259-6580, has the best Sunday brunch buffet in Durango. Moderate.

Out-of-Town

Edelweiss Restaurant, 689 Animas View Drive, Durango, ☎ 970/247-5685 or 800/964-5564, is a mile north of Main Avenue and serves excellent German, Italian, and American cuisine, including hasenpfeffer, scampi marinara, and prime rib. Wash it all down with one of the many imported beers on offer. Dinner Tuesday through Sunday. Moderate.

Café Cascade, 50827 US 550, Durango, ☎ 970/259-3500, offers the most exotic menu in the Durango area – it's also one of the most expensive. But the food and service are first class, and nowhere else can you find an appetizer of fried Louisiana alligator, or entrées of wild boar, stuffed marlin, Muscovy duck, antelope, or quail, along with steaks and fresh seafood. Save your appetite for dinner here; the servings are huge, although half-portions are available. The dining room is casual, spacious, and comfortable. After an active day in the mountains this is a great place to relax and dine, not just eat. The drive here from any direction is beautiful and the setting amidst the soaring peaks is stunning. Located a mile north of Purgatory. Dinner only; reservations highly recommended. Expensive.

MESA VERDE, MANCOS & HESPERUS

There are three restaurants inside Mesa Verde National Park, c/o ARA Mesa Verde, ☎ 970/529-4421. **Far View Terrace Café**, open May through October, and the **Spruce Tree Terrace**, open year-round, offer institutional cafeteria fare such as burgers, sandwiches, or tacos. **The Metate Room**, at Far View Lodge, serves Mexican and American food. Moderate-expensive.

Millwood Junction, 101 West Railroad Avenue, Mancos, ☎ 970/533-7338, is worth the drive. Situated seven miles east of Mesa Verde, or 28 miles west of Durango, this is simply an excellent, unpretentious restaurant, serving inexpensive nightly specials, a gargantuan Friday night seafood buffet, and an eclectic menu of imaginative nouvelle entrées, as well as beef, chicken, or seafood standards. A fabulous, home-made salad bar is a meal in itself, and rich desserts include numerous flavors of home-made ice cream. Some nights there's live music in the bar. Moderate-expensive.

Hamburger Haven, 108 East Grand Avenue, Mancos, ☎ 970/533-7919, is a tiny hole-in-the-wall joint tucked away at the back of the town park. It's far from fancy, but the burgers and Mexican food are good, and the prices are low.

Dusty Rose Café, 200 West Grand Avenue, Mancos, ☎ 970/533-9042, is the newest restaurant in a small town that probably could not support another restaurant. Breakfast, lunch, and dinner, served by a waitstaff in black and white formal-wear, are available, and there is dining indoors or on an outdoor patio. Sunday brunch features crab or eggs benedict, and crab omelettes. The chocolate mousse pie is a must for dessert. Moderate.

Chip's Place, 4 County Road 124, Hesperus, ☎ 970/259-6277, is a straightforward, friendly café attached to the modest, one-story Canyon Motel. Chip serves giant burgers, including an award-winning Super Chili Cheeseburger (it's been inducted into the Hamburger Hall of Fame), sandwiches, tender steaks, and homemade fries, along with daily specials. The restaurant is about a half-mile east of the Hesperus Ski Area on US 160. You won't leave hungry, nor much poorer than when you walked in. Inexpensive.

OURAY & RIDGWAY

Just as the lodging industry grows around here, so do the dining options. Practically deserted a few years ago, Ouray is booming and the number of restaurants is on the increase. Ridgway was practically invisible for years, a blip on the road to Telluride. It too is establishing itself with several decent restaurants. A few of the better ones are the following:

The Outlaw, 610 Main Street, Ouray, ☎ 970/325-4366, serves aged Colorado beef, prime rib, or seafood, and also offers a High Mountain Cookout, May through October. This includes a jeep ride to a mountain stream for a steak, seafood, or chicken barbecue. Moderate.

Bon Ton Restaurant, 426 Main Street, Ouray, ☎ 970/325-4951, is downstairs from the St. Elmo Hotel and, like the hotel, is impeccably restored in the Victorian style. It serves good Italian food and has a good wine list. Dinner is served nightly, champagne brunch on Sundays. Moderate-expensive.

Buon Tiempo Restaurant, 206 Seventh Avenue, Ouray, ☎ 970/325-4544, is a good Mexican restaurant in the historic Western Hotel. Moderate.

The Catamount, 220 South Lena Avenue, Ridgway, ☎ 970/626-5044, is one of the few places to eat in Ridgway, serving prime rib, curry chicken, raspberry pork chops, and seafood pasta. Breakfast is available daily and there is a weekly Sunday brunch. Moderate.

Adobe Inn, 251 Lidell Drive, Ridgway, ☎ 970/626-5939, is well thought of for its Mexican food. Inexpensive.

True Grit Café, 123 North Lena, Ridgway, ☎ 970/626-5739. Presumably, they do serve true grits. Inexpensive.

RICO, DOLORES & CORTEZ

Old Germany Restaurant, 200 South 8th Street, Dolores, ☎ 970/882-7549, serves German dishes, along with imported beers and wines. Moderate.

Dolores River Line Camp, nine miles north of Dolores on CO 145, ☎ 970/882-4158, is a western chuckwagon dinner and western show (songs, jokes), serving well-cooked beef, potatoes, beans, and biscuits. Summers only. Reservations required. Moderate.

Nero's Italian Restaurant, 303 West Main Street, Cortez, ☎ 970/565-7366, serves the best Italian food you'll find in Cortez. Moderate.

Francisca's, 125 East Main Street, Cortez, ☎ 970/565-4093, serves Mexican food, vegetarian plates, and renowned margaritas. Moderate.

M&M Truckstop and Restaurant, 7006 Highway 160, Cortez, ☎ 970/565-6511, serves hearty truck-stop fare: eggs, pancakes, burgers, sandwiches, and steaks 24 hours a day. It's one of the best places to eat in town. Inexpensive.

SILVERTON

It's hard to recommend one over any other of Silverton's dozen or so restaurants. This is a very small town and restaurants stay open because they are able to attract tourists, mainly passengers from the Durango-Silverton train, who spend around two hours in town and never come back. The food available here does not, shall we say, enhance the charm of this interesting old community.

You might consider a picnic, driving south on US 550 to Café Cascade, or sample the local equivalent of cuisine at the following:

The French Bakery Restaurant, 1250 Greene Street, ☎ 970/387-5423, is a restaurant and bakery that converts in winter to a restaurant and ski rental shop. Inexpensive-moderate.

Romero's, 1151 Greene Street, ☎ 970/387-9934, serves tolerable Mexican food, which tastes better after a few margaritas. Inexpensive-moderate.

The Shady Lady Restaurant & Spirits, 1154 Blair Street, ☎ 970/387-5352, is notable more for its earliest incarnation in the 1880s as a bordello than for its food today. You can, however, tour the upstairs rooms. Inexpensive-moderate.

Zhivago's Restaurant, 1260 Blair Street, ☎ 970/387-5357, offers one of Silverton's only vegetarian plates. Inexpensive-moderate.

TELLURIDE

For a small town, there are a lot of places to eat. Perhaps this is more surprising when you consider that there is not even a real supermarket in town. There are, however, several good smaller markets, the best of which is **Rose Victorian Food Market**, 700 West Colorado Avenue, ☎ 970/728-3124, right next door to the Visitors Center, on the right side of the street just as you enter town. Rose's makes great sandwiches for picnics and the stock for supplying your condo is surprisingly imaginative and complete.

The Village Market, 157 South Fir Street, ☎ 970/728-4566, is downtown, next to Baked & Brewed in Telluride.

Campagna, 433 West Pacific Avenue, ☎ 970/728-6190, serves Italian food in an old, historic home. Moderate-expensive.

Floradora, 103 West Colorado Avenue, ☎ 970/728-3888, has burgers, Southwestern dishes, sandwiches, soup, and a salad bar. Inexpensive-moderate.

Baked & Brewed in Telluride, 127 South Fir Street, ☎ 970/728-4775, is a busy local hang-out, serving fresh baked-goods, even decent bagels. Counter service for sandwiches and pizza. Now serving micro-brewery beer. Inexpensive-moderate.

Angel's Athenian Senate, 124 South Spruce Street, ☎ 970/728-3018, has Greek, Italian, and vegetarian food. Moderate.

La Marmotte, 150 West San Juan Avenue, ☎ 970/728-6232, serves classical country and light nouvelle French cuisine in Telluride's old Ice House. Expensive.

San Juan Brewing Company, 300 South Townsend, ☎ 970/728-0100, is a brew pub and restaurant. Moderate.

Sofios, 110 East Colorado Avenue, ☎ 970/728-4882, serves Mexican and Southwestern dishes, fruit smoothies and espresso. Moderate.

Swede Finn Hall, 427 West Pacific Avenue, ☎ 970/728-2085, has seafood, regional game, and vegetarian dishes. Nine beers are on tap, and pool tables are available for rent by the hour. Moderate-expensive.

The Excelsior Café, 200 West Colorado Avenue, ☎ 970/728-4250, serves cheap eats, a Telluride rarity, for breakfast and lunch. Inexpensive.

T'Ride Country Club, 333 West Colorado Avenue, ☎ 970/728-6344, offers cook-your-own steaks and seafood. Moderate-expensive.

New and untested, but recommended are the following:

Fat Alley Barbecue; **McCrady's**, sumptuous seafood; **Border House Salsa Café**, Mexican; **Garfinkle's**, full menu, beer, live music; **Lito's**, Mediterranean cuisine. Moderate-expensive.

Camping

There are hundreds of public and private campgrounds throughout southwestern Colorado, ranging from free, primitive wilderness sites without water or restrooms, to deluxe RV parks. For RV hookups, campers will most frequently have to rely on private campgrounds. Public fee-charging campgrounds generally provide a collection box for the $5-$10 overnight site fee. You just drive in and secure an empty campsite by your presence. Contact local offices of the Forest Service or BLM for campground maps and updates on availability of campsites, fees, facilities, fire and firewood gathering regulations.

SAN JUAN NATIONAL FOREST

There are 38 developed campgrounds in the San Juan National Forest that are fully operational from late May to mid-September. The most popular campgrounds are near major lakes, highways, and communities. These include large campgrounds near **Lemon** and **Vallecito Reservoirs** (nine campgrounds, 266 campsites), and small campgrounds at **Purgatory** (14 campsites), **Silverton's South Mineral Creek** (23 campsites), along the West Fork of the Dolores River at **Burro Bridge** (14 campsites), at **McPhee Reservoir** (see below) and north of Mancos at **Target Tree** (51 sites), or **Transfer** (13 campsites).

Many campgrounds subscribe to a reservation system. ☎ 800/283-2267 for information. Take this information with a grain of salt; many people have reported vacation-ruining problems with this reservation system. The best and still most reliable method of securing a campsite is by being the first person to arrive at the site; the rest of the San Juan forest campgrounds are available on a first-come, first-served basis. Fee campgrounds include a table and fire grate, restrooms, drinking water, and trash pick-up. There is a 14-day limit at all campgrounds.

Among the better-equipped campgrounds, the ones at **McPhee Reservoir** in Dolores offer a wide range of services. At the McPhee

Recreation Area on the west side of the reservoir, there are 80 camp-sites, restrooms, showers, five sites with electrical hook-ups, a group camping area, picnic sites, and a trailer dump station. All are situated among pinyon, pine, and junipers on a bluff overlooking the 450,000-acre reservoir. Another camping area is at the **House Creek Recreation Area**, on the east side of the reservoir, 15 miles north of Dolores. It offers, tables, grills, water, toilets, and trash disposal.

FOR MORE INFORMATION

Dolores District of the San Juan National Forest, ☎ 970/882-7296.

Forest Supervisor, San Juan National Forest, 701 Camino del Rio, Durango, 81301, ☎ 970/247-4874.

For a free copy of the *San Juan National Forest Campground Guide,* ☎ 970/247-4874.

BLM/WILDERNESS

Camping is permitted in designated wilderness areas, although no formal campgrounds exist and no services are available.

There are three campgrounds along the **Alpine Loop Backcountry Byway**, administered by the Bureau of Land Management. Other free BLM campgrounds include the following:

Anasazi Heritage Center, three miles west of Dolores on CO 184, has five sites, with water and flush toilets, at 7,200 feet.

Dolores Overlook, 10 miles east of Dove Creek on County Road J, has eight sites without water, at 7,200 feet.

Emerson, 17 miles northeast of Dolores off CO 145, offers four sites with water, at 7,500 feet. Fishing.

OURAY, RIDGWAY & TELLURIDE

Numerous national forest campgrounds are administered by the **Uncompaghre National Forest**, Norwood Ranger District Office, 1760 Grand Avenue, PO Box 388, Norwood, 81423, ☎ 970/327-4261, or the **Ouray Ranger District Office**, 2505 South Townsend Avenue, Montrose, 81401, ☎ 970/249-3711. These include Ouray's popular **Amphitheatre** (33 campsites) and **Silver Jack** (60 campsites), north of

Ridgway. **Ridgway State Recreation Area** offers developed camping and access to watersports.

There are many beautiful camping areas in the vicinity of Telluride, but the most accessible is the one right in town at **Telluride's Town Park**. It has 42 campsites with showers and restrooms, but no RV hook-ups.

CORTEZ, MESA VERDE & MANCOS

Hovenweep National Monument has a small campground. There is a restroom, but no drinking water. In summer, make sure you have insect repellent – biting bugs can be pretty nasty. The **Ute Mountain Tribal Park** has a primitive campground surrounded by one of the most evocative prehistoric Indian sites in the Southwest. Water is available, but all your other needs should be organized in Cortez before you head out here. Reservations are required. For information, ☎ 970/565-3751, ext. 282. **Morefield Campground**, at Mesa Verde National Park, has 477 campsites, including some with hookups. Facilities include restrooms, showers, laundry, groceries, gas, and dump stations. **Lake Mancos Recreation Area,** ☎ 970/883-2208, is six miles northeast of Mancos on a lake set at 7,800 feet. It includes campgrounds, picnic sites, boat ramps, hiking and horseback trails.

Index